Also by Peter S. Cohan

The Technology Leaders: How America's Most Profitable
High-Tech Companies Innovate Their Way to Success

Peter S. Cohan

Net Profit

How to Invest and Compete in the Real World of Internet Business

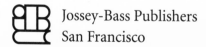
Jossey-Bass Publishers
San Francisco

Jossey-Bass books and products are available through most bookstores. To contact Jossey-Bass directly, call (888) 378-2537, fax to (800) 605-2665, or visit our website at www.josseybass.com.
    Substantial discounts on bulk quantities of Jossey-Bass books are available to corporations, professional associations, and other organizations. For details and discount information, contact the special sales department at Jossey-Bass.

 Manufactured in the United States of America on Lyons Falls Turin Book. This paper is acid-free and 100 percent totally chlorine-free.

Library of Congress Cataloging-in-Publication Data

Cohan, Peter S., 1957–
    Net profit: how to invest and compete in the real world of
internet business / Peter S. Cohan. — 1st ed.
        p. cm. — (The Jossey-Bass business & management series)
    Includes bibliographical references and index.
    ISBN 0–7879–4476–9 (alk. paper)
        1. Internet industry. 2. Electronic commerce. I. Title. II. Series.
HD9696.8.A2 C64 1999
004.67'8'068—dc21   99–6217

FIRST EDITION
HB Printing   10 9 8 7 6 5 4 3 2 1

The Jossey-Bass
Business & Management Series

Contents

To my forebears:

Sophie and Suzanne Cohan for their creativity

Joseph and Paul Cohan for their business sense

and

Samuel and Charles Hieken for their fascination

with technology.

This book is a testament to you all.

—ᴧᴧ— Preface

The Internet has proven itself to be the most significant economic and social phenomenon of the latter half of the 1990s. The financial markets have been replete with tales of investment killings made in a day, simply because a company appended .com to its business model. One of the oddest of these tales is the story of Zapata Corporation, a fish extract company started by a former U.S. president, whose stock doubled in a day when it announced that it was spinning off its Internet business.

To managers and investors schooled in the notion that the value of a company is related to its future profits, the Internet is a perplexing phenomenon. So many of the publicly traded Internet companies have scant revenues and substantial net losses: Why then are these companies worth so much more than many other companies that are much larger and earn substantial profits? And in asking this question, managers and investors are struck with two conflicting emotions. One is the desire to get a piece of the Internet action. The other is a nagging fear that the whole thing is a house of cards that is doomed to unravel at some unspecified point in the near future.

The purpose of this book is to cut through these emotions to get at the reality of the Internet phenomenon. This book is not another exhortation to large companies about why they need to put their businesses on the Web. Nor does it elucidate ten new economic principles received during a trip to the top of Mt. Sinai. This book is about the companies that are working to make economic sense of the Web. It is about understanding the underlying dynamics of the industry segments in which these companies compete. And it is about a search for the business strategies that distinguish the market leaders from their peers.

In thinking about these questions, we can benefit from taking a look at something that happened one hundred years ago. In the 1890s, oil was discovered in Titusville, Pennsylvania. Hundreds of independent drillers rushed to the site to get their share. And as more oil was introduced into the market, the price fell dramatically, wiping out all but the most well-capitalized drillers. Into this boom and bust cycle strode John D. Rockefeller. He saw that the industry could not survive unless there was a way to dampen these wild fluctuations in supply.

So Rockefeller began investing in refineries. These refineries were one of the key choke points, or levers of economic control, in the oil industry. Refineries bought crude, processed it into salable end products, and then found a downstream market for those products. But refineries were only one part of the system that needed to be brought under control. If a driller or refiner produced a commodity but couldn't move it to the market, that commodity had no value. So Rockefeller began using his power to fill up railroad cars with a steady supply of oil products. And he used that power to negotiate volume discounts on railroad transportation. It was worth it to the railroad barons to give Rockefeller a discount on transportation costs in exchange for the profitability of a fully packed train. The result was an industry that was perfectly engineered to provide cheap energy to the masses.

One of the key elements of Rockefeller's strategy was his ability to use Standard Oil stock as acquisition currency. He could buy up rival refineries with his highly valued stock. And he discouraged new entrants into the business by keeping his transportation costs so low that no other firm could meet his prices and make a profit at the same time.

What does Standard Oil have to do with the Internet? Just as oil exploration had very low entry barriers, so does the Web. In every segment, the cost of entry is low, which means that virtually every segment of the Web business has hundreds, if not thousands, of small players. And just as Rockefeller did with the oil industry, some of the leading Web players have analyzed the industry to find its choke points. The leaders in the Web industry have adapted their business strategies so that they can control the key choke points in the Web business.

Just as Rockefeller did with Standard Oil, the companies who are making money on the Web are the ones who have shaped their strategies to take advantage of the most powerful economic levers in their industries. Cisco Systems dominates network equipment because its control of the architecture at the brains of a corporate network forces all other equipment to work with the Cisco router. Kleiner Perkins dominates Internet venture capital because it has the best relations with technology sources, top-performing management teams, and first-class stock underwriters. AOL dominates the ISP business because it has attracted the highest number of eyeballs through its Web content and promotional skills; advertisers are willing to pay the most money to get access to the largest audience.

For those who are exposed to the torrents of hype, it is easy to conclude that the Internet will change everything. The foregoing comparison of the Internet and the oil industry is intended to persuade you that although the content of the Internet business is unique, its form follows historical patterns. This book uses the methods of industrial organization economics to analyze specific Internet business segments. The result is a map that will help investors and managers chart a profitable course through the apparent chaos that is today's world of Internet business.

TARGET AUDIENCE

The value of this book depends on who you are. As we will see further in Chapter One, I wrote this book for people like me. I invest in Internet start-ups, advise managers of Internet businesses on how best to compete, help companies figure out how to use Internet technology to improve their business, and use the Web for research. Given the newness of the Internet in business, I was not too surprised to find that there were no books available that would help me do these things. So I decided to write one.

If you are an investor, this book will help you in two ways. First, it will provide a framework for evaluating potential Internet investments, which I call the Net Profit Retriever. As we will see in Chapter One, this friendly canine helps investors home in on three key issues that help determine whether or not an Internet company is worthy of investment. Second, this book will help you by defining nine mutually exclusive and collectively exhaustive Internet business segments and applying the Net Profit Retriever analysis to these segments. You should finish the book with a keen understanding of specific winners in the nine Internet business segments. More important, you should be comfortable with a method of analysis that you can apply to the world of Internet business as it undergoes its inevitable process of change.

If you are running an Internet business, this book will offer two more benefits. I say two *more* benefits because it is rare to find an Internet business manager who is *not* an investor in his or her own company. The first additional benefit is what I call the Web Business Pyramid. This framework reflects a Darwinian process in which Internet companies either gain ever more economic leverage or are merged out of existence. The Web Business Pyramid offers Internet business managers a way to figure out where they are, where they want to go, and what their strategic options are for getting there. Internet business managers also get the benefit of case studies of companies in related segments and a process for using the case insights to develop effective competitive strategies.

For non-Internet business managers, the book offers another framework: the Web Applications Pyramid. Non-Internet business managers can use this framework to help them assess the costs and benefits of engaging in electronic commerce (e-commerce). The book offers case studies of firms ranging from clothing retailers to the high-tech companies on which the framework is based. The book also describes the vendors of products and services that companies will need to evaluate as they move forward with their e-commerce initiatives.

For the Internet consumer, the book will get beyond the hype about Yahoo and Amazon.com. It will open up a wider world of industries and companies that could present great investment opportunities. The book will also review several services that could offer consumers new ways to shop and do research. Consumers will also find useful techniques for evaluating stocks and Internet services.

ORGANIZATION OF THIS BOOK

Chapter One presents the foundation on which the book is built. The chapter explores some of the remarkable stock market dynamics of Internet companies. It highlights the strategic questions we can use to evaluate the economic underpinnings of these market dynamics. It presents the three conceptual frameworks that we use to answer these strategic questions for investors (Net Profit Retriever), Internet business managers (Web Business Pyramid), and non-Internet business managers (Web Applications Pyramid). It defines the nine Internet business segments that are the focus of this book. Finally, it develops the principles we will use to understand the markets, strategies, and management teams that determine the profit potential of these nine segments.

Chapters Two through Ten explore the nine Internet business segments. Each chapter defines the Internet business segment, analyzes the market and its profit potential, presents case studies, describes the implications for managers, and concludes with a Net Profit Retriever assessment.

The chapters focus on each Internet business segment based on its level in the Web Business Pyramid. Chapters Two through Four analyze the three Powerware businesses; Chapters Five through Eight examine the four Brandware businesses, and Chapters Nine and Ten explore the Lossware businesses. The descriptions that follow include each chapter's unique features.

Chapter Two examines the first of three "Powerware" Internet business segments (those with economic leverage): network infrastructure. It presents cases of the industry leader, Cisco Systems, and a challenger, Nexabit. It describes the strategies and management techniques that keep Cisco at the forefront of this rapidly growing and highly profitable industry, and it traces the rise of Nexabit, whose core product is aimed at the heart of Cisco's success.

Chapter Three scrutinizes the second Powerware segment: Web consulting. The chapter presents a case study of Sapient Corporation, a leading firm in the fixed price/time sector of Web consulting. The case explores how Sapient has historically sustained greater than 60 percent growth by managing smart people, limiting project risk, and acquiring the skills it needs to keep up with the changing needs of its clients.

Chapter Four explores the third Powerware segment: Internet venture capital. It presents an overview of this highly cyclical industry and explores the interplay of forces that drive its fluctuating returns. The chapter presents cases of two very different industry leaders: Kleiner Perkins in Silicon Valley and Sculley Brothers in New York City. These cases focus on such critical capabilities as picking industries, building management teams, managing risk, and structuring investment deals.

Chapter Five presents the first of four "Brandware" Internet business segments (those that are investing to build the dominant brand in their category): Internet security. It begins with a case study that illustrates the importance of Internet security. The chapter shows how CheckPoint Software Technologies and Network Associates are pursuing very different strategies to achieve industry leadership.

Chapter Six presents the second Brandware segment: Web portals. This chapter explores the market forces that drive the extraordinary price fluctuations of many publicly traded Web portals. It describes how Web portals evolved from search engines to gateways into the Web that are designed to attract visitors and advertisers. The chapter presents case studies of Yahoo and Excite that describe the alliances, new services, and management techniques that serve as weapons in the battle for leadership in the Web portal market.

Chapter Seven examines the third Brandware segment: e-commerce. This chapter shows which product categories generate the greatest volume on the Web. It distinguishes between two e-commerce channels— business-to-consumer (b-to-c) and business-to-business (b-to-b)—and explores the five principles that drive their current and anticipated profitability. This chapter illustrates these principles with a b-to-c case in online stock trading and a b-to-b case from Cisco Systems.

Chapter Eight presents the fourth Brandware segment: Web content. This chapter defines three distinct categories of Web content companies. It analyzes the distinct market forces that create such widely varying profitability among the different categories, demonstrating why general technology consultants enjoy economic leverage while some Internet-only content providers are being merged out of existence. This chapter presents cases from each of the categories, profiling the strategies of such firms as CNET, Mecklermedia, CMP Media, International Data Group, Gartner Group, and Forrester Research.

Chapter Nine presents the first of two "Lossware" segments (those segments in which losing money is the first unavoidable step in the struggle up the pyramid): Internet service providers (ISPs). This chapter explores the low entry barriers, intense rivalry, high customer bargaining power, and intense threat of substitutes that shape the current and future low level of ISP industry profitability. This chapter presents cases on AOL, MindSpring, and EarthLink that illustrate the critical importance of customer service and mass marketing to consumers for firms seeking to survive the inevitable shakeout in the ISP industry.

Chapter Ten presents the second Lossware segment: Web commerce tools. It explores the dominant role that Microsoft plays in this segment as it swoops down on companies that take the initiative to create fast-growing new markets. This chapter defines and evaluates four distinct categories of Web commerce tools: browsers, search engines, Web advertising management, and e-commerce enabling software. It presents cases within each category, discussing Netscape, Microsoft, AltaVista, Inktomi, DoubleClick, NetGravity, Sterling Commerce, and Open Market. The chapter describes the implications of these cases for Internet business managers. It concludes by applying the Net Profit Retriever tests to the Web commerce tools segment.

Chapter Eleven applies the concepts developed in Chapters Two through Ten to suggest Internet business opportunities. This chapter reviews the most profitable Internet business opportunities and analyzes the reasons for their profitability. It also looks at unprofitable

Internet businesses to pinpoint what to avoid. The chapter uses the foregoing analysis to develop criteria for screening new Internet business opportunities. It concludes by exploring new businesses in the area of matching employers and employees, asset buyers and sellers, and entrepreneurs and financiers.

Chapter Twelve develops a framework that non-Internet business managers can use to evaluate whether or not to "Webify" their business. This chapter begins by exploding some of the most common myths about e-commerce. It suggests principles based on the positive and negative experiences of companies that have worked with the Web. The chapter uses the Web Applications Pyramid to frame an analysis of the costs and benefits of moving up the pyramid. It presents a ten-step process that managers can use to Webify their business. The chapter presents the case of U.S. Cavalry, a retailer of military uniforms and accessories that migrated from retail stores to paper catalogs to electronic catalogs. This chapter addresses some of the most common challenges that companies face in adopting e-commerce and concludes by suggesting steps that managers can take to benefit from e-commerce.

Chapter Thirteen concludes the book by discussing the implications of the previous chapters for Internet business managers and investors. It recaps the Web Business Pyramid and prescribes the strategic options available to managers as their company progress from Lossware to Brandware to Powerware. The chapter discusses the specific challenges facing Internet business executives and presents a methodology for tailoring competitive strategy. The chapter shifts gears to focus on six rules for Web investing. It suggests tips to help venture capitalists build successful Internet businesses and describes screens that public equity investors can use to select high-return Internet investments. This chapter concludes with a reminder of the importance of economic leverage, closed-loop solutions, and adaptive management to success in the real world of Internet business.

ACKNOWLEDGMENTS

This book could not have been written without the help of many people. I am grateful to all the investment professionals and executives who offered me their views on the topics discussed here, including Jonathan Cohen (Wit Capital); Anthony Ursillo (Loomis Sayles); John Sculley (Sculley Brothers); Roger McNamee (Integral Capital Partners); John

Morgridge, Pete Solvik, Charlie Giancarlo, Doug Allred, Rick Justice, Barbara Beck, and Ed Kozel (all of Cisco Systems); Jerry Greenberg, Nikki Fisher, Chris DeBrusk, Doug Abel, Chris Davey, Anthony Jules, and Christina Luconi (all of Sapient); Ellen Scheibert (Cambridge Technology Partners); Garry Betty (EarthLink); George Bell (Excite); Bob Davis (Lycos); Tim Koogle (Yahoo); Scott Mednick (Think New Thoughts); Joe Firmage (formerly of US Web); Alan Meckler (Mecklermedia); Deborah Rieman (CheckPoint Software Technologies); Bruce Wilson (Cybercash); Chip Mahan (Security First Network); Doug Colbeth (Spyglass); Marc Shinbrood (Axent Technologies); Thomas Noonan (ISS Group); Rob Burgess and Norm Meyrowitz (Macromedia); Jamie Cohan (Andromedia); Warner Blow and Kevin Sibbring (Sterling Commerce); Gail Goodman and Betsy Zekakis (Open Market); and Stratton Sclavos and Richard Yanowitch (VeriSign).

I also appreciate the help of my colleagues Bruce Henderson (Matrix USA), Jeff Coburn (Coburn & Company), Geoff Fenwick (Balanced Scorecard Collaborative), Tom Lynch (Lazard Freres), Eric Stang (ADAC Laboratories), Peter Laino (Monitor Clipper Partners), Jake Wesner (Perot Investments), Mordechai Fester (Cisco Systems), Jay Spahr (BankBoston), Ken Smith, and Howard Seibel. I am very grateful to Cedric Crocker, Julianna Gustafson, and Byron Schneider of Jossey-Bass for their support and encouragement throughout this project. Without Alan Venable's brilliant editing, this book would not have been possible.

Finally, I would like to offer special thanks to my wife, Robin, who patiently tolerated the seemingly endless weekends of writing and revisions.

Marlborough, Massachusetts   PETER S. COHAN
April 1999

—◇— The Author

Peter S. Cohan is president of Peter S. Cohan & Associates, a management consulting firm. Cohan worked at CSC/Index with James A. Champy, coauthor of *Reengineering the Corporation*, and at the Monitor Company, a strategy consulting firm cofounded by Michael E. Porter of the Harvard Business School. Cohan also worked as an internal consultant in the banking and insurance industries.

Cohan is the author of *The Technology Leaders* (Jossey-Bass, 1997), which was selected by *Management General* as one of the top ten management books of 1997. *Management Today* cited Cohan as one of "the Next Generation of Gurus," and he has been profiled in Stuart Crainer's *Ultimate Book of Business Gurus* (AMACOM, 1998). Cohan is a frequent commentator on high-technology companies for CNBC's *Today's Business* and *The Money Wheel*. Bigtipper.com ranked Cohan 1998's Top Tipper, based on the performance of his CNBC stock recommendations. He has been a guest speaker at *Economist* seminars, *Fortune* conferences, Stanford University's Industry Thought Leaders seminar, Singapore's National Science and Technology Board, and "LeaderTalk" from PBS.

Cohan received an M.B.A. from the Wharton School, did graduate work in computer science at the Massachusetts Institute of Technology, and earned a B.S. in electrical engineering from Swarthmore College. Cohan can be reached via e-mail at Peter-Cohan@msn.com.

Net Profit

CHAPTER ONE

Net Profit

_~m~_ **I**f your stockbroker called and tried to sell you stock in a company with $48 million in sales and $144 million in net losses, how would you react? If the broker told you that the market was valuing the company at 344 times the most recent year's sales, would you buy? If he claimed that the company's stock had increased 880 percent since its initial public offering, would you believe him?

WOULD YOU LIKE TO BUY
THE BROOKLYN BRIDGE?

There was a company with those numbers recently, and it's not all that extreme an example—for an Internet business. The company is called At Home. At Home connects consumers and businesses to the Internet via the cable TV infrastructure. As of December 30, 1998, At Home had partnerships with eighteen cable systems. Through these partnerships, At Home had potential access to thirteen million homes; that's how many homes there are with the cable TV infrastructure that is needed to use At Home's service. However, as of December 30, 1998, At Home served only 331,000 cable modem subscribers across North

America, an overall penetration of 2.5 percent. At Home's business has since evolved due to AT&T's acquisition of its parent, TCI. Subsequently, At Home acquired Excite, a Web portal, which we will examine in Chapter Six.

How can a company like this be worth over $16.5 billion? Analysts who favor the stock would argue that At Home's subscriber base had quintupled and that its revenues were up fivefold in 1998. The analysts would point out that At Home's business model was unusually defensible thanks to its partnerships with cable systems that would give At Home a lock on potentially tens of millions of homes to which it could sell a myriad of interactive services.

More skeptical analysts would point out flaws in this logic. The skeptics would argue that At Home was spending hundreds of millions of dollars to add tens of thousands of subscribers, a woefully inefficient means of adding to revenues. Furthermore, the skeptics would point out that At Home faced a formidable array of competitors. The 50 percent of U.S. homes with PCs already have an Internet connection. Although At Home's service was faster, it was also more expensive and would require many subscribers to incur the costs and inconveniences of switching from their existing e-mail systems.

IS THE INTERNET A WEB OF ILLUSIONS?

The At Home case raises many fundamental questions about Internet businesses. How big is the market, really, for At Home's services? Who are At Home's real competitors? Do At Home's target customers perceive that its services offer a much better value proposition than those of competitors? How well does At Home's strategy defend it from competitors, such as "traditional" Internet service providers (for example, AOL), long distance and local telephone companies, and potentially others (such as satellite service providers)? How well can At Home's management team deal with these questions? And how can At Home's stock market valuation be justified?

In my work, I think about these kinds of issues from four different yet related perspectives. As an investor in private and public Internet companies, I need to evaluate these kinds of issues before deciding whether or not to invest. As an adviser to Internet business managers, I base my strategy recommendations on these kinds of issues. As a consultant to non-Internet business managers who may want to "Webify" their business, I need to understand these kinds of issues from the perspective of a potential customer. And as an Internet user, I want to understand these kinds of issues to help pick the best Web services.

To help others understand Internet business from these four perspectives (the investor, the Internet business manager, the non-Internet business manager, and the consumer), I decided to write a book that would address six key Internet business issues:

1. What are the Internet business segments? What industries has the Internet spawned? This book will be discussing businesses that supply the working tools, infrastructure, and funding and management of the Internet; other businesses that let people connect to the Web; and still other firms who provide services over the Web or use it to conduct transactions. We'll see how these and other different Internet industry segments affect one another.

2. Which Internet business segments are profitable now? Which are likely to be profitable in the future? Which are likely never to be profitable?

3. What are the most important forces that drive the current and future profitability of these Internet business segments?

4. What strategies do the leading companies in these Internet business segments follow?

5. How can the stock market valuations of companies in these Internet business segments be explained?

6. What are the implications of these findings for investors, Internet business managers, non-Internet business managers, and Internet consumers?

To answer these questions, I embarked on a three-pronged research program. First, I interviewed the CEOs, key executives, and important customers of scores of public and privately held Internet-related companies. Second, I spoke with Internet business experts, including Wall Street analysts, institutional investors, professors, and management consultants. Third, I analyzed publicly available information on Internet business, including articles from general business publications, trade magazines, Web-based information sources, and financial filings with the Securities and Exchange Commission (SEC).

As I researched the book, I developed several frameworks to help the investor, the Internet business manager, the non-Internet business manager, and the consumer address the aforementioned six business issues. These frameworks helped me evaluate Internet investments, analyze Internet business strategies, and decide how the Web can best be used to improve non-Internet businesses.

FRAMEWORKS FOR ASSESSING INTERNET BUSINESSES

Following are three practical frameworks with which we will make business sense of the Internet. The first is aimed mainly at the investor, the second at Internet business managers, the third at non-Internet business managers. But no matter what hat you are wearing, you will probably find that all three frameworks enlarge your Internet business understanding. Even if you are simply someone who wants to understand the Internet as an important new aspect of American culture, you will benefit from understanding these frameworks. I call them

- The Net Profit Retriever
- The Web Business Pyramid
- The Web Applications Pyramid

The Net Profit Retriever

They say that if you want a friend on Wall Street, get a dog. Many Wall Street tycoons own Golden Retrievers. To invest in Internet companies, we need a *Net Profit* Retriever.

The Net Profit Retriever can put its nose to the ground and sniff out Net profits. Figure 1.1 shows how the Net Profit Retriever does its job. The Net Profit Retriever works like a finely tuned investment filter. Put any Internet company in front of it, and The Net Profit Retriever will tell you whether the company is likely to be a good long-term investment.

The Net Profit Retriever has a particularly sensitive nose for sniffing out good Internet companies. Instead of the normal number of nostrils, it has three. One nostril sniffs for the industry, the second for the company's strategy, and the third for its management. If the scents of all three are right, the Net Profit Retriever barks three times to tell you that the company is a worthy investment.

What exactly does it take to get the Net Profit Retriever to bark three times? First, the Internet company must be competing in an

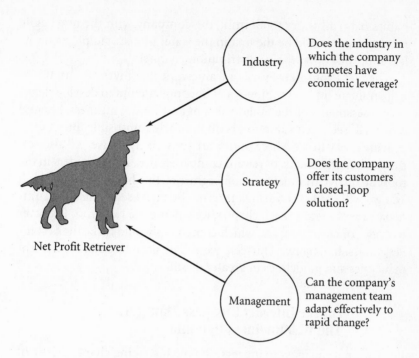

Figure 1.1.   The Net Profit Retriever.

industry with economic leverage. Economic leverage means that the companies in the industry sell a product that is so important to its customers and in such scarce supply that these companies can charge a very high price. If an industry comprising ten companies controlled all the world's water supply, that industry would have virtually unlimited economic leverage.

Second, the company should offer its customers a closed-loop solution. A closed-loop solution means that the company provides all the services a customer needs to get the economic benefit for which the customer bought the product or service in the first place. In our fictional water industry, the company that finds the source, purifies the water, pipes it to your home, pulls the glass from the cabinet, drops in the ice cubes, fills it with water, and serves it to you with dinner is offering a closed-loop solution.

Third, the company's management must be able to adapt effectively to rapid change. This ability is particularly important because Internet time is said to be measured in dog years. (Good thing we have a Net Profit Retriever.) If people suddenly decided to change their drinking habits from all water to all milk, the company with the most agile management would be the first in the water industry to plug a limitless supply of milk into its distribution channel.

The Net Profit Retriever is a framework that investors can use to help evaluate Internet businesses. It does not attempt to develop definitive assessments of the dollar value of an Internet business, because as we will see, such valuation is often nearly impossible. But it does provide a way to see where profits are most likely. As we will also see, the stock market tends to reward companies that are the leaders in the most attractive Internet business segments. In Chapters Two through Ten we will study the various Internet business segments; in a summary near the end of each chapter, we will use the Net Profit Retriever to draw conclusions about which companies would make the best investments. In Chapter Thirteen, we will explore Internet investment principles and guidelines in greater depth.

For the Internet Business Manager: The Web Business Pyramid

For Internet business managers, the most striking characteristic of Web businesses is the rapid pace of change. Internet business managers need a framework that can help them think about where their company should head and how it should get there. Investors should take note also, so that they understand where their investments are headed. The Web Business Pyramid, depicted in Figure 1.2, is such a framework.

The pyramid shape implies a process of aspiration and attrition. Most Web businesses start out at the bottom of the pyramid. Few survivors make it to the top.

LEVEL I: LOSSWARE. Lossware refers to Web businesses that are destined to lose money. At this level, barriers to entry are very low; that is, it is easy for new firms to enter the market. Customers have no switching costs, meaning that it is easy for them to take their business elsewhere. Vendors spend virtually all their money in what seems like an unending loop of marketing and other expenses. The result of the spending is most often competitive parity, not competitive advantage. Many firms do not survive this level. In fact, there may even be some whole segments of the industry that do not survive this level.

One such industry segment, which we will explore in Chapter Ten, is the Web browser business. Web browsers let people navigate the

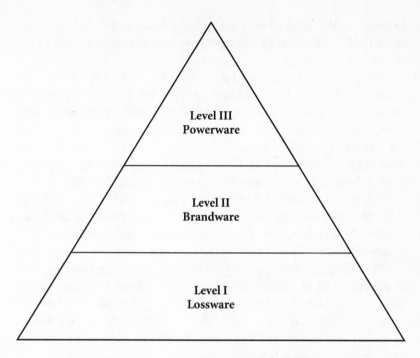

Figure 1.2. The Web Business Pyramid.

Internet. In the early 1990s, browser technology was widely available. To create new Web browsers required only a few programmers. Netscape was the first to achieve dramatic commercial success with the browser. However, there were few barriers to entry. Microsoft built a competing product and gave it away for free. The Web browser business effectively ceased to exist. Its entire cost of development and marketing became a marketing giveaway, and nothing remained that could be used to earn revenues.

LEVEL II: BRANDWARE. Brandware is a group of businesses that have the potential to be profitable if the most heavily promoted brand survives and the weaker ones fold. In Brandware businesses, the industry is still highly fragmented, implying that the cost of entry is quite low. However, in Brandware businesses it is becoming clear that customers are really not interested in sifting through the offerings of seventy different vendors. Customers tend to buy from whichever vendor has the most compelling marketing message. Customers also want to buy from a vendor that is likely to survive the inevitable industry consolidation.

Inherent in this level of the pyramid is the notion of a shakeout. By definition, fewer vendors will survive to climb to the top level of the pyramid.

Web portals, to be discussed in Chapter Six, exemplify a Brandware business. Yahoo is a familiar example. This industry segment started off as a few companies trying to simplify the Web's massive complexity by providing users with a site that would help them search the Web for various content. Web portal firms started generally as search engine firms. Like the Web browser firms, search engine firms gave away the service for free. In short, Web portals started off as Lossware.

Web portals evolved into Brandware because it became clear that there was the potential to get companies to advertise on them. Managers of the search engine companies recognized that the value of their business increased in relation to the number of visitors to their Web site. So the companies began trying to create switching costs between themselves and advertisers and site visitors. These efforts, including chat sites, personalization, news, shopping, and a host of other services, were intended to get visitors to spend enough time at the sites to make them attractive targets for advertisers. Thus arose the idea that Web portals are brandable.

However, Web portals are expensive to maintain. Fierce competition for visitors and advertising has forced a few of the smaller players to sell out to media companies with deep pockets. It is possible that a small number of large Web portals will survive. And because these survivors may "control" access to large numbers of visitors whose tastes and interests are well understood, they may be able to achieve economic leverage over advertisers.

LEVEL III: POWERWARE. Powerware refers to businesses that generate consistently high returns. Powerware businesses enjoy economic leverage and offer customers closed-loop solutions. The economic leverage comes from offering a valuable product or service that is in scarce supply because most competitors have been squeezed out; and the closed-loop solution is delivered to raise the switching costs between vendors and customers to such a high level that new entrants are effectively locked out.

In some cases, Brandware evolved into Powerware. Such an evolution has occurred in venture capital, as Chapter Four explains. Originally, the venture capital industry consisted of a fairly small number of firms. The ones that made winning investments tended to emerge as survivors when pension funds and endowments came along to make the next round of investments.

Internet venture capital firms help build Internet companies by providing capital, hiring management teams, and gaining access to the public equity markets. Venture capital firms have used their own willingness to risk capital in start-up companies and the cyclical nature of capital markets as levers to grab control over two additional elements of economic value creation: management talent and access to premier underwriters. As a result of this control, leading venture firms have powerful economic leverage.

Chapters Two through Ten are organized using the Web Business Pyramid framework. These chapters analyze the evolving profit dynamics of the Internet business segments and explore the requirements for competitive success in each. Chapter Thirteen takes the framework further, showing how competitive strategies evolve as a firm progresses up the pyramid.

For Non-Internet Business Managers: The Web Applications Pyramid

For non-Internet business managers, the most important challenge is to understand the incremental costs and benefits of moving their business to the Web. Non-Internet business managers need a framework that can help them evaluate these costs and benefits depending on their company's current level of "Webification" and its business objectives. The Web Applications Pyramid, depicted in Figure 1.3, is such a framework.

Many companies are in the Level I, online brochure stage. They put product literature, annual reports, and other information traditionally in print form on their Web site.

Some companies have begun to use the Web as a means of collecting order forms. The order information gathered via the Web is then printed out and used as an input into an unchanged order fulfillment process. Because these companies do not integrate the ordering information into their back-end processes, they are at Level II, front-end transaction applications.

Whereas many companies have implemented applications near the base of the pyramid, very few companies have built the kinds of applications that are at the top. It is rare for a firm to start with Level III. More often, firms work their way up through the levels. They learn

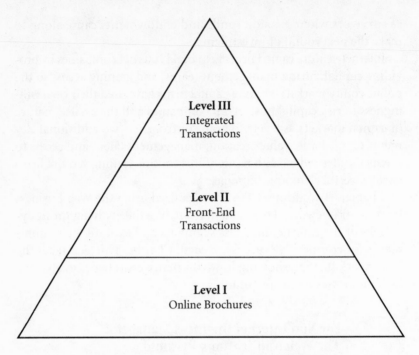

Figure 1.3.   The Web Applications Pyramid.

important corporate lessons at each level that enable them to perform more effectively when they move up.

As we will see in Chapter Seven, a few companies, such as Dell and Cisco, have installed integrated transaction applications that tap into the full power of the Web. For example, these applications use the Web to exchange information with customers. The information is tightly linked with the internal operations of the company. These applications are referred to as Level III, integrated applications.

This framework is developed fully in Chapter Twelve, which helps the non-Internet business manager focus on how best to use these Web applications to improve his or her business performance.

NINE INTERNET BUSINESS SEGMENTS

An Internet business is a company that derives some or all of its revenues through the Internet. From my research, I have concluded that there are nine Internet business segments, each of which is a distinct industry with unique competitors, customers, profit dynamics, and requirements for competitive success. The nine Internet business segments are

1. Network infrastructure
2. Web consulting
3. Internet venture capital
4. Internet security
5. Web portals
6. Electronic commerce
7. Web content
8. Internet service providers
9. Web commerce tools

Let's define each of these Internet business segments in turn.

Network Infrastructure

Network infrastructure is the hardware that directs traffic over the Internet. It consists mainly of devices called routers, switches, hubs, bridges, and network interface cards. Vendors of this equipment include Cisco Systems, 3Com, Ascend (now part of Lucent Technologies), Cabletron, Network Equipment Technologies, Fore Systems, and Bay Networks (now part of Nortel Networks).

Web Consulting

Web consulting firms help organizations use the Web to improve their competitive positions. They accomplish this, first, by working with client executives to understand their business objectives. Then the Web consultants design and implement Web-based systems that help the clients achieve their objectives. Web consultants include Sapient, Cambridge Technology Partners, and US Web.

Internet Venture Capital

Internet venture capital firms provide capital, recruit managers, and help grow Internet companies so that they can go public and generate high investment returns. Internet venture capital firms include Kleiner Perkins, Integral Capital Partners, Institutional Venture Partners, and Sculley Brothers.

Internet Security

Internet security firms provide software and services that help protect organizations' information networks from unauthorized intrusion and tampering. They accomplish this by providing such services as ethical hacking, in which an authorized individual attempts to break into a firm's information network to identify security weaknesses. Internet security firms also sell a variety of software products that are designed to plug such weaknesses. Internet security firms include CheckPoint Software Technologies, Network Associates, Axent Technologies, and Security Dynamics.

Web Portals

Web portals give Internet visitors a place to begin their exploration of the Internet. They do this by offering search engines, e-mail, information services, chat, and other services. Some firms in this segment are attempting to make the Web their primary mode of transaction. Others are adding Web channels to existing conventional modes of business. Web portals seek to attract as many visitors as possible so that companies will view the Web portal as an attractive place to advertise. Web portals include Yahoo, Excite, Lycos, and Infoseek.

Electronic Commerce

Electronic commerce (e-commerce) is the selling of products and services using the Internet. E-commerce firms let people trade securities, buy books and CDs, purchase computer hardware and software, obtain air tickets, reserve hotels, conduct online auctions, and purchase many other products and services. E-commerce firms include E-Trade Group, Amazon.com, Travelocity, eBay, Onsale, and Peapod.

Web Content

Web content firms produce news about and analysis of the Internet. They hire reporters and consultants who collect information about the Internet, and transmit the Internet-related information and analysis through a variety of media, including magazines, newspapers, TV, radio, trade shows, and the Internet itself. Most Web content firms also produce content about other technologies besides the Web. Web content firms include Mecklermedia (now part of Penton Media), CNET, Gartner Group, Ziff-Davis, and CMP Media.

Internet Service Providers

Internet service providers (ISPs) provide individuals and organizations with connections to the Internet, using a variety of media that includes telephone wires, cable TV, regular TV, and eventually low earth orbiting (LEO) satellite networks. ISPs include Earthlink, Microsoft Network, Prodigy, At Home, and MindSpring.

Web Commerce Tools

Web commerce tools help organizations conduct business over the Web. These tools include advertising management services and software, Web browsers, multimedia broadcast tools, search engines, and online catalogue software. Web commerce tool vendors include DoubleClick, NetGravity, Andromedia, Netscape, Macromedia, Inktomi, Sterling Commerce, and Open Market.

PRINCIPLES OF NET PROFIT

Subsequent chapters will delve into the details of each of these Internet business segments. Here, let's preview some important themes and principles that will emerge. As the Net Profit Retriever suggests, a successful Internet company is likely to be one that satisfies three basic criteria: positioning within a leverage-point industry; a strategy that delivers a closed-loop solution to customers; and management that adapts well to change. The following principles are grouped within those three broad concepts.

Profit Drivers and Leverage

Here are seven ways that the Internet changes industry structure:

1. *The Internet is an n-to-n, not a broadcast, medium.* The Internet is evolving as a mass medium like TV, radio, or newspapers. However, whereas TV, radio, and newspapers are primarily one-to-n (one speaking to many) broadcast media, the Internet is an n-to-n (many

speaking to many) medium. This means that every person connected to the Web can be both a source and a receiver of content from others on the Web. More important, this difference in network topology reflects a more fundamental difference in its view of human behavior. In a broadcast medium, people are more passive recipients of content. In an n-to-n medium, people contribute to the content and therefore exert more control over it. This control increases the bargaining power of buyers, thereby reducing the profitability of the supplier.

2. *Internet buyers behave differently than buyers influenced by other media.* People who buy goods via the Internet are much less susceptible to being "sold" by vendors. Internet buyers are self-directed. They decide that they want to make a purchase and use the Internet to collect information. This information arms them so that they can make a better deal for themselves than they would have otherwise. Better buyer information also increases the bargaining power of buyers and cuts into the supplier's profitability.

3. *Customers who purchase over the Internet are loyal to their own interests.* Jupiter Communications, a research firm, estimates that the turnover of customers who visit the more popular Internet sites, such as Yahoo and Excite, is roughly 10 percent *per month* ("The Jupiter/ NFO . . . ," 1998). This exceptionally high level of customer churn makes it very difficult to build customer loyalty, and therefore an ongoing battle rages between Web portals and Internet users. Web portals spend heavily on marketing to attract Internet users. Internet users are always seeking better sources of information to give them an advantage in their negotiations. This dynamic reduces a supplier's profits.

4. *Barriers to entry are very low in most segments.* In most Internet business segments, there are more vendors than the market can support. For example, there are roughly forty-five hundred ISPs in the United States alone. To get into the business, the capital and technical requirements are very limited. To *stay* in the business, however, the marketing and sales expenses are very high, and the prices that an ISP can charge are often capped at about $20 per month. Only the network infrastructure segment has very high barriers to entry.

5. *Mobility barriers are also low in most segments.* For every strategy that seems to be working, there are very few ways to keep competitors from copying the strategy almost instantly. For example, Web portals such as Yahoo, Excite, and Lycos all adopted a strategy of mak-

ing it easy for visitors to personalize their Web sites in early 1998. This feature let visitors pick the specific stock prices and news categories they wished to see when they visited the Web portal. The success of this feature for one vendor prompted the others to copy it within a very short period of time.

6. *It is more profitable for Internet businesses to serve organizations than individuals.* Consumers use the Internet to collect information that gives them a better deal, thereby pressuring the suppliers' profits. Companies are more profitable customers because they move more slowly than consumers. Companies would rather create a standing purchasing process one time than reconsider and renegotiate every time they place a new order for the product or service. Companies therefore tend to take a long time making the initial purchase decision for a new type of product; they then attempt to standardize their own processes around the product or service of the winning supplier. Even when a new technology comes along, they are reluctant to switch suppliers.

7. *Giving away products and services to build market share is a common strategy.* The Internet started off as a government project. As such, the culture of the Internet evolved under the assumption that the Internet would always be sustained by a source of funds other than commercial profit. As a result of this culture, the Internet continues to harbor a certain anticommercial bias. This bias is reflected in the very low prices that are charged for software and information that is available over the Internet. In most cases, software and information are given away or sold cheaply as a means of establishing a commanding brand presence as quickly as possible.

The effectiveness of this strategy depends on whether it leads to customer lock-in. Customer lock-in takes place when a vendor of a new technology is able to encourage most early adopters to use the product at the beginning of its life cycle. If the product wins a large share of the early adopters, the rest of the market will also be forced to adopt that product in order to interact with the early adopters.

If a firm can give away its product to establish market leadership and subsequently leverage that leadership position into a profitable business, then the strategy makes economic sense. However, if the leadership position is eroded by another competitor who imitates the strategy and leverages its marketing clout to take away the first firm's market leadership, then the giveaway strategy fails.

Strategies Favoring Closed-Loop Success

Here are five strategies for achieving closed-loop success:

1. *Start with the market, not the technology.* The biggest problem with many high-tech firms is that their leaders fall in love with technology and lose sight of the market. This is no less true of Internet business executives. The winning firms are looking first at the market to see whether potential revenues can be large enough to justify an investment. The challenge in many Internet markets is that although current revenues may be rather small, rapid growth rates and compelling market trends may yield a big market in the foreseeable future.

2. *Use Web technology to enable a better business process.* Running an ineffective business process on the Web will not make it any better. A successful Web firm is creative about how the Web technology can enable a more effective business process. Amazon is a well-known and compelling example of how Web technology can improve a business process. With one hundred people in a loft in Seattle and no warehouse, the company was able to grab two million book customers in a few years. At the heart of this success was a great idea about how the Web could provide a much better way for people to buy books. Amazon embodied a radical concept of how a book distributor could strip away non-value-added costs without subtracting from the value to customers.

3. *Raise switching costs.* Look for customers who have an incentive to keep coming back to one vendor. Find as many ways as possible to keep those customers coming back to your company. As we will see in Chapter Two, Cisco Systems has built a Web-based system that creates many tight linkages with its customers. One part of the system lets customers solve their own customer service problems. Another part lets customers buy network equipment without human intervention. Another lets them check the status of the manufacturing, delivery, and payment.

4. *Build barriers to entry.* Amazon has built formidable barriers to entry into its segment of selling books over the Web. Barnes & Noble (B&N) has built a Web site in an attempt to leverage its big brand in the "bricks and mortar" part of the business. But B&N will not be able to lower its cost base to that of Amazon. Amazon has made tremendous use of its first-mover advantages. But, as we will see in Chapter Seven, B&N struck back in November 1998 by acquiring Amazon's book supplier, Ingram Book Group.

5. *Partner to get the capabilities needed to close loops.* At Home's phenomenal market capitalization was based mostly on the value of its eighteen partnerships that gave it potential access to ten million captive customers. The stock market was valuing each dollar of 1998 revenues at $344 of market capitalization. Without the partnerships, At Home would be a technology with no apparent access to customers.

Principles of Adaptive Management

Here are five management principles that are critical for surviving the rapid changes in the world of Internet business:

1. *Be paranoid.* The biggest threat to an Internet business often comes from within. Management complacency is particularly threatening to firms with market leadership in profitable segments. Unless management has specific mechanisms in place to counter such complacency, there is a real danger that a new technology can quickly erode an incumbent's lead. As we will see in Chapter Two, Cisco Systems has created such mechanisms.

2. *Make the customer the firm's magnetic North Pole.* As we will see in our discussion of CheckPoint in Chapter Five, the survival of an Internet firm depends on the firm's maintaining constant contact with customers. This does not mean that customers dictate the strategic direction of the firm. It does mean that the firm must lead its customers while adapting to customer feedback regarding the firm's strategic direction. If a firm does not track its customers' spending patterns, it is almost guaranteed to bet wrong on its future strategic direction. One way to make everyone in the company care about customers is to link a big chunk of employee compensation to improvement in independently administered customer satisfaction survey scores.

3. *Managing growth depends on hiring and retaining smart people.* As we will see in our discussion of Sapient in Chapter Three and Yahoo in Chapter Six, an Internet firm can only keep up with incredibly rapid growth if it is able to attract, retain, and maximize the productivity of a large number of smart people. Internet companies with work environments in which smart people thrive are the ones best positioned to sustain market leadership.

4. *Banish the not-invented-here syndrome.* As we will see in our discussion of Cisco Systems in Chapter Two and Yahoo in Chapter Six, an Internet firm cannot simultaneously lead its market and invent all its technologies in its own research lab. Many new technologies are invented outside the firm. An Internet business therefore has a choice: it can wait until its own research lab can come up with a better version of the technology, or it can license or acquire the latest technologies that its customers want to buy. The winners don't stand on ceremony; they get the technologies that customers want to buy—before their competitors can gain a foothold.

5. *Be prepared to reinvent the company.* As we will see in our discussion of Spyglass and Netscape in Chapter Ten, an Internet firm must be prepared to completely reinvent its business model. What looked like a good business can quickly become a money pit if competitors like Microsoft decide they want a piece of it. Internet business managers who are able to think up and implement credible contingency plans have a much greater chance of surviving in the Darwinian world of Internet business. As Netscape's experience demonstrates, reinventing a company does not *ensure* its survival.

OVERVIEW OF THE BOOK

Figure 1.4 shows how each of the nine Internet business segments fits within the Web Business Pyramid. Chapters Two, Three, and Four analyze the Powerware segments: network infrastructure, Web consulting, and Internet venture capital. Chapters Four, Five, Six, and Seven evaluate the Brandware segments: Internet security, Web portals, e-commerce, and Web content. Chapters Nine and Ten assess the Lossware segments: Internet service providers (ISPs) and Web commerce tools.

As we will see, a Lossware business can become a Brandware business fairly quickly. Thus we use these categorizations to help organize the chapters rather than to draw permanent conclusions about the economic fate of specific companies in the segments.

Chapter Eleven recaps important principles and develops ideas for new businesses that are likely to be spawned as a result of the Internet. Chapter Twelve develops the Web Applications Pyramid further as a way to help non-Internet business managers assess how best to use the Web. Chapter Thirteen elaborates on how firms can move up the Powerware pyramid and goes into more detail about private and public equity investing. Welcome to the world of Net profit!

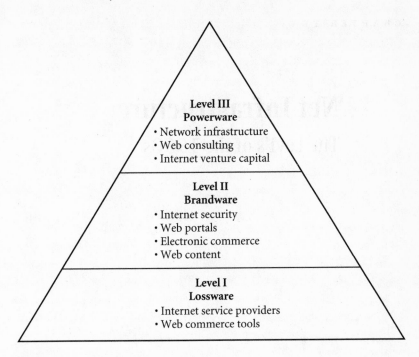

Level III
Powerware
• Network infrastructure
• Web consulting
• Internet venture capital

Level II
Brandware
• Internet security
• Web portals
• Electronic commerce
• Web content

Level I
Lossware
• Internet service providers
• Web commerce tools

Figure 1.4.   Internet Business Segments and the Web Business Pyramid.

CHAPTER TWO

Net Infrastructure
The Levi's of the 1990s

T his chapter analyzes the most profitable of the Internet business segments: the design, manufacture, and distribution of network infrastructure. It assesses the size, growth rate, and profitability of this segment and explores why this segment is so profitable and likely to remain so. The chapter describes how the most profitable company in the segment, Cisco Systems, sustains its superior performance. We compare Cisco's strategy with that of Nexabit, a privately held firm that is launching an attack on the core of Cisco's technological stronghold. The chapter presents four tests for finding a start-up infrastructure company that is likely to be a good investment, and the Net Profit Retriever assesses the network infrastructure segment.

GOLD IN THE HILLS

In the 1850s, California was a popular destination for adventurous Americans. The reason? Gold. Or at least reports of gold discoveries that filtered back East. One thing is clear: although the telephone had not yet been invented, the principle behind the children's game of telephone certainly was operating here. In telephone, a group of, say, ten children line up. The first child whispers a phrase in the second one's ear. The second child passes the message on to the third, and so on. Finally, the tenth child receives the message and announces it to the rest. Invariably, the first child's message has been hopelessly garbled by the time it arrives at the tenth child.

By the time the reports of gold in California reached back to the East, they were wildly exaggerated. The result was that swarms of prospectors found their way to California, and most of them went broke. Many used up their money on picks, shovels, maps, and mules. In the end, the ones who made the money were not the prospectors but the suppliers of their needs. This is how Levi Strauss got started.

Fast-forward to 1998. The state-of-the-art in economic hype is yet again emerging from California. When asked about Internet hype, a leading venture capitalist says that if anything, the Internet is under-hyped. Of course, this venture capitalist has made billions of dollars off the Internet. He picked the right business plan, and he provided capital, a management team, a sense of urgency, and access to the underwriters of initial public offerings. It is not difficult to see why he is so enthusiastic. How has he made billions? He's selling the Levi's of the 1990s.

If a firm wants to be part of the Internet, it needs network infrastructure. Network infrastructure is not very exciting for the average person, but it is exciting to the investor who was lucky enough to invest in it at the beginning. For example, if you had purchased Cisco Systems stock when it first went public in 1990, your investment would be up by more than 50,000 percent, adjusted for eight stock splits between 1990 and February 1999. Even in 1999, investment in network infrastructure offers a reasonably attractive and predictable return, although perhaps not as attractive as at the beginning of the decade.

OVERVIEW OF THE NETWORK INFRASTRUCTURE MARKET

To understand the market for Web infrastructure, it helps to know a bit about networks. Think about a university. It has different academic departments. For example, it might have a computer science department and a business department. Each department might need to register students, record grades, keep track of a payroll for its professors, and send out student transcripts. To do these things, the department might have a number of PCs connected together, with some data stored on individual PCs and other data on servers. The department might have these computers connected in a local area network (LAN).

But what would happen if one department wanted to send a file to another department? For example, if a student in the computer science department were applying to the M.B.A. program, the administrator in the computer science department might be authorized to send a record of the student's transcript electronically to the business school. And what if, in trying to send that file, there were a small technical problem? What if the computer science department used a different kind of network than that of the business school?

There are a number of potential solutions to the problem. One solution is to make every department change its computer networks so that all departments use the same network for sending data across departments. Another solution is to invent a machine that can translate from one network to another.

Such a device—the router—was invented over ten years ago. The router is a leverage-point technology for the network infrastructure market. Now the router is the basis for the network equipment industry, of which network infrastructure is a big component. According to Cahners In-Stat Group (1998), the network equipment industry reached $26.5 billion in 1997 and grew to $30.8 billion by the end of 1998. This 16 percent growth represents a slowing of the 30 to 50 percent growth rates that the industry has enjoyed over the last ten years. The industry not only has been growing fast but also has been a very profitable place to do business. The average return on equity for industry participants exceeds 30 percent, among the highest in American industry.

The network equipment industry consists of two key product categories: central control devices and edge connectors. Central control devices are stacks of computer hardware boxes bundled with software; they cost anywhere between $10,000 and hundreds of thousands of dollars. One type of central control device is a router that connects LANs within an organization and connects wide area networks (WANs)—a larger networks of LANs—across the campuses of large organizations. Routers analyze packets of information and figure out the fastest way to send the information to its destination. Routers can also send packets of information among networks that use different network protocols.

Alternative forms of central control devices include switches, hubs, and bridges. Of these devices, switches have proven to be the most significant market. Switches are generally used to connect the LANs within an organization's network. Switches have most of their intelligence in specialized computer chips that enable the switches to work much faster and to cost less than routers; switches generally cost from several thousand to a few tens of thousands of dollars per device. Central control equipment is used by large and small organizations, telecommunications companies, and ISPs.

Edge connectors are installed inside PCs, laptop computers, printers, and other devices to connect them to an organization's network. The most common type of edge connectors are network interface cards (NICs). NICs are rectangular in shape, contain maybe ten computer chips, are about as big as an adult's hand, and cost a few hundred dollars. NICs represent a very large market with a low profit margin. Any device that seeks access to a larger network will need some kind of edge connector.

The Internet infrastructure business is roughly a third of the network equipment market. This segment is attractive because it is growing very fast and is extremely difficult for new competitors to break into. There are four significant competitors dividing up the pie: Cisco Systems, 3Com, Bay Networks (now Nortel), and Cabletron.

3Com controls the lower-margin edge connector product category; it benefited from its June 1997 acquisition of modem maker U.S. Robotics. Cisco Systems controls the higher-margin central control devices. Bay Networks and Cabletron are second-tier competitors in the central control device product category.

Why are central control devices so profitable? Why are edge connectors unprofitable? How is their profitability likely to evolve?

PROFIT DRIVERS IN THE CENTRAL CONTROL DEVICE PRODUCT CATEGORY

The forces that enhance the profitability of the router and switch business far outweigh the forces eroding it. These forces are likely to continue to support the high profitability of the central control device product category.

Barriers to Entry

The three most significant barriers to entry are technological innovation, access to distribution, and customer switching costs. Firms that offer faster, more reliable, more secure technologies that work with other vendors' products can deter competitors that are unable to deliver comparable levels of technological innovation. The sales force of the leading firm, Cisco, makes it very difficult for competitors to take away Cisco's customers. Cisco's sales force is aided by the technical architecture of its machines, which make it easier for customers to stick with Cisco equipment when they need to expand their networks.

Bargaining Power of Customers

Customers are in a fairly weak bargaining position. As we will see later, the one bargaining chip that customers had during the early history of the router industry was that they could threaten to buy new network equipment that purported to offer faster performance at a lower cost. Cisco was able to mute this source of customer bargaining power through its program of acquiring companies that made the new technology that customers wanted to buy.

Rivalry

Rivalry in this segment was very intense; however, Cisco achieved dominance, and its competitors were weakened in the process. In 1994, two Cisco competitors, SynOptics and Wellfleet, combined to form Bay Networks. At the time, Bay Networks' revenues were roughly 10 percent higher than Cisco's. Four years later, Cisco revenues were three-and-a-half times those of Bay Networks. In 1998, Bay Networks was acquired by Nortel Networks. 3Com has been unable to penetrate the central control device segment, being left with selling devices literally on the margin of the network. Cabletron has been unprofitable and has experienced significant executive turmoil. This intense rivalry has driven out most of the credible competitors.

Two forces could affect the level of rivalry in the future. New companies are likely to develop new technologies that will offer customers better performance at lower costs. Cisco is likely to acquire the best of these technologies and integrate them with its existing operating system.

And as Cisco goes after new markets, such as network devices that can handle voice and data, it will find itself competing more with such firms as Lucent Technologies and Nortel Networks. These competitors are in much better financial condition than were Cisco's earlier rivals. The battle for these new markets could be intensely rivalrous.

PROFIT DRIVERS IN THE EDGE CONNECTOR PRODUCT CATEGORY

The forces that erode the profitability of the edge connector product category are very powerful. These forces are likely to continue to depress the profitability of the edge connector business.

Barriers to Entry

The barriers to entry in the edge connector business are relatively low, and the channels of distribution are indirect and highly fragmented. As a result of this situation, a new entrant with the capital and a product that conforms to industry standards can gain access to distribution. Nevertheless, edge connector customers and distributors prefer to deal with companies that offer good service and support. Therefore, these customers and distributors prefer to deal with well-regarded vendors such as U.S. Robotics, a company that 3Com acquired in 1997. Although barriers to entry are not very significant, a reputation for good service and support is important for a firm seeking to survive over the long term in the edge connector product category.

Bargaining Power of Customers

There are many different vendors of edge connectors that conform to industry standards. Furthermore, these devices are quite inexpensive and are subject to volume discounts. Bargaining power between vendors and customers is clearly tilted toward the customer.

Rivalry

Rivalry in this segment is extremely intense. Edge connectors are seen as commodities. Success depends on a firm's managing its supply to minimize unit and inventory carrying costs while providing timely order fulfillment. The firm with the lowest costs can cut prices to gain market share and still leave some room for profit, but this cost-driven battle for market share is likely to keep profits low.

CASES

Cisco Systems: The Best Infrastructure Firm

Let's study the case of Cisco Systems, the obvious model for success in network infrastructure. As we look at Cisco, think about how the

Net Profit Retriever would evaluate Cisco's strategy and management.

Cisco Systems dominates the strongest segment of the network infrastructure business. As we noted earlier, Cisco Systems stock has been a very attractive investment since its initial public offering. More important, the company is likely to continue to dominate a highly profitable and rapidly growing segment, so Cisco Systems could be an attractive investment far into the future. Furthermore, Cisco Systems is an extremely well-managed company. As Cisco's markets change, no company is better positioned to adapt to that change and exploit its profit opportunities.

Cisco thinks of itself as being the leader in the network infrastructure business. Prior to the mid–1990s, when the Internet was primarily a tool used by universities and the government, Cisco thought of itself as being in the business of helping to build networks. As the Internet grew into a popular business tool, Cisco was well positioned to supply the network equipment and services needed to make the Internet work for business.

Cisco is now the leading supplier of network equipment and services to enterprises and ISPs. It sells the hardware and services that large enterprises use to build intranets, extranets, and connections to the Internet. Intranets are networks that people inside an organization access to share information that is proprietary to the company. Extranets link the company to its suppliers and customers.

Understanding the inner workings of Cisco can help investors identify what it takes to create a successful network infrastructure company. Why is Cisco so successful? Cisco dominates a leverage-point industry by offering its customers a closed-loop solution. Cisco got to this point through six sources of advantage. Any firm that can match or outperform Cisco in these activities will have a compelling claim on investors' capital.

1. Learning from failure

2. Building switching costs through interoperability

3. Customer advocacy

4. Acquisitions that add value to customers

5. Aggressive direct sales

6. Hiring and maximizing the productivity of entrepreneurs

LEARNING FROM FAILURE. The most important reason for betting on Cisco's future is that its management team has created an organization that can learn from failure. Cisco's senior executives have personally experienced the most common problems that have beset successful high-technology companies. For example, they have seen how an engineering-driven culture can ignore the needs of customers, thus causing the best salespeople to defect to companies that are making the technology that customers need. Cisco's executives have built an organization that is wired to avoid such mistakes.

According to John Morgridge, Cisco chairman, the salesperson is really the most powerful person in a high-tech company. In Morgridge's experience, the sales force controls the relationship between the corporate customer and the company that makes the equipment that the salesperson is selling. As long as the equipment vendor offers a product that customers want to buy, the sales force can continue to earn their commissions. But if that vendor stops making a product that customers want to buy, the salespeople will decamp to the company that does (John Morgridge, interview with the author, May 1997).

This bit of insight has profound implications for why Cisco Systems has been able to dominate the most profitable segment of the network equipment business. Using this logic, Morgridge was able to break out of a very common way of thinking about managing a high-tech business. Traditionally, high-tech companies believed that the only way to develop new technologies was with their own engineers. If the technology didn't come from that company, it was not going to be good for the customer to buy. A corollary to this reasoning was that a high-tech company would never acquire another high-tech company.

Cisco has gained other useful insights from systematically studying the failures of companies like Wang and Digital in order to identify what went wrong and to develop ways to keep the same things from happening at Cisco. Cisco found that if you go back to every technology company that went bad, you can trace the problem to its inability to listen and properly identify problems. Companies that failed became religious about one technology and one solution.

This theory was put to the test in 1993 when Boeing, one of Cisco's largest customers, told John Chambers, Cisco's CEO, that Boeing was about to place a large order for switches with another vendor. At that point, Cisco made routers and controlled about 80 percent of the router business; it did not make switches. Cisco was the first company to market routers and, as we will see later, used aggressive marketing and customer switching costs to build a dominant position. The conventional wisdom in high-tech would have dictated that Cisco avoid the switch business because it hadn't invented the switch. But Cisco bucked the conventional wisdom.

Morgridge and Chambers realized that Cisco was in danger of going the way of Wang Computer and other East Coast high-tech firms that failed to adapt to changing customer needs. They could see that in some instances, switches could replace routers. They decided they didn't want Cisco to become yet another high-tech company that leaves its sales force with a product line that customers don't want to buy. Although Morgridge and Chambers were not afraid that all of Cisco's customers would stop buying routers, they wanted a way to sell switches to Boeing. So Cisco paid $95 million to buy Crescendo Communications, the company from which Boeing was about to buy the switches. Since then Cisco has made thirty such acquisitions of companies with a variety of technologies.

At the time of the Crescendo acquisition, Cisco had to overcome an internal fear that switches would cannibalize routers. The salespeople needed to be convinced that selling routers and switches was going to be worth their while. Ironically, the customers in this case were ahead of the sales force. And it turned out that the sale of switches ended up creating more demand for routers by increasing the number of LAN networks that needed to be connected via routers. By March 1999, Cisco sold $4.0 billion worth of switches derived from Crescendo and two other switch companies that Cisco acquired. In the end, Cisco customers (through faster, cheaper networks), sales staff (through higher commissions), and shareholders (through more valuable Cisco stock) all won big as a result of the Crescendo acquisition.

Although this discussion highlights other sources of advantage that we will discuss later, it features a higher-order capability: Cisco's ability to learn from failure. It shows how Cisco executives learned from what they believed had caused Wang to fail and took action to keep themselves from going down the same path.

BUILDING SWITCHING COSTS. Another reason that Cisco is able to dominate the market and keep out new entrants is that companies that buy network infrastructure equipment want all the different pieces to work together; they want "interoperability." Whether a company buys different network equipment from different vendors, identical equipment from different vendors, or everything from one vendor, it wants the different pieces to work well together.

Internet technologies go by many different names: Frame Relay, ATM, Fast Ethernet, and FDDI, among others. Without getting into technical detail, we can say that these technologies are all aimed at helping organizations build computer networks that perform well and don't cost too much. To perform well, a network must transmit data fast, must have close to 100 percent uptime, must have very tight security, and must transmit data among different communications protocols. To be cost-effective, a network must have a relatively low total cost. The total cost includes not only the cost of purchasing the network equipment but also the cost of making the new equipment work with the old. Often the latter costs more than the former.

Some technologies, such as Fast Ethernet, may be slower than others, such as ATM, but because they are technically similar to legacy networks built using the earlier Ethernet standard, they may be more cost-effective. Cisco made a conscious decision that it would not try to dictate to customers the technology they should use in their networks. Whereas many Cisco competitors might make products that used ATM technology, for example, Cisco chose to make sure that whatever product a customer used, it would work with other Cisco products in that customer's network.

To achieve this interoperability, Cisco developed a piece of software called Internetwork Operating System (IOS). So for a new competitor to have even a hope of getting into the business, it must develop products that can interoperate with Cisco using standard protocols. Although IOS is open to competing products, it works most efficiently when it is connecting Cisco products.

And if Cisco's relationship with customers and its IOS did not create sufficient switching costs, there is yet a third switching cost. Cisco has trained its customers to pick a vendor that can offer them an "end-to-end solution." Customers dislike constantly repeating an elaborate request for proposal (RFP) process with multiple vendors to pick the best of each piece of networking technology from different vendors and then figuring out how to make all the pieces work together. Cisco's end-to-end, closed-loop approach enables customers to avoid these hassles.

Cisco has trained its customers to want end-to-end solutions and, by offering outstanding customer service, has made it easy for customers to do business with one company—Cisco. End-to-end solutions lead to fewer network breakdowns. CEOs really only notice networks when the networks stop working. Thus, if the end-to-end supplier can really deliver on its commitments, an end-to-end solution offers the network manager the best chance of keeping his or her job.

CUSTOMER ADVOCACY. Customer advocacy is deeply embedded in Cisco's culture. As we saw earlier, many high technology companies are run with the idea that the engineers know what is best for the customer. By contrast, Cisco is run with the belief that the customer is the magnetic north pole of the company. This belief gives Cisco an important advantage.

A brief look at Cisco's early history illustrates the power of customer advocacy. According to *Fortune,* Cisco was founded in 1984 by Leonard Bosack and Sandy Lerner, married, academic administrators at Stanford University. Bosack ran the computers for the Stanford computer science department. Lerner operated the computer system at its business school. The two computer systems were unconnected and unable to communicate with each other or with any of the other computer systems around the Stanford campus (Nocera, 1995).

Bosack and Lerner devised a way to connect the different networks and create one big Stanford network. Bosack developed a crucial innovation: a high-speed, relatively inexpensive "router"; a device that forwards data packets from one computer site to another. Router software allowed the packages to be read by any kind of computer on the network. Since Stanford was funding its own router effort, the university refused to give Bosack and Lerner permission to make routers for Stanford.

Bosack and Lerner took Stanford's refusal as a challenge to start their own company. Bosack and Lerner mortgaged their house for seed capital. They borrowed against their credit cards. Lerner took a job with Schlumberger to support herself and her husband, while also working for Cisco when she could. Friends met in their living room to build routers and write software.

This startup mentality helped to forge Cisco's culture. Cisco is known for its absolute willingness to give customers what they want, rather than what it thinks they should have. Cisco likes to say that it has no religion when it comes to technology. This trait began in Cisco's early days, when customers were mainly friends and peers at other universities who wanted the same kind of networking capability that Stanford had. Customers often worked collaboratively with the Cisco engineers to build these early systems. Lerner placed so much emphasis on keeping customers happy that she established Cisco's customer-support group, calling it the "customer advocacy" group (Nocera, 1995).

Beginning in 1994, Cisco's concept of customer advocacy began to spread to Cisco's use of the Internet to improve customer service and enhance profits. Cisco has used the Internet to achieve great results. For example, in its fiscal 1998, Cisco generated $5.7 billion in revenue, or 67 percent of its total, from transactions conducted via electronic commerce. Furthermore, Cisco estimates that its internally developed Web applications have added over $500 million per year to the firm's profits.

How did Cisco achieve these results? According to Fortune, Cisco's Technical Assistance Center, which provides after-sales service, was Cisco's first department to use the Internet. By 1994 the Technical Assistance Center was unable to hire sufficient staff to keep up with customer service demands. If Cisco could not hire new engineers fast enough or enhance the productivity of its current ones, it would have to reduce its sales of routers and switches (Tully, 1998).

Brad Wright, the center's head, thought that the solution was to automate routine customer service activities on the Internet so that buyers could serve themselves. With the support of Doug Allred, Cisco's Senior Vice President of Customer Advocacy, Wright asked several of his engineers to develop programs that could answer customer questions online. Within ninety days, Wright's team had Web-ified the most frequent questions. The team also created a way for customers to download support software from Cisco's Web site.

The reaction to Wright's system was extremely positive. Many customers began using the Internet to obtain twenty-four-hour service. Calls and faxes to the Center declined. While Cisco's sales increased more than fourfold since 1995, its engineering support staff merely doubled, to eight hundred. Without automated sales support, Cisco estimated it would require over one thousand additional engineers. Cisco estimated savings of $75 million a year from the engineers it did not need to hire. Cisco calculates another $250 million in savings by distributing support software via the Web rather than loading it onto disks and mailing them to customers.

The spirit of customer advocacy resulted in another successful use of the Internet to improve Cisco's ordering process. In early 1995, Linda Thom Rosiak, the newly appointed head of customer service, was concerned about Cisco's ordering process. The source of Rosiak's concern was the time it took to move orders from Cisco's customers to its plants or suppliers.

The delays resulted from the many errors in the orders, which arrived by fax. All Cisco products are custom-built. Each has common elements, including memory, power supply, software, and cables. While Cisco offers choices for each, many of the combinations do not work together. For example, customers often do not chose enough memory to handle their choice of software. Customers also found that the prices for the thirteen thousand parts in Cisco's thick catalogs were not always up-to-date. Forty percent of the orders that Cisco received had the wrong prices or configurations. Cisco's response was to fax the incorrect orders back to the customers. The result was that customer shipments were delayed by weeks as the errors were sorted out. Rosiak realized that putting the sales process on the Internet would eliminate these problems. Customers could complete their projects much faster, and Cisco would avoid the cost of hiring new people to find the errors.

To make her vision a reality, Rosiak worked with Cisco's chief information officer, Peter Solvik. Solvik assigned Rosiak some of his own engineers to design programs that linked customers to Cisco. The first one, called Status Agent, let customers use the Web to track the status of their orders. The next posted the prices of all Cisco products. The third was software that performed online configuration of Cisco products in a customer-friendly fashion.

In 1996, Cisco began offering routers and switches for the first time over its business-to-business Web site, Cisco Connection Online (CCO). Customers click onto a program called Configuration Agent, which walks them through the major components of a router. If they choose the wrong combination of circuit boards, for example, the program notes the error and helps them to make an acceptable choice. Once a workable configuration is selected, its current price appears automatically.

Customers found that CCO makes order processing more efficient. At Sprint it used to take sixty days from the signing of a contract to the completion of a networking project. Due in part to the efficiency of CCO, it now takes thirty-five to forty-five days. Sprint has also been able to reduce the number of people in its order-processing group from twenty-one to six.

Cisco is also saving money on order-processing workers. In the Summer of 1998, Rosiak employed roughly three hundred service agents handling all customer accounts. She estimated that she would need nine hundred without the help of CCO. The difference represents estimated annual savings of $20 million (Tully, 1998).

The notion of customer advocacy extends even to Cisco's Information Systems (I/S) department. In 1991, Cisco's I/S department budget was low, at 0.75 percent of revenue. Adapting the I/S activity to the rapid growth in Cisco's business was a major challenge. As we saw in the case of his collaboration with Rosiak, Pete Solvik allowed all business managers to decide how much they wanted to spend on I/S. This was a major difference in the way that I/S budgeting took place since traditionally, I/S had decided its own budget.

Solvik unleashed the process of investing in technology to help business units put business practices in place. Business unit managers are tied to the success of customers. And the success of the business unit managers depends in part on the success of I/S. Solvik has changed the way I/S works with the business units so that Cisco gets a higher return on its investment in his department (from an interview with Pete Solvik, Chief Information Officer of Cisco Systems, May 1997).

ACQUISITIONS THAT ADD CUSTOMER VALUE. As mentioned earlier, since purchasing Crescendo Communications in 1993, Cisco has made thirty acquisitions. The number of acquisitions and partnerships continues to grow. The primary reason for these acquisitions has been Cisco's desire to provide its customers with the technology solutions they need. Cisco prefers to develop the technology to meet customer needs. However, if another company has developed that technology, Cisco will seek a business partnership to benefit the customer. If neither developing the technology in-house nor partnering to deliver the technology is possible, then Cisco may consider an acquisition.

When Cisco starts to look at potential acquisitions, it considers three issues: (1) How will the potential acquisition fit in with Cisco? (2) What are the advantages and disadvantages of the potential acquisition? and (3) How compatible is the culture of the partner with Cisco's culture? Using Cisco's initial answers to such questions, the company develops a hypothesis about how successful the acquisition will be within Cisco. Cisco tests and refines this hypothesis as the company goes through the acquisition process (Charles Giancarlo, senior vice president of global alliances at Cisco Systems, interview with the author, May 1997).

Cisco has developed five tests to guide its search. First, the acquired management team should share Cisco's vision of the industry. Second, the acquired company's product lines and sales forces should not overlap with Cisco's. Third, the acquired company should be geographically close to Cisco's headquarters. Fourth, the acquisition should create short-term wins, such as an increase in stock price after the announcement of the deal. For example, when Cisco announced the StrataCom acquisition, Cisco's stock price went up 10 percent following the announcement. In contrast, when Ascend, a Cisco competitor, announced its 1997 merger with Cascade, both company's stock prices dropped. Fifth, the products of the acquired company should also create long-term wins. Cisco uses employee retention, new product development, and return on investment to gauge the success of its acquisitions.

Cisco has had tremendous success integrating its acquisitions and therefore enjoys an excellent reputation among companies that are potential acquisition candidates. Cisco employees through acquisition have a very low voluntary attrition rate because Cisco acquisitions are well integrated. In fact, companies that are being pursued in hostile takeovers often see Cisco as a white knight. As a result, Cisco receives calls from companies that are being pursued in these situations.

Cisco's capability with acquisitions suggests three criteria that investors can use to evaluate whether a network infrastructure company, or any Internet company for that matter, is good at acquisitions. First, an investor should check to see if the stock price of the acquirer and the target went up after the announcement of the deal. Second, an investor should assess whether or not the acquired company added to the acquirer's earnings within two years after the deal closed. Third, the investor should talk to industry experts to find out the acquirer's skills at post-merger integration (Giancarlo interview, May 1997).

AGGRESSIVE DIRECT SALES. Direct sales has always been a strategic strength for Cisco. Cisco account representatives listen carefully to customer needs and work closely with engineering or technical support to provide customers the best available solutions. Firms that sell their product through a distributor, instead of directly, lose this flow of information. For example, some competitors in the industry sell indirectly, through such firms as Tech Data or Merisel. These firms do not automatically make the end users' product requirements available to the firm that actually produces the equipment.

According to Rick Justice, a vice president of sales, Cisco's sales force is a strategic factor in Cisco's success because in high-tech markets, the battle is not won in the research labs but on the street. This realization is reflected in the fact that Cisco's chairman, John Morgridge, and CEO, John Chambers, both have backgrounds in sales. In fact, because of their sales backgrounds, they understand what motivates the best salespeople. They realize that the best salespeople are intensely competitive. And to win the battle for high-tech markets, you must compete for the best salespeople (Rick Justice, interview with the author, June 1998).

Through its culture of customer advocacy, Cisco encourages salespeople to stay in constant touch with customers. If the sales force is listening, it will learn critical information from customers—information they need if they are to be successful.

To reinforce the importance of listening to customers, Cisco CEO John Chambers keeps track of how often Cisco executives meet with customers at Cisco's executive briefing center. When client executives come to the center, they listen to presentations by Cisco executives and then give the presentations a rating. John Chambers consistently receives the highest ratings from customers. Because Chambers makes giving these presentations a priority, all the other Cisco executives do so as well. The message that customers receive from this level of executive attention is that their business is important to Cisco, from senior management down.

Cisco's way of working with customers is influenced by John Chambers' business experience. Chambers worked for IBM when it led the world with mainframes. Then IBM lost its lead to minicomputers. Chambers saw the same thing happen again when Wang lost its market in word processors to the PC. In both cases, the leaders lost the formula. They stopped listening to customers. IBM and Wang started thinking that they knew the answers. Cisco knows that if it stops listening to customers, it will meet the same fate. As such, customers come first, even before internal corporate issues. For example, at executive committee meetings, if an immediate problem arises with a customer, an executive may leave the meeting to solve the customer's problem. Although this hampers internal processes at Cisco, it does so while creating a satisfied customer.

At senior staff meetings, the first item on the agenda is a report on critical customer accounts. If a customer is experiencing a network outage, this topic will take precedence over a discussion about revenues and profits. Chambers also receives e-mail and voicemail on the status of critical accounts nightly. This daily involvement with customers sends a message to the rest of the company that if customers are important enough for the CEO, they are important enough for every other person in the company; everyone must listen to customers and respond.

Cisco also knows what motivates the best salespeople: competitive salaries, superior technology, and a respected management team. Cisco pays them a low base salary but a high commission that provides them the opportunity to have the highest cash compensation in the industry based on performance. Cisco differs from other technology companies that are uncomfortable paying salespeople more than engineers or senior executives who are not involved in sales. Cisco realizes that if it spends $1 million to motivate a salesperson who adds $50 million to revenues, the company is enjoying a tremendous return on its investment. Other employees at the company agree with this philosophy, because they recognize that they depend on the sales force to get the order; and because all Cisco employees are stockholders, everybody benefits from the success of the sales force.

Cisco attempts to attract and retain the top 10 percent of the employees in the industry throughout the company. Cisco compensates heavily and interviews exhaustively. The most successful salespeople are fiercely competitive and able to work effectively with people at all levels of the organization, from the engineers to the CEO.

Recently a team of two Cisco account executives built a customer relationship from nothing to $50 million in revenues in twelve months. The account executives visited with the client and realized that given its needs and the state of technology, there was a vast opportunity for the customer to improve its competitiveness. However, the account executives saw that in order to deliver on this opportunity, Cisco would need to change its way of doing business. The account executives presented the opportunity to people inside Cisco and ended up creating a new project management capability to deliver what the client needed. After working twenty-hour days for six months, the account executives were able to close the sale. This success was well publicized inside Cisco, reinforcing the idea that every customer contact by the sales force represents a chance to "win the lottery" (Justice interview, June 1998).

HIRING AND MAXIMIZING THE PRODUCTIVITY OF ENTREPRENEURS. Another great strength of Cisco is its ability to hire entrepreneurs and get them to work very hard on behalf of the company. Along with Microsoft, Cisco is one of the leading proponents of the idea that acquiring a company is a way to hire smart people in bulk.

One example of this approach to "hiring" is Cisco's acquisition of Granite Systems. In November 1996, Cisco paid $220 million to acquire Granite Systems, a forty-person startup founded by Andy Bechtolsheim, one of the original founders of Sun Microsystems. He developed the Sun workstation while studying at Stanford University. He ultimately left Sun with $50 million in stock. Soon thereafter, he founded Granite Systems to develop a computer chip to run a very fast networking technology called Gigabit Ethernet. As the networking industry began to see the opportunity in Gigabit Ethernet, Cisco acted fast to acquire what it perceived to be the leading team in the industry.

Bechtolsheim's Cisco Systems stock is worth several hundred million dollars. Within Cisco, he is a good leader who works 16 hours a day, seven days a week. When asked why he works incredibly long hours, Bechtolsheim gives an unexpected answer. He says he has a personal compulsion to be the first person to get a winning product onto the market just as that market is emerging, and at Cisco he has found the best environment anywhere to support that personal compulsion. At other firms, internal selling might consume six months to make a simple product change. At Cisco, such a change can take a week.

Cisco CEO John Chambers also works exceptionally long work hours. Why? For the excitement, not for the money. Cisco people perceive themselves to be building an industry as important as the telephone network of the late 1800s. The business environment is wild and woolly—like the railroad or telephone industry. It is very exciting to be at the center. It's a different challenge. People enjoy creating something. Cisco people feel that they are creating a whole new industry—the next IBM, the next AT&T. After the new industry is created, many of the Cisco executives will probably go back to a startup that represents the beginning of yet another new industry. But they see their time at Cisco as a once-in-a-lifetime opportunity.

It is this chance to participate in creating the future that makes Cisco such an exciting place for entrepreneurs to work. As long as Cisco continues to create an environment that attracts and motivates such people, Cisco will control much of the supply of talent that otherwise might have helped a competitor.

Nexabit: Router Challenger

Founded in fall 1996, Nexabit is a Massachusetts-based router start-up that presents a potential challenge to Cisco Systems. Backed with $25 million in venture funding from Hambrecht & Quist, Fidelity Ventures, and Microsoft cofounder Paul Allen's Vulcan Ventures, Nexabit has developed a router that the company claims can run one hundred times faster than Cisco's and is priced competitively. Nexabit's router is designed to be used by ISPs that handle the largest and most rapidly growing volumes of high-bandwidth Internet traffic such as videos or color images.

Nexabit's management team has a track record for building high-performing, cost-competitive systems components. Its chairman, Ray Stata, is an MIT graduate who founded Analog Devices, a publicly traded $1.1 billion (1997 sales) manufacturer of application-specific computer chips used for controlling the operation of such products as camcorders. Its CEO, Mukesh Chatter, a networking and telecommunications engineer, started neoRAM before joining Nexabit.

Independent analysts admit that the Nexabit router has not been fully tested, but agree with Chatter's performance claims. For example, according to *Red Herring* (Henig, 1998b), Nexabit has divulged its architecture to David Passmore, an independent consultant with his own firm, NetReference. Although Passmore acknowledges that Nexabit has not proven its software's ability to handle rapid network traffic growth, he notes that neither have router start-ups Avici or Juniper. Passmore says he is comfortable with Nexabit's claim that its product can go one hundred times faster than Cisco's.

Is Nexabit's faster router performance enough to threaten Cisco? Customers and industry experts claim the answer is no. As we noted earlier, customers want to deal with a network infrastructure firm that can offer a system that will help increase their network's speed and reliability. Potential Nexabit customers are large telecommunications firms and ISPs that will test its router in real-world circumstances. These potential customers would also demand that Nexabit deliver excellent technical service in the event of a network service interruption.

For his part, Passmore acknowledges that a firm like AT&T is more likely to trust an established company like Cisco or Lucent. He also points out that Cisco has learned through experience how to tune its products so that they perform well in real-world situations. Ultimately, Passmore suggests that the best technology does not win in the network infrastructure business—marketing and sales win (Henig, 1998b).

Cisco is responding to Nexabit in its usual way: by investing internally and looking outside to evaluate the start-up's capabilities. For Nexabit's part, it is unlikely that it will be able to match Cisco's sales, marketing, and support capabilities. If Cisco decides that Nexabit offers the best high-speed router technology available externally or internally, Cisco will probably acquire Nexabit.

IMPLICATIONS

How can investors profit from the network infrastructure industry? One obvious option is an investment in Cisco Systems. However, there are likely to be other companies in the industry that could constitute even better investments. Many investors are in a position to finance start-ups as angels or as venture capitalists. These investors should look for companies that satisfy the following four tests, which we will apply to Nexabit:

1. *Does the company have a product that is targeted at a large and growing market?* It is crucial for investors in start-up network infrastructure to resist the siren song of the technologists. If it is hard to quantify the size and growth rate of the market into which the start-up's product is to be sold, then stay away. If, as in Nexabit's case, the start-up's product is offering a quantum improvement in the performance of a product that is currently being sold into a big market, go on to the second step.

2. *Has the company's product received positive reviews from independent analysts?* It is positive news for a potential investor if the start-up's managers make positive claims about the product that are verified by independent tests. It is up to the investor to assess whether the tests are measuring product performance variables that are important to customers. However, if the product passes muster in independent tests, the investor should go on to the third step. Nexabit seems to be doing well on this step, although more test results would be helpful.

3. *Does the company have a strong management team that can attract and motivate talented sales and engineering staff?* As we will see in Chapter Four, a big market and a good product are important ingredients to a successful start-up. However, the management team is perhaps the most important. The way to evaluate a management team is to get objective verification of its past performance. Has the CEO actually raised a company from the ground up to $100 million in sales? Has the CEO attracted and retained high-quality sales and engineering people? Do the members of the management team have a record of impeccable integrity? Have the members of the management team demonstrated

their ability to work effectively in teams? Does the CEO have a record of creating an environment in which creative people feel they can work effectively?

If these questions can be answered in the affirmative, then investors should consider getting out their checkbooks. However, given Cisco's power in the network infrastructure industry, investors should consider a fourth test. There is not really enough information available on Nexabit to answer this third question—particularly in the area of sales, marketing, and service.

4. *Could the company's product complement Cisco's product portfolio?* Many start-up companies in the network infrastructure industry end up choosing to be acquired by Cisco instead of going public and competing with Cisco. An investor should study Cisco's product portfolio and compare it to the start-up firm's product. If the start-up firm has a product that could complement Cisco's product portfolio, then this may open up acquisition by Cisco as a viable exit option. Depending on the outcome of Cisco's evaluation, Nexabit could be such a company.

A network infrastructure company that passes all four of these tests is probably worth investing in. Nexabit satisfies tests one and two and might satisfy three and four as well. In this case, it might also be wise to compare Nexabit to its competitors Juniper and Avici before making an investment decision.

THE NET PROFIT RETRIEVER'S ASSESSMENT OF THE NETWORK INFRASTRUCTURE SEGMENT

Cisco Systems wins the Net Profit Retriever's approval. Its industry has economic leverage, it offers its customers a closed-loop solution, and its management adapts effectively to rapid change.

1. *Economic leverage.* As organizations have gone online, the router has occupied an increasingly critical role in the daily operations of the Internet. With 80 percent of the router market, Cisco has few challengers. With few vendors of valuable routers and with great customer dependence, the industry in which Cisco participates has tremendous economic leverage.

2. *Closed-loop solution.* Network equipment buyers no longer wish to spend time evaluating the best supplier for each component of their

network. Buyers want to purchase their network equipment from one vendor who can assure that all the different components will work together (interoperate). Cisco gives buyers the closed-loop solution they need—keeping up with their changing business needs. This makes it difficult for new competitors—with single-component solutions— to break into Cisco's customer relationships.

3. *Adaptive management.* Cisco's acquisition strategy and its compensation program prove that its management team adapts well to change. Acquisitions have played a critical role in helping Cisco keep up with changing technologies. If the new technologies perform well, buyers want them. As we saw with Cisco's acquisition of Crescendo, Cisco uses acquisitions to keep up.

Cisco's compensation scheme also encourages the company to adapt to change. In addition to giving all its employees stock options, Cisco pays them bonuses only if they improve quarterly customer satisfaction scores that are calculated by an independent source. Therefore, Cisco improves the way it works so as to enhance its customers' satisfaction.

CHAPTER THREE

Web Consulting: It's All About Commitment

~~~

Corporate CEOs don't have any consuming passion for information technology (IT). In fact, they seem to have a very ambivalent attitude about IT. They know IT can get them into trouble if they neglect it, and they know that they don't understand how it works. But they have also seen examples of how it can add to profits, and when IT adds to a competitor's profits, then CEOs know that they need to spend money on it just to keep up.

The growth of electronic commerce (e-commerce) invokes similar responses from CEOs. For market sizing purposes, e-commerce is defined as the sale of goods or services for which the customer uses the Web to place the order. With revenues of $73.9 billion in 1998 forecast to grow to $1.2 trillion by 2002, e-commerce is likely to make the CEO feel a mixture of profit lust, fear, and skepticism. The profit lust comes from thinking about how to get a piece of the market. The fear is that some other competitor will get there first and take away customers in the process. And the skepticism is that this is all a bunch of hype designed to sell more boxes and wires that never quite seem to pay off.

In response to these anxieties, up steps the Web-enabled systems integration consultant. Let's call these consultants *Web systems integrators*. Ideally, what Web systems integrators do is help the CEO identify an opportunity to profit from e-commerce and then make it happen. The CEO doesn't want to know about HTML and Java; the CEO wants to spend a fixed amount of money and get a big financial return. Web systems integrators try to create that return.

How exactly do Web systems integrators differ from other computer consultants? Whereas other computer consultants might specialize in developing systems with a particular technology, Web systems integrators must be conversant in a wide range of technologies. The reason that Web systems integrators must have this interdisciplinary skill is that their customers demand it. Unless the Web systems integrator can get the Web front end to tie in smoothly to the back-end operations of a company, the client will not realize the full potential from the firm's investment in Web technology.

This chapter explains why Web systems integration represents such a profitable place to invest and compete. It describes the services that Web systems integrators offer, and discusses the size, growth rate, and profitability of the Web systems integration market. The chapter explains why the Web systems integration segment is so profitable now and likely to remain so in the future, and we look at a case study of Sapient to learn what it takes to succeed in the Web systems integration business.

OVERVIEW OF THE WEB CONSULTING MARKET

Web systems integration is a professional service delivered to organizations who want to use the Web to improve their economic performance. Web systems integrators start by understanding the business objectives that their client's senior executives want to achieve with the Web. The Web systems integrators help direct a cross-functional client team to change the client's business processes so as to achieve those business objectives. To change these business processes, Web systems integrators use a structured methodology that translates business objectives into new systems and new ways of working. Web systems integrators work with clients to build new systems and processes, and test what has been built to make sure it will work effectively in the real world.

Market Size and Growth Rate

Web systems integration is a large and rapidly growing market. According to International Data Corporation, the worldwide market for Internet consulting was $4 billion in 1997 and is anticipated to grow to $33 billion by the year 2002, a 60 percent compound annual growth rate ("Sapient Corporation Announces . . . ," 1999).

Major Players and Types of Players

The systems integration business preceded the commercial emergence of the Web by over thirty years. Multibillion-dollar firms, such as Electronic Data Systems, Computer Sciences Corporation, Andersen Consulting, American Management Systems, and IBM, began offering systems integration services before the advent of minicomputers, PCs, and the Internet. Andersen Consulting is privately held, and Perot Systems had an IPO in February 1999. The other large firms are publicly traded. The fact that some systems integrators have grown so large without going public suggests that they generate so much cash that the primary reason for systems integrators to go public is to provide shareholders with a convenient means of diversifying their investment portfolios.

These multibillion-dollar firms are at one end of the scale. At the other end are thousands of relatively small systems integrators whose annual revenues range from $1 million to $400 million. Most of these smaller firms are privately held, although a few of them, such as Diamond Technology Partners, Keane, and Sapient, are public. The key point here is that the barriers to entry into the systems integration business are quite low, and it is therefore quite common for people to leave the large firms and start their own smaller ones.

Despite the large number of industry participants, only the largest firms are considered capable of doing the largest systems integration jobs. Large organizations generally feel most comfortable hiring large systems integrators to execute multiyear, multibillion-dollar systems projects. Nevertheless, these large systems integrators have not been taking over or specializing in the field of Web systems integration. As we will see later in this chapter when we examine the case of Sapient, Web technology has created demands for capabilities that most of the traditional systems integrators seem to lack.

Paradigm Shift in the Systems Integration Industry

The way that systems integration services are delivered is undergoing an important shift. In the past, systems integrators all charged clients on a time-and-materials basis. While telling a client that they would try to finish a project within a particular budget and time frame, they would actually bill for the amount of time they spent working for the client. If the project was not completed within the budget, the systems integration firm would keep getting paid as long as it was still working on the project.

In the early 1990s, some firms developed a fundamentally different strategy. These innovators began to sign contracts that obligated them to complete the project within a fixed time for a fixed price. This fixed time/price (FT/P) strategy clearly benefited clients by giving them a huge increase in value.

As we will explore in greater detail later, it was highly unlikely that many time-and-materials firms would copy the strategy. They would rather sit back and watch the innovators quickly go out of business as they failed to deliver on their commitments. This hope of the time-and-materials companies actually masked a fear that their secret source of profits would be wiped out. The time-and-materials firms won bids by setting low initial contract prices, but they made their profits by charging higher rates for the use of resources that exceeded contracted levels.

For the client, the time-and-materials approach was not a source of great satisfaction. The failure of a time-and-materials project to achieve the client's business objectives was often a reason the company's chief information officer lost his job. And the client typically ended up spending more money than it had budgeted for a system that did not end up delivering the return the client had anticipated. In short, the time-and-materials approach to systems integration tended to benefit the consultant more than the client.

But an FT/P working arrangement is ultimately better for the better consultants as well. Many consultants are highly motivated by the idea that their work helps the client become more successful. It is particularly frustrating for these idealistic consultants to find themselves working in a time-and-materials environment where sticking to the letter of a contract is more important than finishing the client's project on time and within budget. These consultants gain a great sense of motivation from working in an environment where the most important value is delivering on commitments.

PROFIT DRIVERS

The forces that enhance the profitability of Web consulting are likely to be stronger than the forces that diminish it.

Inherent Attractiveness of FT/P Versus Time-and-Materials

In recent years, the firms offering the better client value proposition have enjoyed higher profits and faster growth. For example, in 1997 the average net profit margin for the traditional time-and-materials firms was 5 percent, whereas the FT/P group earned almost twice that, an average of 9 percent. Time-and-materials consultants are increasing revenues at an annual rate of 15 percent as compared to a 70 percent annual rate for the FT/P players. Time-and-materials consulting profits are growing at an anemic 0.2 percent as compared to a 75 percent rate for the FT/P companies. Admittedly, it is easier for the FT/P companies to grow faster simply because they are smaller. But their faster growth is due also to the superiority of FT/P. Now that clients have an alternative in FT/P, they are moving their business there quite aggressively.

The basic reason for the profitability of the FT/P strategy is that it gives both the consulting firm and the client a strong need to make the project work. Typically, the consulting firm will not take on the project if the client is not willing to explicitly have the same level of commitment to making the project viable. After the client has committed real resources and time to defining the real business objectives of the project, both the consultant and the client know whether the project is worthwhile; and if a mutual decision is made to proceed, it is unlikely that either party will back out.

Despite the best efforts of the client and the FT/P consultant, in some cases projects are not completed on time and within budget. As we will explore later, these situations are handled on a case-by-case basis. In general, the FT/P consultant will try to anticipate the problem and negotiate a solution that is acceptable to both parties. Because the FT/P consultant wants to sustain its reputation for creating client value, the consultant may choose to incur all or part of the cost over- run, depending on the arrangement that has been negotiated with the client. Given the stress that investors place on high earnings growth, these situations pose an obvious trade-off between long-term reputation and short-term profits.

The FT/P approach to Web systems integration is changing several elements of market structure that are likely to enhance the profitability of the business. Most important, delivering consistently on the promise of FT/P is very difficult. Therefore, the number of firms that can cite a track record of doing so is quite small, and thus the number of competitors is small. And as the leaders continue to attract new clients, they have the potential to generate a lead that could be difficult to surmount—unless they fail to sustain their record of timely delivery.

The paradigm shift from time-and-materials to FT/P has had a significant impact on the forces that are likely to drive the profitability of the Web systems integration business in the future: rivalry, barriers to entry, and the bargaining power of buyers.

Rivalry

Rivalry among systems integrators remains intense. The FT/P firms are likely to continue to take market share away from the time-and-materials firms. The reason is that FT/P firms are organized to deliver greater certainty of outcome and cost at a price that is likely to be much lower than the time-and-materials firms can charge. The time-and-materials firms make most of their profits on the extra fees they charge when projects go over budget, so they are unable to compete with the FT/P firms by imitating FT/P strategies. If the time-and-materials firms did try to imitate the FT/P firms, they would further imperil their profit margins.

In the future, the locus of rivalry will be among firms in the FT/P ring. As implied earlier, rivalry among FT/P firms will be on the basis of their reputation for delivering on their promises. Firms that can fulfill their promises to deliver a project on time and within budget will find themselves gaining market share at the expense of firms that fail to deliver.

The firms that deliver will also experience growing revenues, profit, and stock prices. Given that a large part of employee compensation in the Web systems integration firms comes in the form of stock options, the firms that sustain a reputation for delivering on their commitments can attract and retain a larger share of the best employees. Conversely, the firms that are unable to deliver on their commitments will lose their best people to firms that can.

Barriers to Entry and Mobility Barriers

The challenge of delivering on the FT/P commitment constitutes a significant barrier to entry. For new entrants, the ability to build systems on an FT/P basis will present an ever greater challenge as customers begin to demand this way of working from all systems integrators. For the manager of a small firm, taking on the FT/P commitment looms as a "bet the company" strategy.

An additional barrier for new entrants is the challenge of building Web front ends that are integrated with back-end operating systems. Although there are many firms that design Web pages, there are far fewer that can build a compelling Web front end and also link that front end to the client's back-end systems in a way that will jump-start the client's profit growth.

For systems integrators who operate on a time-and-materials basis, changing to FT/P is extremely difficult. As we discussed earlier, the time-and-materials firm tends to put in a low bid to win a contract and then makes up the difference on the prices that they charge to deliver resources over and above the contracted amount. The FT/P approach is seen by time-and-materials firms as a hugely risky proposition that slashes already low profit margins. So it is unlikely that the time-and-materials firms will jump into the FT/P approach unless they begin to experience a precipitous and sustained drop in revenues.

Moderate Customer Bargaining Power

Customer bargaining power is likely to decline from high to moderate as the market share of FT/P firms increases. The factors that increase customer bargaining power are likely to be offset by the factors that decrease that power. On the one hand, the FT/P commitment certainly shifts more of the risk of project failure onto the Web systems integrator. On the other hand, if a Web consultant feels that a new client is not sufficiently committed to a project, then that consultant may decline to sign a contract. Thus, if a company expects a guaranteed outcome at a guaranteed price, there will be fewer firms from which to choose.

CASE
Sapient: Managing People and Risk

To continue to take advantage of the high growth rates and profit margins available to leaders in this segment, Web systems integration firms must meet three challenges. First, leaders must make careful choices about which new client engagements to take on and how to manage the inherent risks of these projects. Second, they must hire and develop people who can handle the tremendous responsibilities that accompany rapid growth. Third, they must develop a way to meld the design skills needed to build effective Web front ends with the technological know-how required to integrate these front ends with a client's operational systems.

Which firms are facing up to these challenges? One FT/P firm that leads the industry in profitability, if not in revenues, is Sapient Corporation. An analysis of Sapient's strategy reveals insights into how to make money in the Web consulting segment.

Sapient Corporation is a $160-million (for the year ending December 31, 1998) systems integration firm with 1,450 employees; it earned a 13 percent net margin, the most profitable in the industry. Jerry Greenberg and Stuart Moore, Sapient's cofounders and co-CEOs, both worked at Cambridge Technology Group (CTG). They saw an unmet need in the market: clients for IT services were increasingly frustrated because they were not getting what they wanted. If they could figure out how to satisfy clients' needs, Greenberg and Moore reasoned, they would have a good business. This idea motivated them to start a company with the goal of delivering client-server systems projects in a fixed time and for a fixed price. Since then, Sapient has grown its revenues and profits at a historical annual rate in excess of 60 percent, several times the industry average. After doing its first Web project in 1994, Sapient estimates that well over 45 percent of its 1998 engagements were Web-related.

Although Sapient has not achieved its FT/P goal on every project, its record compares favorably to the records of its peers, and the company remains committed to meeting the needs of its clients, even in the face of adversity. In the case of one difficult project, Sapient persisted, despite great client skepticism, to finish the project, choosing to absorb the cost overrun. To Sapient, it was more important to maintain its reputation than to stop the financial bleeding from that particular contract.

Sapient's strategy is consistent with the value of keeping commitments. One of the most important strategic choices Sapient makes is that of deciding which customers to work with. Sapient seeks out clients who are determined to create sustainable business processes to create value for their customers through their work with Sapient. Sapient wants to work with companies that are willing to commit the right people—from senior executives to subject-matter experts—to make the big changes needed to make new processes and systems work. Sapient also works with clients that are creating entirely new industries—a phenomenon that is increasingly common in the Internet business. In short, Sapient wants to work for companies that are leaders in their industries or have the potential to be. Sapient looks for client engagements in which it can build its credibility by quickly delivering results valuable to the client and its customers (Chris Davey, senior vice president at Sapient, interview with the author, May 1998).

To implement this risk-sharing strategy, Sapient does two things extremely well. Through two internal organizations, it recruits and develops excellent people (the People Strategy Organization, or PSO), and it approaches its work with discipline (the Quality Design and Delivery organization, or QUADD).

After looking at these organizations, we will also examine how Sapient's acquisition of Studio Archetype reflects Sapient's effort to integrate the skills of user-centered design, brand, research, and strategy with the technical skills of the systems integrator.

GREAT PEOPLE: THE PSO. Sapient's value as a company depends on its ability to create a "virtuous cycle" that we discussed in Chapter One. The starting point of this virtuous cycle is the base of clients who are willing to give Sapient a strong recommendation to other potential clients. If the recommendation turns the potential client into an actual client, Sapient must yet again deliver on its FT/P commitment. Sapient's ability to deliver depends on its ability to staff the project with people who can meet the commitment. Thus, Sapient's continued growth depends on its people.

With its historical growth rate of more than 60 percent, Sapient's virtuous cycle is highly dependent on its ability to create the right working environment. In order to fulfill new contracts, Sapient must hire and retrain the best people. Each new hire has the potential either to increase or to undermine the success of the enterprise. If Sapient does not maintain the quality of its people, and if, consequently, client projects fail too often, Sapient's reputation for keeping its commitments will be diluted. If its brightest consultants see Sapient as having lost its distinctiveness, they will leave, the task of recruiting new people to replace them will become harder, and Sapient's ability to deliver great service will decline.

Clearly, recruiting and developing the right people are two of the most important responsibilities at Sapient. These responsibilities fall into the bailiwick of Sapient's People Strategy Organization (PSO). Until the latter part of 1998, the PSO was run by Anthony Jules, a thirty-year-old Sapient vice president. Jules earned B.S. and M.S. degrees from MIT in computer science (Anthony Jules, interview with the author, May 1998).

While in the MIT graduate program, Jules realized that he knew nothing about business. He left MIT after finishing his master's degree and went to join Sapient. After a year, he realized that he was fascinated by the idea of building businesses. Jules felt that he had been put on the planet to build things, be they machines, relationships, or businesses. After five years at Sapient, Jules is happy he made the choice. Sapient looked to him like a place where he could learn a substantial amount, and it has been "like drinking from a firehose."

At Sapient, Jules has been a software developer, a system architect, and a project manager. Jules started Sapient's San Francisco office. In 1995 he left to look at some outside business ideas. In 1997 he returned to Sapient as vice president of the PSO.

Sapient recognized that it could achieve growth through an intentional strategy. The objective of the PSO was to put the processes and systems in place to handle the people issues associated with growth. Two unique aspects of Sapient shaped the PSO. First, Sapient had always been very feedback oriented, both from clients and employees. Even when Sapient had fewer than one hundred employees, the company would conduct employee surveys to help identify what was bad and good about the company and what needed to change. Second, Sapient had a strong culture, one of commitment to making every project succeed; there was a need to articulate that difference to people who were coming into the organization.

Sapient looks for people who will fit its unique culture. It is biased toward people with leadership ability and an interest in learning and growing. Sapient people are excited about being open and interacting with others. And Sapient wants people who care deeply about being successful and who are interested in solving clients' business problems.

Within this context, the PSO developed a way to be strategic about hiring people and to anticipate the firm's hiring needs. Sapient hires about 30 percent of its people from college and 70 percent from industry. The PSO has separate teams that are responsible for hiring from these sources.

College hiring is seasonal. The busiest times for college hiring are in January and in the summer. The college hiring campaigns begin a year ahead of time and aim at recruiting people with bachelor's degrees in computer science and in liberal arts. Sapient spends time getting its name in front of candidates. The culmination of the recruiting process is Sapient's Super Saturdays.

Super Saturdays are one-and-a-half-day sessions at a Sapient office, to which twenty to fifty college recruits are invited. The candidates go on a tour and listen to presentations. They participate in team exercises and undergo three or four interviews. The objective of these sessions is to let recruits know who Sapient is, what the company can offer them, and what behavior Sapient rewards. Sapient holds Super Saturdays eight times a year at its offices in San Francisco, Atlanta, and Cambridge, Massachusetts.

Sapient is looking to hire leaders. Seth Bartlett is a young employee who exemplifies Sapient's notion of leadership. A liberal arts graduate, Bartlett deeply wanted to work at Sapient. In college he had demonstrated an aptitude for leadership, and he had a chance to use this talent during a troubled Sapient project. As assistant project manager, he worked hard to make the team and the client comfortable in a very stressful situation. Despite severe challenges, Bartlett kept the Sapient-client team focused on what was important. He had an unstoppable desire to understand the client's business. He focused on the client's goals and persisted in asking what the team would do next to achieve the goal. The result for Bartlett was that he received glowing recommendations from the client and from his Sapient colleagues. Next, Sapient gave Bartlett the assignment of hiring thirty-five new college graduates with great leadership ability. Bartlett found forty-two people, made offers to each, and thirty-eight accepted.

To close the deal on recruits who fit its culture, Sapient does not use money, though it pays at or above the market rate for the position. It offers stock ownership to all employees. Its recruiting edge is the combination of cash, stock, and opportunity that Sapient provides to people who share its values.

After recruits are hired, they spend their first week at Sapient in a Bootcamp that gives new employees an experience of the company's culture and values. They go through the week completing different exercises that illuminate aspects of Sapient's unique culture.

For example, Sapient has a different expectation of hierarchy. At other companies, the higher a person's title, the more he or she is allowed to do. Sapient, however, expects every person to be part of a team that consists of people whose strengths and weaknesses complement each other—for example, vice presidents will take direction from directors when the directors have the leadership skills required to meet client needs. In order for an experienced hire to function well at Sapient, the company needs to dismantle that person's mental model of hierarchy.

Sapient does not believe that age necessarily correlates with leadership ability. For example, the former head of Sapient's Atlanta office is a very talented individual less than thirty years old. He carries himself and runs his business with the acumen of a much older person. He has leadership skills and a deep understanding of business. He is a trusted adviser to clients. His good sense for people and judgment in making business decisions inspire trust.

The Bootcamp sessions also encourage teams to communicate with each other. In one team exercise, called mapping, people draw a picture of themselves that helps others understand them. Often the mapping exercise allows deep insights into a person's life or reflects the high level of trust that has developed between members of the team. For example, during mapping sessions some people have revealed that they were adopted or from divorced parents. The Bootcamp also emphasizes important Sapient values such as leadership, openness, relationships, growth, and client-focused delivery (Christina Luconi, co-owner of the PSO at Sapient, interview with the author, May 1998).

Sapient also differs from other firms in its attitude toward burnout. Rather than trying to squeeze the most out of its employees and then spitting them out, Sapient stresses sustainability. It wants its people to feel that they can sustain what they are doing.

One Sapient management tactic for achieving sustainability is to have team members spend time at the beginning of a project setting expectations with their teams. Because Sapient people are so dedicated to their work, they often must be pushed to articulate their nonwork commitments. For example, they are encouraged to discuss their preferred work schedule, their need to pick children up from day care during the week, and their commitments to classes outside work. By articulating these obligations at the beginning of a project, team members enhance their ability to work together in ways that complement each other's schedules, which in turn promotes a sustainable work life.

As mentioned earlier, Sapient is very feedback oriented. In fact, Sapient team members receive client feedback after each phase of a project has been completed, and bonuses are linked to the results of this feedback.

DOING THE RIGHT THING WELL: THE QUADD ORGANIZATION. Sapient's PSO attracts great people to the company, but getting the right people is only part of the solution. Sapient's Quality Design and Development organization (QUADD) gets the right people doing the right things in the right way. Let us look at the evolution of QUADD within Sapient and discuss how QUADD helps manage the risks inherent in Sapient's business.

In order to deliver on its commitment to build systems within a fixed time period and for a fixed cost, Sapient decided to create an organization devoted to inventing and using methods that would enhance its own productivity. More specifically, this organization would consolidate disparate efforts in the company to improve methodology and disciplines. For example, QUADD would find ways for teams to invent, use, and share experiences. The ultimate goal of these efforts was to lower the risk that Sapient undertakes each time it signs an FT/P contract.

Sapient's rapid growth demanded that the company develop consistency in executing its projects. Doug Abel, QUADD's leader, loosely adopted the Capability Maturity Model for software development, which originated at Carnegie Mellon University. This model emphasizes the importance of creating a process that delivers results predictably. Abel believed that disciplined practices in the conduct of software development projects was a key component in keeping Sapient from repeating mistakes and to encouraging Sapient's adoption of practices that worked (Doug Abel, vice president of Sapient, interview with the author, June 1998).

For custom software development, Sapient does its work using a structured, workshop-based approach to projects. Sapient's process is evolving as it does more Web, package development, and strategic consulting work. Sapient's traditional approach, called the QUADD process, consists of four stages: RIP workshop, design workshop, implementation, and production. The Rapid Implementation Plan (RIP) workshop is designed to rapidly identify the client's needs, develop a strategy and action plan to meet those needs, and create consensus, momentum, and excitement around the solution. The design stage focuses on describing in significant detail the proposed process changes and required information technology architecture. The implementation stage involves developing, testing, and transitioning to the new applications or enhancements to packaged software applications. The production stage primarily involves the maintenance, enhancement, and support of the system after the client has begun using it in daily operations.

———

It is said that nothing concentrates the mind like a gun pointed at one's head. This expression comes to mind when thinking about the risks associated with an FT/P systems development project. If project costs exceed the contracted price, FT/P systems development firms will lose money and damage their reputations.

Keeping a project within the contracted price requires managing two sources of risk: business and technical. Sapient focuses intensely on overcoming all obstacles that get in the way of delivering value to the client. Sapient uses three techniques to manage business risk: the RIP workshop stage of the QUADD process, client teams, and the project review process. If the system works when it goes into production, then the firm has managed technical risk well. Sapient manages technical risk through the work of QUADD's internal consultants, through the quality review process, and through active learning.

Managing Business Risk. First, the RIP workshop stage of the QUADD process involves everyone, from client executives to end users, as well as Sapient project team members. Session participants meet at Sapient's offices for as long as a week. These sessions typically have one of two outcomes: the participants agree on a clear vision, objectives, business case, and prototype for the project, or the participants agree that the project is not worth doing. Often, the willingness to make an investment in this planning session is an indicator of future commitment. If a potential client is not even willing to devote a week of its key people's time to a week-long meeting at Sapient's site, they are unlikely to have the commitment required to complete an important project on-time and on-budget.

After the RIP workshop produces a clear set of project objectives, Sapient then creates a client team. Sapient has a unique approach to structuring client teams. A client team is a group of Sapient and client employees who work together to complete the client's project. Depending on the requirements of the project, this team may consist of a project manager, an architect, developers, and subject-matter experts.

Web teams may also include information architects, content experts, designers, strategy consultants, and branding specialists. The team works with the client from the time the project is sold to the delivery of the solution. The project manager is responsible for ensuring that the team is working well and that there is good communication with clients; he or she also focuses on making sure that the project scope delivers the business value that the client is seeking. On a typical technology implementation, the architect is responsible for making sure that the system architecture will work well and will adapt as the client's business changes.

Also part of the client team are Sapient directors, who may have responsibility for multiple projects or clients. The directors work with the teams and the clients to clear away organizational impediments to the completion of a project. The directors are also typically involved in the original selling of the project. Often they help facilitate executive consensus around the solution and encourage client executives to invest the time of their people to ensure that the business objectives of the new system solution can actually be achieved.

Sapient's client team approach differs from the approach used by some of the larger time-and-materials systems integrators. The time-and-materials firms tend to bring in different teams of experts for each phase of a project. For example, there are sales specialists brought in to close a deal, then industry experts for the analysis phase, then a separate team for the design phase, and so on.

Although this approach has the advantage of bringing specialists to clients at each stage of the process, it also has substantial disadvantages. For example, each functional team must hand off the project to the next team when it has completed its work. The handoffs frequently result in miscommunication. When the scope of a project changes during the development stage, for example, the changes in scope must be handed back to the design, analysis, and concept teams that preceded the development stage. These backwards handoffs cause the project to take more time and money than originally anticipated.

By contrast, Sapient's client team approach virtually eliminates handoffs. Although the teams may not always embody the level of technical or functional expertise that large time-and-materials systems integrators enjoy, Sapient brings this expertise to teams through director oversight and internal consultants from the QUADD organization. Clients benefit from access to a team that is focused on meeting their needs. The directors and consultants also serve an important mentoring role that helps develop Sapient people to take on new responsibilities as the company grows.

The unique way that Sapient structures its client teams helps manage a project's business risk. The structure of the cross-functional team increases the flow of communication between client and Sapient team members throughout the process; it encourages an ongoing, systematic discussion of what is working and what is not and helps to remove barriers to achieving the project's objectives.

Finally, Sapient manages business risk through its project review process. Project reviews are of two types: progress reviews and quality reviews; we will discuss the second type a bit later in this chapter. The progress reviews are intended to get a general sense of the health of the project. The review teams assume that the project team can be trusted to highlight the issues on which the team needs help. Each progress review team typically includes a vice president, a director, and other team members. The review teams are designed to encourage a mentoring relationship between the senior members and other team members. The reviewers meet with the project manager and architect each month. The project manager highlights specific problems where the project needs help. For example, the project manager might point out that the project team is concerned that the client is becoming less satisfied because of differing expectations. The reviewers might suggest ways to enhance the levels of communication with the client to ensure that each side's expectations are well understood.

Sapient's techniques for managing business risk accomplish two objectives. They ensure that Sapient and its clients undertake projects only when there are clear business objectives and benefits. They also enforce rigorous and open communication among all members of the client team so that problems are identified and addressed before they derail the project or lead to client dissatisfaction.

Managing Technical Risk. QUADD's internal consulting group tests out new technologies or techniques that might be helpful to project teams and identifies potential problems with new technologies before they are used in client settings. The internal consulting group develops best practices for Sapient in a controlled environment to help limit technical risk. It develops frameworks for reducing risk and conducting common operations. It attempts to create a model that tests what can potentially be achieved by client teams. The focus of the group is to continuously develop ways of executing client projects that capture the best of Sapient's experience combined with the most effective technology.

The internal consulting group builds standard architectures and tools that can be shared across projects. The internal consulting group also identifies ways to increase productivity by the use of standard, off-the-shelf tools. In choosing the tools around which to standardize, Sapient looks for a supplier that is persistent in improving its products and that appears to have the financial strength to be viable over the long term.

Another technique Sapient uses to manage the technical risk within a project is the quality review process. This process is more intrusive than the peer review process described earlier. Quality reviewers external to the project ask questions and verify results; they look at code and ask more detailed questions. The quality review helps identify technical problems before too much time has elapsed.

Sapient also manages technical risk through a process it calls active learning. Active learning contrasts with passive learning, whereby Sapient teams would invite others from the organization to learn about what worked and what did not work in a just-completed project. Active learning, in contrast, does not wait until the end of the project to spread learning. In fact, review teams and technology consultants go from project to project as the work is being done. These roving reviewers spread the best practices among the projects in "real time." Although it is difficult for Sapient to quantify the benefits of active learning, there are four or five teams that begin using a new, more effective technology during the course of their projects. Using passive learning, these team members would most likely have learned about the new technology only after the other project teams were disbanded (Abel interview, June 1998).

BLENDING CREATIVE AND TECHNICAL CULTURES: THE STUDIO ARCHE-TYPE ACQUISITION. In recent years, the proportion of Sapient's revenues from projects related to the Web has increased to over 45 percent. In order to do an effective job on Web-related projects, Sapient found that it needed to supplement its skills in management consulting and technology implementation with other skills made critical by the Internet. Sapient had always been strong at integrating systems and building client-server solutions. To build complex Web solutions, Sapient began to partner with firms that had additional creative and branding skills.

As Sapient's Web-related business grew, it became increasingly obvious that the company would need either to acquire or partner with a number of design firms. Sapient also realized that it would need to develop an approach that could ensure that creative and technical people work well together. It saw that visual designers approach problems in a fundamentally different way than technical people. Consistent with the value it places on learning, Sapient decided to create integrated teams that would lead to the best results for its clients.

Sapient tackled the first issue by acquiring a Web developer, Studio Archetype. Founded in 1988, Studio Archetype is based in San Francisco, with offices in New York and Atlanta. With 140 employees at the time of the acquisition, Studio Archetype creates brand identities and interactive products and services.

Because of Studio Archetype's outstanding reputation, Sapient felt that its combination with Sapient's technology expertise would create a firm with skills that would benefit Sapient's clients. So, Sapient acquired Studio Archetype in August 1998. Under the acquisition agreement, Sapient issued about five hundred thousand common shares (worth around $24 million at the time of the announcement) in exchange for 100 percent of Studio Archetype's equity.

Sapient clearly believes that this acquisition establishes its presence in the Web systems integration business. Sapient increasingly found that its clients were demanding closed-loop solutions to help them maximize the return on their e-commerce initiatives. Sapient perceived that Studio Archetype's expertise in brand consulting and user-centered design was superior to that of any other firm Sapient had considered.

Sapient saw that Studio Archetype complemented Sapient's capabilities in strategy development, business consulting, and technology implementation. Most important, both firms shared a common vision of being the very best at what they do in order to help their clients develop "revolutionary" products and services ("Sapient Acquires . . .," 1998).

That Studio Archetype's founder, Clement Mok, assumed the new role of chief creative officer at Sapient reflects the significance of this acquisition to Sapient. Mok is responsible for setting the creative vision and strategy for Sapient. Mark Crumpacker, Studio Archetype's

CEO and executive creative director, became president of Studio Archetype and continues to oversee all of Studio Archetype's operations. How effectively these new roles will work out for Sapient and its clients remains to be seen, but industry and financial analysts have praised the match.

IMPLICATIONS

What general principles come out of this analysis? What makes a Web consulting business profitable? What competitive strategies do Web consulting firms pursue to achieve market leadership? And what insights does our discussion of Sapient's strategy offer into how to spot potential in other Web consulting firms?

1. *Exploit the economic leverage of Web consulting.* There are no stable maps of the Web business. Managers and investors must look for activities or technologies that occupy the strategic high ground. Web consulting is a leverage point because it directs the work of three constituents. It offers strategy to CEOs, commitment to corporate IT staff, and greater revenues to technology vendors. Web consulting's leverage will increase as more organizations begin to realize the value of Webifying their businesses.

2. *Stick with FT/P consulting.* The firms in the FT/P segment of the Web consulting business are not eager to see the time-and-materials companies begin to replicate their approach. Fortunately for the FT/P companies, the time-and-materials companies continue to view FT/P as a very risky strategy. Although the risk is indeed high, the perception of risk is much more significant than the actual risk. The relative profitability of the two strategies bears this out. But the perception of risk and the difficulty of changing the organization are what keep the time-and-materials company out of the business.

As the Sapient case illustrates, an even higher barrier to entry and a challenge for firms who are already in the arena is the FT/P commitment. Firms that can deliver on the commitment attract more business. By attracting more business, their stock price goes up. As their stock price goes up, it becomes easier to attract and motivate new people who can perform the new client work. Conversely, firms that can not deliver on their commitments lose business. Their stock prices drop, and they lose their good people.

3. *Find companies that offer closed-loop consulting and implementation.* Companies hire Web consultants to provide an economic payoff. Companies are not looking for an education in HTML and Java.

They don't want simply to put their corporate brochures on their Web site. Companies want a Web consultant to show them how they can change their business processes to create value for their customers. Then companies want the Web consultants to make the new business process work using Web technology that brings a rapid payoff.

4. *Look for virtuous cycles based on the firm's ability to recruit and deploy the best talent.* Success in the Web business depends on a firm's ability to create a virtuous cycle. For example, Sapient's cycle starts with its base of clients who are willing to refer Sapient to potential clients. The positive reputation among clients is a result of Sapient's ability to attract great people who solve their business problems. As long as Sapient can continue to attract more of these people and direct them properly, it can build its base of satisfied clients.

5. *Look for consulting firms that create switching costs—through their own successes.* Companies do not like to spend time undergoing complex purchasing processes every time they need the services of an outside vendor. Companies prefer to go through the process once and then keep doing business with the same vendor as long as the vendor keeps up with their changing needs. For example, when Sapient finishes a risky project that has a big positive impact on client operations, the client will have a hard time switching to a competing consultant the next time around. And each time Sapient succeeds, the cost of switching to another vendor rises.

6. *Look for consulting firms whose management team's average age is under thirty-five.* Web consulting is a game for people with tremendous energy and determination. It is unlikely that a senior team over thirty-five years old will be able to sustain that energy level. Over thirty-five, most people are trying to balance their work and personal lives. Web consulting is not a business for people whose lives are balanced. It simply demands too much of a time commitment. If a firm's management team is over thirty-five, it is probably too old to keep up with the industry's pace.

THE NET PROFIT RETRIEVER'S ASSESSMENT OF THE WEB CONSULTING SEGMENT

Sapient is an example of a Web consulting firm that passes the Net Profit Retriever's three tests. Its industry has economic leverage, it offers its customers a closed-loop solution, and its management adapts effectively to rapid change.

1. *Economic leverage.* As we noted in the principle 1 in the previous section, Web consulting is an industry with economic leverage. Principle 2 points out that the FT/P commitment actually enhances the economic leverage of firms that fulfill it. The reputation of Web consulting firms for delivering on that commitment is the ultimate barrier to entry. Firms on the right side of that barrier will grow and enjoy economic leverage because they control a valuable resource in increasingly high demand.

2. *Closed-loop solution.* Sapient is an example of a Web consulting firm that offers a closed-loop solution to organizations that want to Webify their business to increase profits. As principle 3 suggests, the closed-loop solution requires three skills: business sense to suggest systems that increase a client's profits, creativity and expertise to develop a user-centered Web solution, and technical and change-management skills to build those systems on time and within budget. Prior to its acquisition of Studio Archetype, Sapient had the first and third skills in-house; now it has the second as well.

3. *Adaptive management.* Sapient's management also adapts effectively to change. To meet client needs, Sapient can acquire and integrate companies that add new capabilities. Sapient also hires and retains large numbers of great people to support its 60 percent historical annual growth. Finally, Sapient spreads insights about new technologies and best practices through its active learning process.

CHAPTER FOUR

Internet Venture Capital: Money Dictates

J ohn Doerr, the dean of Internet venture capital, has been saying for years that, if anything, the Internet may be under-hyped. Doerr also enjoys pointing out that he is a coconspirator in the largest legal creation of wealth in history. At the end of 1997, Doerr's firm had invested in 250 companies that combined had generated annual revenues of $61 billion, employed 162,000 people, and were worth $125 billion in stock market value (Doerr, 1998). With a personal net worth estimated by *Forbes* between $100 million and $250 million, Doerr has at least one hundred million reasons to be enthusiastic about the Internet (Jeffers, 1997).

Doerr's firm, Kleiner Perkins Caufield & Byers (Kleiner Perkins), has earned very high investment returns. According to the *San Francisco Chronicle* (Sinton, 1998), in 1997 Kleiner Perkins earned a return of eleven times its investment in fifteen of its companies that went public in 1997.

VentureOne, a San Francisco venture capital research firm, also highlighted Kleiner Perkins's performance in 1997 when initial public offerings (IPOs) by venture-backed companies dropped 41 percent—to 134 from 227 in 1996 (Sinton, 1998). It ranked Kleiner Perkins first in three of four categories:

1. *Number of IPOs.* Kleiner Perkins invested in fifteen new public companies. By contrast, Weiss Peck & Greer Venture Partners and Hambrecht & Quist, both of San Francisco, and Norwest Venture Capital of Minneapolis had seven IPOs each.

2. *IPO proceeds.* Kleiner Perkins portfolio companies raised a total of $556.3 million in public stock offerings. (Next best was Goldman Sachs, whose six companies raised $483.9 million.)

3. *Board representation.* As a sign of their involvement with their investments, Kleiner Perkins partners were directors of nine of the fifteen companies in which Kleiner Perkins had invested that then went public. (InterWest Partners, TA Associates, and Domain Associates held five seats each.)

A key area where Kleiner Perkins did not place first was average after-market performance—the increase in stock price since its initial offering price. Of forty-one venture capital firms tracked by VentureOne that invested in at least three companies that went public last year, ten exceeded Kleiner Perkins's average gain of 55.2 percent at year-end.

Kleiner Perkins's best performer was At Home, the firm we discussed in Chapter One. Kleiner Perkins's initial $7.4 million investment increased in value to $374 million as of December 31, 1997. Figure 4.1 highlights the returns of six of the fifteen companies that went public in 1997 in which Kleiner Perkins held initial stakes.

Most of the companies in the figure are in the e-commerce, ISP, and infrastructure segments of the Web business. For example, Amazon.com is in e-commerce, At Home is an ISP, and MMC Networks, a designer of high-speed networking chips, is part of the infrastructure segment we discussed in Chapter Two. NeoMagic, a firm that designs, develops, and markets software that speeds up the multimedia performance of notebook PCs, is an example of a successful non-Web investment. Making over eleven times their investment, Doerr and his partners clearly are making money on the Web.

But what exactly is the nature of their business? How big is it? How fast is it growing? What kinds of investment returns are typical? What trends drive future profitability? And what does it take to be a leader?

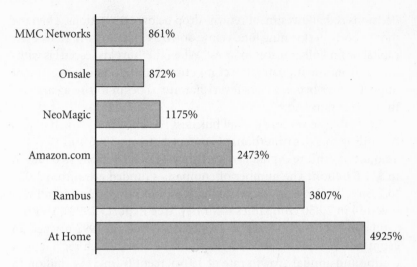

Figure 4.1.   Investment Performance of Selected Kleiner Perkins Investments, from Initial Investment Date to December 31, 1997.
Source: Sinton, 1998.

OVERVIEW OF A CYCLICAL INDUSTRY

The venture capital business is a special kind of investing. Venture capital firms are usually partnerships. The limited partners invest capital in the partnership; the general partners identify opportunities, make the investments, and shepherd the companies to the point at which the limited partners can get their capital out—either through an IPO or by selling the company to another firm. The limited partners receive 80 percent of the proceeds from the exit transactions. The general partners divide the other 20 percent among them. In addition, the general partners receive an annual management fee that ranges between 1 and 2 percent of the assets under management. The management fee is intended to cover the cost of operating the firm.

The venture capital business is quite cyclical. When returns are high, money pours into the venture capital funds. This surfeit of capital to be invested creates a feeding frenzy for the few attractive companies in which to invest. A typical outcome is that the venture capital firms end up either paying too much for good companies or lowering their investment standards. The effect of making these sub-par investment decisions is that investment returns drop below expectations. Then the more poorly performing funds close down as investors withdraw their capital or find other places to invest. When the "surplus" capital is withdrawn from the industry, the competition to fund good investment opportunities becomes less feverish, returns begin to rise again, and the cycle begins anew.

Recently, the venture capital business has been in a growth phase. According to PriceWaterhouse Coopers, between 1996 and 1997 the amount of venture capital invested grew 44 percent from $8.0 billion to $11.5 billion. The number of companies funded grew from 2,021 to 2,669. For 1998, an estimated $14 billion of venture capital was invested in 2,850 companies ("Money Tree Report," 1998). Venture capital investments in Internet-related companies in 1998 reached an estimated $3.3 billion, or 24 percent of the total, which represents a compound annual growth rate of 191 percent from $134 million in 1995. Between 1995 and 1997, Internet dollar investments increased 103 percent, versus 27 percent for all other industries, including other high-technology investments. The number of Internet companies that received venture capital grew 61 percent, compared with 26 percent for all other industries (VCs, 1997).

What's driving the rapid growth in Internet-related venture investing is the extraordinary returns that firms such as Kleiner Perkins have earned. The average returns tend to vary by the company's stage in development and by year. For example, in 1996, the highest one-year internal rates of return, 44.2 percent, were earned by investors in seed and early-stage ventures. However, over a ten-year period, the highest internal rates of return, 22.1 percent, were earned by investors in later-stage companies (VCs, 1997).

PROFIT DRIVERS

What are the key trends that drive the profitability of the business? Some forces enhance industry returns over the short run; others have the potential to diminish returns over the longer run.

Stock Valuations

In the short run, the most important force driving the returns of venture firms is the extraordinary stock market valuations of Internet companies. As we discussed earlier, most Internet companies lack profits and are therefore valued in terms of their revenues. Of course, in some cases even their revenues are quite small in comparison to their stock market valuations. As John Sculley points out, investors view the Internet as a business opportunity that will be bigger than television. They see investing in these companies now as getting in on the ground floor of the next Microsoft. Because these investors are not smart enough to know which business model will work, they try to pick the companies that are first in their industry. The investors assume that the leading companies stand the best chance of figuring out a way to make money on the Internet even if their current business models do not work out (John Sculley, interview with the author, June 1998).

Brand Leverage and Limited Mobility

Branded venture firms like Kleiner Perkins have developed a network of the most skilled start-up managers. Their track record of successful venture creation makes them attractive to entrepreneurs. Their access to capital markets has been strengthened by years of successful IPOs. And they have an exceptional ability to create investor enthusiasm about their companies.

The branded venture capital firms provide a range of services that together make Internet Venture Capital a leverage-point industry. Firms like Kleiner Perkins direct the efforts of several powerful constituents: they direct the work of entrepreneurs and management teams; they share risk (and returns) with other venture firms that invest in their companies; they create new business for law and accounting firms and use these professionals to help screen deals; they provide stories for the media, particularly such industry magazines as *Red Herring* and *Upside*; and they offer a flow of work for investment banks that handle the IPOs of their portfolio companies. Brand power raises mobility barriers. Although a group of experienced venture capitalists may be able to start a new small firm, there are significant barriers to matching the strengths of branded firms such as Kleiner Perkins.

COUNTERVAILING FORCES

Offsetting the positive forces, there are countervailing trends that tend to reduce returns.

Low Barriers to Entry

The venture capital business, like many other segments of the money management business, has low barriers to entry. Anyone with credible experience working in the venture capital business can start a new firm. The new entrants need a track record of successful investments, and they must also be able to convince investors to park some money with them; but the recent climate for IPOs has rendered these abilities more common.

According to Neil Weintraut, a partner in 21st Century Internet Venture Partners in San Francisco, the feeding frenzy has gotten so crazy that, at times, venture capital firms have taken on the characteristics of the start-ups. Weintraut jokes that it feels as if there are as many start-ups of venture capital firms as there are start-ups in which to invest (Littman, 1998).

Competition for Talent

Another negative trend is that the tremendous demand for management teams in Silicon Valley is raising the compensation costs paid to start-up management teams. Because they are aware of their value, executives are demanding higher levels of equity participation.

Smaller Equity

A third negative trend is that venture firms are being pressured to write bigger checks in exchange for a smaller equity stake in the best new ventures. According to Ruthann Quindlen of Institutional Venture Partners, high-tech valuations have increased as much as 40 percent over the last several years, especially in communications and software. According to VentureOne, the median valuation of companies that have received an initial round of venture capital financing increased from $13.1 million to $21 million in the third quarter of 1997 (Littman, 1998).

Competition from Angels and Corporations

Competition is coming not only from within the ranks of the venture capital firms but from two other sources as well. First, there are the angels—wealthy individuals who enjoy writing checks to get a piece of a start-up. Often angels have become wealthy through their stock options as employees of a major high-tech company. They therefore have both the ability to help young companies and experience in the industry. From the perspective of an entrepreneur, angel money tends to come with fewer strings attached; unlike some venture capitalists, angels tend not to force the company to replace its top management team or make radical changes in strategy.

According to entrepreneur Kamran Elahain (Littman, 1998), a co-founder of six companies, many people in Silicon Valley are investing $50,000 or $100,000. A new company can thus raise $250,000 from a small number of angels, although the angels perform less due diligence and so are taking considerable risks.

Eric Ver Ploeg is CEO of start-up Angara Database Systems. The firm sells software that allows companies to work faster on subsets of huge databases. Ver Ploeg raised $100,000 in April 1997 from a wealthy real estate developer. Ver Ploeg often finds it easier to convince an angel than a venture capitalist. He finds them more willing to like a concept, even if the entrepreneur has yet to develop a clear marketing strategy (Littman, 1998).

Perhaps we should regard angels as complementing the work of traditional venture capitalists. As the venture funds grow, the extra cost and time of managing smaller investments has become an annoyance for venture capitalists. Increasingly they are making fewer but larger investments—at least $2 million. It takes as much or more time to work with early-stage start-ups as it does to work with the later-stage companies.

How do the most skilled angels work? One such angel is Madhavan Rangaswami, or M.R. According to *Computer Reseller News* (Mehling, 1997), in early 1996, M.R. decided to leave the intense pressures of the computer industry before it was too late. He cashed in his forty-to-one stock options in Dutch software maker Baan Co. (which he helped take public), quit his seventy-hour workweeks as vice president of worldwide marketing, and retired to his home in the Catalina Mountains in Tucson, Arizona.

There he started a family, took vacations and long hikes, and began to ask himself what he had accomplished beyond a successful career. However, he could not quite withdraw from the industry completely. He was looking for a way to balance the excitement of Silicon Valley with having a personal life.

With his cash and twenty-five hundred industry connections, he became an "active angel." He invests his funds and expertise in young, underdeveloped companies that need financial, management, and marketing help. M.R. may be the best-known "active angel." With Constatin Delivanis, former chief executive of two high-tech start-ups, M.R. cofounded the Sand Hill Group to support start-up and emerging companies.

M.R. actively works with the companies in which he invests, sometimes giving marketing advice, helping them choose management people, or preparing them so that they can raise money from the larger venture capital community.

Typically, M.R. seeks out companies with less than $5 million in sales, works to double the firm's value, then sends management out for venture capital funding. This strong base gives the founders more control. Most small entrepreneurs favor this approach because they believe it is less intrusive than the traditional venture capitalist approach.

M.R. currently works with three other enterprise software clients: i2 Technologies, a public company based in Irving, Texas, which has been growing at more than 100 percent per year since hitting revenue of $25 million in 1995; Aspect Development, in Mountain View, California; and MarketFirst, Santa Clara, California.

In addition to the angels, corporations are also getting into the venture capital business by setting up their own venture funds. Intel and Microsoft are the most well known of this new class of venture capitalists, but there are at least two dozen others, including Cisco Systems and Adobe Systems.

CASES
Kleiner Perkins: Closed-Loop Solutions

The most successful firms in venture capital have developed a closed-loop solution for creating new ventures. Rather than requiring an entrepreneur to go to one firm for capital, another firm for recruiting, and a third firm for investment banking, the providers of closed-loop solutions offer a one-stop shop. The closed-loop solution yields very high returns on capital for investors and tremendous success in the product and capital markets for entrepreneurs.

Kleiner Perkins's strategy can give us useful insights into how leading firms provide a closed-loop solution for the creation of new ventures. Key elements of that solution include the following:

• Reputation
• The Kleiner "keiretsu"

- Negotiating strategy
- Risk management
- Process for making investment decisions
- Vision of the Internet

REPUTATION. Kleiner Perkins's current generation of partners inherited a franchise based on reputation and values. Wes Sterman, founder of Heartport, a Kleiner-backed company that has developed minimally invasive coronary-bypass surgical procedures, believes that the firm's backing brings instant credibility to a company. Kleiner Perkins's reputation is based on its fame and the outstanding performance of its portfolio companies.

John Doerr's highly reputed marketing skills influence the success of Kleiner Perkins's portfolio companies. Doerr uses his own visibility to encourage investors to focus attention on Kleiner Perkins companies. For example, when Morgan Stanley led the August 1995 IPO for Netscape, Doerr persuaded Netscape to go public just as the equity markets were discovering the Internet. The press coverage of the offering helped increase sales of Netscape's Web browser. Going public as early as possible also helped Netscape generate cash to use for acquisitions that have proved useful for capturing innovations developed outside the company.

THE KLEINER "KEIRETSU." At the core of Kleiner Perkins's relationship network are the more than 250 companies in which it has invested. People hire Kleiner Perkins for its knowledge and its ability to effect change in a variety of industries. Expanding from its core companies, Kleiner Perkins has built extensive relationships with other companies through alliances and joint ventures.

This relationship network is called the Kleiner keiretsu after the Japanese system of extensive cross-ownership within a family of companies, with a bank coordinating activities at the center. Kleiner Perkins acts as the bank in this case, encouraging its companies to work with one another whenever possible; providing introductions; and suggesting marketing agreements, research collaborations, or joint ventures.

According to *Red Herring*, Kleiner Perkins encourages the companies within its network of talented entrepreneurs to help each other by forming buy-sell, licensing, or endorsement arrangements. For example, Destineer is a company that Kleiner Perkins and Mobile

Telecommunications Technologies started in 1990 to develop a one- and two-way nationwide messaging service that would use narrow-band Personal Communications Services frequencies. Because Wireless Access, another Kleiner Perkins company, was developing advanced pager technology, Kevin Compton, a Kleiner Perkins partner, suggested that Mobile Telecommunications Technologies and Wireless Access work together. Mobile subsequently invested in Wireless Access, and the two companies, along with Motorola and Destineer, codeveloped protocol, networking, and chip technologies that have been incorporated into SkyTel, Mobile's paging network (Gove, 1998).

The Kleiner keiretsu began in the early 1980s, when two start-ups, Lotus and Compaq, formed an alliance. This alliance was arranged by Kleiner Perkins's co-investor in these companies, venture capitalist Benjamin Rosen. Doerr brought in Kleiner start-up Businessland, one of the first retail computer chains, to market Lotus software and Compaq PCs. Today, the Kleiner keiretsu forms alliances among its Internet companies (Gove, 1998).

According to *Fortune,* an important source of people for the Kleiner keiretsu was a single engineering building at Stanford where John Doerr spent some time in the early 1980s: Margaret Jacks Hall, then home of the computer science department. Three start-ups based on the technology developed there now have a combined market value of more than $50 billion. Around 1980, Doerr, then a newly hired venture capitalist at Kleiner Perkins, started visiting. On the second floor, a professor named Jim Clark was working on a project that would become Silicon Graphics. On the fourth floor, Andy Bechtolsheim, then a Ph.D. candidate, was building a prototype workstation for the Stanford University Network, or SUN, which would become Sun Microsystems. In the basement, a research computing director named Len Bosack, together with Sandra Lerner, his wife and counterpart at the business school, was coming up with ways to link the various computer networks woven throughout campus, an effort that became Cisco Systems (Aley, 1997).

NEGOTIATING STRATEGY. Kleiner Perkins partners have a reputation for being hard-nosed. They negotiate tough financial deals. Their argument is that they offer more to entrepreneurs, so they should receive higher returns.

The firm prefers to invest at either the seed or first-stage level, but it will also put money into already profitable companies that are close to going public, such as Shiva or Intuit, the developer of personal finance software. It will also occasionally invest in struggling public companies that represent potential turnarounds, such as Platinum Software.

Kleiner Perkins rarely participates in a deal unless it is the lead investor and receives a board seat. Kleiner Perkins seeks to negotiate fairly with its entrepreneurs because it believes that overly harsh deals make it difficult to build a great company or make a great investment. In addition, it insists on focusing attention on the risks in a project and using scarce early capital, time, and energy to remove these risks.

John Doerr's negotiating ability contributes to Kleiner Perkins's power in Silicon Valley. John Colligan negotiated against Doerr when his company, Authorware, was being acquired by Kleiner's Macromind-Paracomp in 1992. Despite having negotiated against Doerr over the terms of the merger, Colligan agreed to stay on as president of the new Macromedia, which develops advanced multimedia software. Colligan was so impressed with Doerr that he was glad to get him on his side.

Much of Doerr's influence comes from the hundreds of managers whom he has helped place in important jobs. He spends as much time interviewing marketing and technology recruits for his companies as he does questioning CEOs. Doerr strengthens his network by placing Kleiner CEOs on the boards of other corporate members of the keiretsu. For instance, Gordon Eubanks Jr., the CEO of the software company Symantec, joined the Collabra Software board just three months before that company was acquired by Netscape to enhance Netscape's position against Lotus Notes. Randy Komisar, the CEO of video game maker Crystal Dynamics, is a board member of two companies associated with Kleiner, Total Entertainment Network and MNI Interactive. John Kernan, CEO of Lightspan Partnership, sits on the board of fellow educational software company Academic Systems. And Netscape's Jim Barksdale is a board member of At Home, the Kleiner-TCI joint venture.

The network has been reinforced by the firm's "CEO-in-residence" program, which brings temporarily out-of-work top executives into Kleiner Perkins to review business plans, engage in strategic thinking, and help with recruiting. For example, William Campbell, the former CEO of GO, a pen computing company, became the first CEO-in-residence after AT&T acquired the start-up in 1993. A year later Doerr recruited Campbell as president and CEO at Intuit.

Doerr and his partners also visit computer shows and conferences. Doerr discovered the idea for At Home at the December 1994 Western Cable Show in Anaheim, when he and an executive from TCI discovered a small Motorola telephone-ready cable box that could be adapted to provide a broadband computer link to the Internet (Heilemann, 1997).

RISK MANAGEMENT. Doerr believes that risk comes in four parts. The first is technical risk: Can the technology do what is needed? Second is market risk: Is there sufficient demand for the technology? Third is people risk: Will the people who founded the company stay? Fourth is financing risk: Can the money be raised to finance the venture? (Heilemann, 1997).

Doerr does not consider it a mistake to bet on a technology that does not yet work, because Kleiner Perkins is supposed to take risks. In fact, Kleiner believes that technology risk is much better than market risk, which is the most dangerous of the four. The danger is that after millions of dollars have been invested in a company that is spending a million dollars a month on operations, the venture firm finds out that there is no demand for the product.

Kleiner Perkins has spent a considerable amount of time developing a formula for dealing with risk. Its experience in writing business plans, recruiting management, hiring professional support, dealing with Wall Street, and even setting up equipment leases helps reduce many of the risks. Kleiner Perkins's first law is, "Get the risk up front and out of the way early." The company tries to remove financing risk by putting up its own money and by ensuring that entrepreneurs get access to other sources of capital if they need them.

Despite its effort to manage risk, failure is an inevitable part of the venture capital business. For example, in 1997, Kleiner Perkins closed a failed venture into which investors had put $15 million in four rounds. Kleiner Perkins wrote off its investment. There were forty employees. Other companies in Kleiner Perkins's portfolio offered jobs to over half the team, and the investors circulated résumés to help all the employees get great jobs. As long as employees work hard with the team's prior management and don't lie, the venture industry does not penalize failure.

PROCESS FOR MAKING INVESTMENT DECISIONS. To understand how Kleiner Perkins makes investment decisions, it is helpful to examine an example of one of the firm's first Internet investments—Netscape Communications. According to *Institutional Investor*, Netscape Communications was the first firm to commercialize the Web browser. It was started by Jim Clark, a former CEO of Silicon Graphics, a company that makes high-end computer workstations. When Clark realized he would need to raise venture capital to support Netscape in spring 1994, he visited NEA and Mayfield Fund before he visited Kleiner Perkins. At that time, Clark had recently left Silicon Graphics—which he had founded in 1982 and which had been backed by NEA and Mayfield—because of a dispute over compensation. When he met with these firms, he offered a less than enthusiastic sales presentation. Furthermore, he did not let these two firms meet twenty-four-year-old Marc Andreessen, whom Clark had recruited from the University of Illinois to develop a more advanced version of the Web browser (Mosaic) he had originally created for the university (Peltz, 1996).

Clark also priced the deal aggressively. He told NEA and Mayfield that he was personally putting up $3 million and pricing his concept at another $3 million, for a total initial valuation of $6 million. At that point, Clark wanted to value the start-up at $18 million, three times Mayfield's valuation. In negotiating for a higher initial valuation, Clark was trying to keep a larger share of Netscape for himself and a lower percentage for the venture firms.

Mayfield never called Clark back, and NEA told him they would only offer a multiple of two. Clark, who had already shared an early version of his Internet idea with Doerr in January 1994, felt free to follow up with Kleiner Perkins. Doerr was intrigued by Andreessen—whom he first met a few months later—and impressed by the potential size of the Internet market. Kleiner Perkins had earlier invested in America Online. However, an investment in Netscape would be a bet that millions of users would want to visit the World Wide Web, a larger and more chaotic domain than that offered to users of AOL's proprietary service. (Undoubtedly Kleiner Perkins's ownership of both AOL and Netscape facilitated their November 1998 merger.)

Doerr and his partners quickly decided to accept Clark's conditions. Although the price appeared high at the time, Kleiner Perkins's original $5 million investment was worth as much as $600 million near Netscape's peak stock market valuation in May 1996. And Kleiner Perkins liquidated much of its stake in Netscape between April 1997, when it held roughly 6.8 million shares, and May 1998, when it held only about 412,000 (Netscape Communications, Proxy Material, 1997 and 1998).

Kleiner Perkins follows a certain process discipline in its work. During the week, the firm's general partners spend most of their time out of the office—recruiting, visiting companies, going to conferences, or attending board meetings. But on Monday mornings, by 9:00 A.M. they are gathered at the Sand Hill Road headquarters for the weekly partnership meeting. The partners review existing investments and explore potential new ones. Formal presentations take place at 11:00 A.M. and 2:00 P.M. and rarely go beyond an hour (Peltz, 1996).

The firm's process for accepting or rejecting an investment is efficient. At least two sponsoring partners will have already spent considerable time working on each potential deal. By the time the sponsoring partners present the results of their investigation, the firm can usually make investment decisions the same day. Deal valuation involves experience and simple calculations. Valuation math that is too complex may indicate that the deal is not attractive as a venture investment.

Each deal must pass one crucial test: Would its advocates be willing to sit on the company's board of directors? Considering that each partner directs at least two new investments a year and that the firm holds board seats on 80 percent of its companies, the time commitment can become substantial. For this reason, Kleiner concentrates its investments on the West Coast, within a two-hour flight from San Francisco. For East Coast investments, Kleiner partners with local venture firms, such as Greylock Management in Boston or Venrock Associates in New York.

The partners' meetings have always been conducted efficiently. Tom Perkins, a founder, wanted an atmosphere in which people achieved results. The discussions are always direct and often brutal. All partners have an equal voice. Anyone can veto any deal, and everyone is expected to participate actively. John Doerr's views are often the most powerful, but only because he has earned his partners' respect. Information sciences partner E. Floyd Kvamee considers him inventive and resourceful; Douglas Mackenzie, another member of the information sciences group, sees Doerr as persuasive, open, and approachable.

By the time Doerr brought Netscape to the partners' meeting in June 1994, he and several information sciences partners had already met a number of times with Clark and Andreessen to agree on a business plan. In attempting to convince Kleiner Perkins to invest, the

Netscape executives explained how their Web browser software could become a window on the Internet. They argued that the Web was going to change the way business was done, regardless of Netscape. Although the importance of the Internet may seem obvious now, Bill Gates thought at the time that it was overhyped. In fact, it took him about two more years to recognize the significance of the Internet. (When he did so, he was able to crush Netscape with Microsoft's Internet Explorer.) In contrast, the Kleiner partners had voted to invest in Netscape in just thirty minutes (Peltz, 1996).

VISION OF THE INTERNET. Doerr counters Bill Gates's original perception of the Internet by claiming that its growth potential may be underhyped. Doerr cites a positive spiral that supports the growth of the Web. Growth in the number of connected nodes and the increased speed of these connections fuel demand for more network connections. This growth in demand convinces investors to finance companies that can meet the demand for more network connections and greater bandwidth.

In retrospect, Netscape now appears to be the first step in a major strategic Internet initiative engineered by Doerr. Kleiner Perkins has invested—and plans to invest further—in a host of companies designed to exploit various aspects of what the firm views as a major new marketplace. Each general partner has taken on more than one Internet investment. Doerr comments that PC hardware and software grew into a $100 billion industry in the 1980s but that the Internet could be three times bigger.

Kleiner Perkins now has stakes in more than a dozen Internet companies, including Com21, Concentric Network, Diamond Lane Communications, Excite, At Home, Healthscape, Individual, OnLive! Technologies, Netscape, Precept Software, SportsLine USA, Total Entertainment Network, and VeriSign. The firm has also urged many of its affiliated companies to target the Internet. Sun has not only developed Java, a programming language that could dominate the Internet, but also has entered into alliances with a number of other Kleiner companies, such as Netscape, Intuit, and Macromedia, as well as with Microsoft, which licensed Java.

In the 1980s, Kleiner Perkins made significant investments in the PC business. In the 1990s, it has made a large investment in the Internet. One of the firm's strengths has been its ability to see ahead of the crowd to the next big thing. Another is its willingness to go the next step by making a large bet on its vision. The results shown in Figure 4.1 suggest that so far, Kleiner Perkins's vision of the Internet is paying off.

Sculley Brothers: A Market Perspective

Sculley Brothers operates with a different philosophy than Kleiner Perkins. Its market-oriented approach to investing in and managing companies provides an interesting counterpoint. Although the Sculley Brothers fund is not open to public investors, we look at this case to understand certain principles.

Sculley Brothers is a private investment firm started by John Sculley, former CEO of Apple Computer, and his brothers; it is based in New York City. The firm has four guiding principles. First, because Sculley and his brothers are marketing people, they start with markets and apply three steps of testing: (1) Is the market huge and a possible candidate for investment? (2) For that market, can the firm uncover a powerful business-technology concept that it believes will change the ground rules of that market? (3) Can the firm identify potentially prestigious corporate partners who see strategic value from the partnership?

Once Sculley Brothers has satisfied these three tests, it feels it is in the best position to attract a great management team. Sculley Brothers differs from most venture capitalists in several ways. First, each brother has run a major business and has had senior operating experience in the United States and in other global markets. Arthur Sculley was head of worldwide private banking at J.P. Morgan and also played a key role in setting up its offices in Singapore and Hong Kong. He has spent nine years in Asia. David Sculley was CEO of H.J. Heinz North America and of H.J. Heinz U.K. and was group executive in charge of Weight Watchers and Oreida Potato. John Sculley was founder and CEO of PepsiCo's Foods International, CEO of Pepsi-Cola, and CEO of Apple Computer.

Second, Sculley Brothers invests its own family capital rather than raising a fund. Third, Sculley Brothers takes a far more active role in its companies than does the typical venture capital firm. Sculley focuses on defining market-driven business models, recruiting senior management, building brands, helping put together corporate relationships, implementing roll-ups (consolidating companies in a fragmented industry) and mergers and acquisitions, raising investment capital, and promoting each company to key constituencies and major customers. As does the Kleiner keiretsu, Sculley Brothers tries to cross-leverage opportunities within the portfolio where possible. Its technology portfolio includes companies in the Internet infrastructure, business-to-business (b-to-b) transaction support services, and business-to-consumer (b-to-c) network services segments (John Sculley, e-mail to author, June 10, 1998).

The Sculley Brothers technology portfolio, summarized in Table 4.1, reflects the firm's judgments about which segments of the Internet business have the greatest profit potential. John Sculley thinks that the Web as currently implemented is fairly primitive. In his view, the Web is more like the CB radio than the cellular phone. The Web has yet to develop a real business model because people are not willing to pay for most of the information that they get from the Web. Except for AOL, no company has done an effective job of creating a mass-market online service; and AOL is not a Web-based service—it is proprietary. Ultimately, however, the Web will evolve to capture a mass audience the size of the cable industry, with a potential reach of forty million homes in the United States.

The following are some other insights from Sculley (Sculley interview, June 1998):

• Current Web-based services such as Yahoo and Excite are search engines that are attempting to transform themselves into destination sites. Because consumers spend an average of six minutes per visit at these sites, the model of making money with them from advertising does not appear as attractive as it did a few years back. Therefore, these services are now trying to turn themselves into places where e-commerce takes place, going beyond the original search engine model.

• A current limiting factor on mass market adoption of the Internet is narrow bandwidth. The copper telephone wire now in use was designed to be used by 10 percent of the population, making calls averaging four minutes, at any given moment. Over the next five years, Sculley anticipates that the technology will be put in place to make dramatic increases in bandwidth. In addition, the Web will be able to grow dramatically within the next five to ten years only if the experience becomes more customer friendly.

• It is possible that virtual private networks (VPNs) will become increasingly important. Technology will make it more cost-effective for companies to build their own packet-switched networks to handle b-to-b transactions. There are big markets in the b-to-b area that will benefit from using the Web, VPNs, or both to do their business processes cheaper, faster, and better. As companies find their customers

Company	Description	Partners	Co-Investors	Status
Cambridge Display Technologies	Low Cost, low power high resolution displays	Hoechst, DuPont, Phillips, and Seiko-Epson	Intel, Herman Hauser, Esther Dyson, Lord Young-led group	Pre-IPO
Zapa.com	2D/3D media rich network	Microsoft, Intershop	Intershop, Star Ventures, Gilder	1999 Launch
NetObjects	Corporate Internet site developer	IBM, Lotus, Novell	IBM, Venrock, Norwest, Perseus Capital	1999 IPO
Veon	Broadband hypervideo servers	Comcast, Cablevision, Intertainer, Sun	H&Q, East-West, HK Catalyst, Gemini	Pre-IPO
Intralinks	Highly secured Internet-based document workflow service	JP Morgan, Chase, Citicorp, Bank America, IBM	Patricoff, Perseus Capital, Euclid	Pre-IPO
Peoplescape	Computer-assisted executive recruiting service	Christian & Timbers	Christian & Timbers	Pre-IPO
TalkCity.com	Web community service	NBC, Cox, Hearst, ATT, WebTV	SoftBank, Patricoff, New York Life, Soros, Intel	1999 IPO
GreenTree Nutrition	e-commerce for personal health care products	Yahoo, Women.com, iVillage	21st Century Internet Fund, Intel, Softbank	Pre-IPO
SoftVideo	Video services and training	Stanford University Engineering School	Transcosmo	1999 Launch
Buy.com	e-commerce	Softbank, Ingram	Softbank	1999 IPO

Table 4.1. Selected Companies from Sculley Brothers' Technology Portfolio.
Source: Sculley Brothers, 1998.

demanding that they provide both lower price and better service, Web- or VPN-enabled b-to-b e-commerce will become a huge market opportunity.

• In the b-to-c area, there is little evidence that consumers are willing to pay for the information they get from the Web. The business models that make sense in b-to-c involve transactions for products and services that consumers can purchase more cheaply, more quickly, and more easily over the Web than through traditional channels. Dell Computer's Web site, over which the company sells $10 million of equipment each day, is an example.

• The stock market places tremendous value on companies that are trying to achieve leading market share, regardless of profitability. Amazon has clear market leadership in book selling over the Web and is moving toward similar market position in selling CDS. A more extreme example is Mirabilis, an Israel-based maker of Internet-based chat software with twelve million registered users. Although it had no revenue and never purported to have a business model, it kept building an audience. When Mirabilis surpassed AOL in audience size, the company's CEO believed it would get the attention of the market. In June 1998, AOL bought Mirabilis for $287 million in cash (Sculley interview, June 1998).

IMPLICATIONS

The foregoing discussion suggests five principles for success in the Internet capital business.

1. *Venture capital is not just for institutions anymore.* The traditional notion that venture capital is just for large financial institutions has gone out the window. Increasingly, well-connected angel investors are able to pony up the early-stage cash that can give them a significant stake in an exciting start-up opportunity. And corporations are beginning to see venture investing as a very valuable way to get a window into new technologies. With all these new entrants, the pressure on venture investors to find great deals will continue to intensify.

2. *Invest in great management teams, not just technology.* Contrary to popular belief, great technology alone does not make a successful new venture: technology can change, new competitors can emerge, and markets that were forecast to be huge can shrivel. A successful venture depends on finding or creating a great management team that

has demonstrated its ability to build a large new business despite all these uncertainties. Increasingly, management is the scarce resource in putting together new ventures. The venture capitalists who can put together winning teams will be the ones who earn the highest returns.

3. *Bet on big markets.* As we will see in Chapter Eight, there are entire industries devoted to forecasting how markets that are tiny now will become huge in five years. The challenge for the venture capitalist is to find new businesses that are doing something to make a big change in a market that is huge right now. If the new venture can create a quantum improvement in customer value for a huge market, then it is a safer bet for the venture capitalist. There is much more room for error when a venture is going after a big market. Unfortunately, too many new ventures hear the siren song of technology and lose sight of this critical principle.

4. *Scrutinize and manage risk before investing.* The time to perform exhaustive due diligence is before investing a penny in the venture. The previous three principles suggest important areas in which to look for problems. Is the management team capable? Is there really a big market for the venture's product? Does the company have a compelling customer value proposition? Given the surfeit of capital available for ventures that can pass these three tests, it should not be difficult for such high-potential ventures to raise the capital they need to scale themselves to the point that they can go public.

5. *Nurture the network.* The venture capitalist with the best network wins. The best network includes great managers and managers in training; investment bankers and analysts from leading firms, such as Goldman Sachs and Morgan Stanley; corporate partners who can help a new venture with distribution, financing, or specific technical capabilities; and journalists who can get the word out about a venture just as it is about to go public. The successful venture capitalist is constantly building the network and finding new ways for the members of the network to connect and create new value.

THE NET PROFIT RETRIEVER'S ASSESSMENT OF THE INTERNET VENTURE CAPITAL SEGMENT

The Internet venture capital industry makes the Net Profit Retriever bark three times. Its industry has economic leverage; it offers its customers a closed-loop solution, and its management adapts effectively to rapid change.

1. *Economic leverage.* Venture capital firms talk to thousands of entrepreneurs. They screen out 99 percent of the business plans because the market potential is weak, the technology is not competitive, or the managers are not up to par. They invest in the remaining 1 percent—the firms that pass the screening process. They build management teams. They help form business partnerships. And when the financial performance and market conditions are right, they find investment banks to take the companies public in an IPO. The general partners of these firms typically earn returns that are ten times their investment, and their personal net worth can typically range from $50 million to $125 million and beyond. These results suggest that venture capital is an industry with economic leverage.

2. *Closed-loop solution.* By offering its stakeholders a closed-loop solution, leading venture firms such as Kleiner Perkins have created the dominant brand in its industry. These stakeholders include entrepreneurs, investors, and investment banks. These firms also provide entrepreneurs a closed-loop solution. An investment by firms such as Kleiner Perkins is a stamp of approval in the eyes of talented engineers, salespeople, marketers, and financiers. These leading firms can take a promising technology, help build a very capable management team, offer access to important business partners, and provide contacts with leading investment banks to take the company public when the financial performance and market conditions are right. Although most venture capital firms will claim to offer this closed-loop solution, Kleiner Perkins is the leading brand because it has a track record of consistent execution.

Similarly, leading venture firms offer the previously noted high investment returns to its investors. Investment banks have the confidence that a company with an IPO supplied by leading firms such as Kleiner Perkins will provide them with profitable follow-on business as the company continues to grow.

3. *Adaptive management.* Two facts suggest that Kleiner Perkins's management adapts effectively to change. The most obvious one is that Kleiner Perkins has demonstrated its ability to invest in companies at the leading edge of technology. The success of its investment portfolio suggests that Kleiner Perkins is able to evaluate industries, strategies, and management teams effectively. Given the rapid pace of change in the industries in which Kleiner Perkins invests, it is plausible to assume that its management adapts well to change.

As we will discuss further in Chapter Seven, Kleiner Perkins has taken a leadership role in recognizing the importance of political involvement. John Doerr, Kleiner Perkins's lead partner, has formed TechNet, a consortium of Silicon Valley executives whose mission is to influence public policy toward technology companies. Doerr raises money for such politicians as Al Gore, who has spoken repeatedly about the importance of the Internet. And the Internet business has flourished. Kleiner Perkins's management does not so much adapt to change as lead change.

CHAPTER FIVE

Internet Security: Barbarians at the Gates

I magine that you are CEO of a bank based in New York, with offices in 120 countries and $300 billion in assets. Thousands of miles away, a twenty-seven-year-old is sitting at a computer terminal in his basement apartment in Kiev. He has spent the last twenty-six hours running a computer program called CRACK. CRACK is a little software utility that he downloaded from a Web site. CRACK's role in life is to probe huge computer networks, trying different passwords until it finds ones that unlock valuable data. CRACK completes its work, and the hacker is thrilled: he is looking at a list of one hundred corporate bank accounts, each containing over $5 million, and the passwords for those accounts. And he is about to run another program that will siphon off $1 million from each one into his numbered Swiss bank account.

Fast-forward three months. You are sitting in an audit committee meeting of the board as your auditor describes how $100 million in deposits disappeared from the accounts of your one hundred best customers. As you listen to the report, questions are rushing through your head. How could something like this have happened? Who is responsible? How can we keep this from ever happening again? How can we recover the money? And how will we be able to keep those customers from taking their business elsewhere?

This scenario is fictional but much like what really happened to a major financial institution a few years ago. Detecting and preventing these kinds of attacks is the business of Internet security.

—~~~—

Internet security, Web portals, e-commerce sites, and Web content are four Web industry segments that we will examine in this second part of the book. The average participant in these segments is losing a substantial amount of money. Often, however, the largest of the firms in these segments, such as America Online, E-Trade, and Yahoo, are earning a profit. What these segments all share is an unstable industry structure. The segments are unprofitable now, but they are likely to become profitable in the future.

We will analyze each of these segments and attempt to predict how they will evolve. As we will see, the potential profitability of the segments depends heavily on the emergence of a clear segment leader. If such a leader emerges, it is likely that the segment will consolidate around the business model pursued by the leading firm. Once this consolidation takes place, the segment has the potential to become profitable as money-losing firms are squeezed out of the industry.

The structures of these Brandware industries are fundamentally different than those discussed in the first section of the book. The industries that are typically unprofitable now but likely to become profitable in the future are not leverage-point industries: they are not in a position to direct the efforts of large numbers of third-party developers. They find themselves more in the position of needing to convince their customers that their products and services are worth purchasing. Whereas the demand for network equipment or Web consulting services is coming from customers who feel an urgent need to buy, the same cannot be said about the demand for Internet security, Web portals, e-commerce businesses, or Web content.

OVERVIEW OF THE INTERNET SECURITY MARKET

The Internet security industry exemplifies the structure just described. The market for corporate security systems has ballooned from $305 million in 1995 to an estimated $2.4 billion in 1998, a compound annual growth rate of almost 100 percent. The industry offers four distinct products and services: firewalls, authentication, encryption, and professional services. Firewalls protect an organization's computers from unauthorized access by computers outside the organization. Authentication verifies the identity of a person attempting to gain access to an organization's data or to conduct an electronic transaction. Encryption encodes information as it is sent over a network so that if the information is intercepted, it will not be useful to the interceptor. Professional services include consulting to help organizations identify security weaknesses. As we will see later in this chapter, ethical hacking is a form of paid marketing for Internet security firms that sell software to fix security weaknesses.

The forces driving the increase in the future profitability of the Internet security business are likely to be greater than the forces making it unprofitable. The forces driving increased profit include high growth, the proliferation of distributed networks, the growing demand for integrated security solutions, and the consolidation of the Internet security industry. The forces working to decrease profitability include the perception that Internet security is not as important as other IT issues, such as Year 2000 (Y2K) remediation; the absence of industry standards; and the low, but rising, barriers to entry into the business.

SOURCES OF FUTURE PROFITABILITY
The Growing Market

According to *EDP Weekly,* the Internet security business was expected to grow very rapidly between 1995 and the year 2000. Authentication was expected to grow at 92 percent, encryption at 108 percent, and professional services at 69 percent. According to International Data Corporation, firewalls were forecast to grow from $636 million in 1998 worldwide revenues to $1,845 million in 2002, a 31 percent compound annual growth rate (The Worldwide Firewall, 1998). *EDP Weekly* anticipated that overall spending on information security was anticipated to increase in 1999, with 25 percent of all large organizations budgeting more than $500,000 for information security needs. Between 1998 and 1999, the number of companies spending more than a half-million dollars on information security products and services was expected to increase 73 percent ("Responding to Rising . . .," 1998).

The big increase in spending is driven by the very high numbers of Internet users and the different combinations of Internet traffic. These factors have contributed to a rise in the number of security breaches, particularly from insiders. Of 1,063 information security professionals polled, 54 percent said that their companies experienced an incident of employee access abuse in the last year, a 35 percent increase over 1997. Nearly 20 percent of the respondents suffered a leak of proprietary information, up 58 percent ("Responding to Rising . . .", 1998).

The concern about Internet security exists not only for companies but for consumers as well. According to a *BusinessWeek* survey, 61 percent of Americans who do not currently use the Internet would do so if they felt that their privacy were better protected than it is now. Of those who do go online, 77 percent have never made a purchase via computer. Of those who have, 56 percent are very concerned that credit card information may be misused. Of those who haven't, 86 percent express the same concern. Only 9 percent of consumers would completely trust a privacy policy posted on a Web site; 58 percent would trust it somewhat, and 33 percent not at all ("Online Insecurity," 1998).

The underlying reason for the growth in corporate security concerns and the Internet security business is a big change in the way corporate computing systems are designed. When companies used mainframes to process corporate data, securing information was relatively simple. As companies have enabled greater distributed access through distributed computer architectures, the number of potential unauthorized access points to a company's data has increased. Now a company's data are vulnerable to unauthorized access by external hackers, laptop computer thieves, angry customers, frustrated suppliers, disgruntled current employees, and recently terminated employees.

Instead of residing on a mainframe computer, corporate information is now spread out across networks of smaller computers, called servers, that can be accessed by suppliers and customers via PCs, laptop computers, and other devices. Corporate Web sites linked to the outside world via the Internet give hackers with malicious intent a channel that they can use to break into company networks.

The Internet has added another layer of complexity to the job of the computer security manager. The growth in the number of physical devices on the network has also increased the security challenge. Many organizations must manage and secure servers running a variety of operating systems, such as Windows NT, Novell NetWare, and various versions of Unix. In addition, many corporate networks are based on multiple communications protocols, including Token Ring, TCP/IP, and IPX-based networks. Yet another complication is the variety of media cabling, ranging from copper to twisted-pair to fiber optics, as well as microwave and emerging wireless networks. These systems range across states and around the world, multiplying the number of points at which the organization is exposed.

Consolidation and Closed-Loop Solutions

Changes in how companies store and retrieve data are changing the structure of the market for computer security. In the past, companies could protect their data by purchasing point products—a firewall, some encryption software, or a virus detection utility. The spread of distributed corporate networks has created a demand for integrated product suites. Now companies are demanding closed-loop solutions that allow them to secure the entire network from end to end. To provide these integrated solutions, Internet security vendors are looking for ways to offer customers an entire portfolio of point products, all linked together seamlessly.

A popular way to build these product portfolios has been through acquisitions. For example, Network Associates, itself formed from the merger of McAfee Associates and Network General in 1997, has made several acquisitions to build up a portfolio of security products. Since December 1997, Network Associates purchased Pretty Good Privacy, an encryption and authentication firm, a firewall company, a vendor of software that looks for network vulnerabilities, and an antivirus software firm.

Other firms have also been quite active in making acquisitions. In early 1998, Axent Technologies purchased Raptor, a firewall firm, for $124 million. In March 1998, Axent purchased AssureNet Pathways, a supplier of authentication products. Even Cisco Systems has gotten into the business. Cisco already sells two firewalls and offers encryption technology. In February 1998, Cisco agreed to purchase Wheel-Group, a company that makes software to detect network intruders and vulnerabilities, for $245 million. This trend toward consolidation is likely to continue as long as customers continue to seek integrated security solutions (Boslet, 1998).

Why will these trends help drive up the profitability of the Internet security industry? To the extent that customers begin to spend more money on integrated security solutions, they may find themselves becoming more dependent on a single vendor who can offer them the best closed-loop solution. And as this demand-side trend intensifies, the number of vendors who can deliver what customers need is likely to decline. The surviving vendors are thus likely to find themselves in a stronger bargaining position just as customers' perceived need and budget for integrated security solutions increase.

FACTORS HOLDING PROFITS BACK
Low Priorities

Of course, the future is likely to hold some clouds for the industry as well. As we discussed before, security is important, but it is not clear that security is as important as remediation of the Year 2000 (Y2K) problem. As long as companies are required by SEC regulations to report on the status of their Y2K remediation efforts, IT departments are likely to devote most of their resources to solving the Y2K problem. Because not all firms will actually solve their Y2K problems in time, it is possible that security software vendors could take a back seat to Y2K in the budgeting process for a while after 2000.

According to the *EDP Weekly* survey of information technology executives ("Responding to Rising . . .," 1998), despite increasing budgets, the most important obstacle to security is a lack of adequate funding, mentioned by 58 percent of respondents. The second-biggest obstacle is a lack of end-user awareness, cited by 50 percent of all respondents. Of course, a very costly and widely publicized Internet security breach could change this set of priorities in favor of the security vendors.

Low, But Rising, Barriers to Entry

Another factor that is militating against the profitability of the industry is the low barriers to entry. Although many of them are quite small, there are an estimated five hundred firms in the Internet security market, and the cost of entry is very low. All that is required to start a new firm is a group of engineers with the technical know-how to develop a security product or deliver professional services, and the capital to pay for their upkeep. Considering today's proliferation of venture capital, these requirements are not very steep, so there are likely to be many small, new entrants. At the same time, the exit barriers are quite low. As a result many companies are being taken out of the industry through consolidation or by simply running out of cash.

Entry barriers to the Internet security business are rising. Many of the small, new entrants will not become significant industry participants. The increasing complexity of all but a very small number of firms in the industry will achieve critical mass. Nevertheless, a few of the new entrants could introduce a disruptive technology that would imperil the market position of today's industry leaders.

High Sales and Marketing Costs

The success of 1998 IPOs by VeriSign and Internet Security Systems adds substantial financial firepower to those Internet security firms that are fortunate enough to gain access to the public equity markets. Access to capital provides a powerful incentive to sacrifice short-term profitability for market share. In fact, the extraordinary market valuations of companies in this sector are predicated on the assumption that the companies will eventually become the de facto industry standard in a huge and rapidly growing industry. Conversely, when IPO markets dry up, nonpublic Internet security firms are forced (because of the need to sustain high marketing spending) to seek additional private capital or sell out to competitors who are better capitalized.

It is this surplus capital earmarked for eventual market dominance that fuels a third antiprofit force in the industry, namely a trend of high and growing sales and marketing expenses. An analysis of the income statements of the companies in the Internet security business reveals two insights. First, sales and marketing expenses consume a bigger share of revenues than does any other cost component. Second, the share is growing. Clearly, marketing costs place powerful downward pressures on profits for the average Internet security firm, as they do for firms in other segments of the Internet industry.

Here is how it works. Cash flow shapes the evolution of high tech industries such as Internet security. The surplus of venture capital pours into the select group of companies that are deemed potential winners. These nominees for the role of de facto industry standard scramble to line up customers and alliance partners. When the companies generate annual revenues higher than $5 million, they go public. This generates additional capital that is funneled into a more intensive effort to land more customers and alliance partners. In the "endgame" of this ongoing race for the top, it becomes clear to the industry who is accumulating new customers and alliances exponentially and who is struggling to keep the lights on. Eventually the winners acquire the losers.

Investors are guessing that the winners in the endgame will be able to reap high profits in a huge and rapidly growing market, but these profits have not yet fully materialized and no one really knows yet if they ever will. Still, our analysis suggests a future of increasing industry profitability. As the perceived industry leaders emerge, sales and marketing expenses may decline as customer switching costs grow. The impact of this evolution should be greater profitability for the average participant in the Internet security business.

SPOTTING FUTURE PROFITS

As the previous sections have implied, for the Internet security industry segment, as for the Web portal, e-commerce, and Web content segments, the question is not so much how to make profits today but how to spot future profitability. Here are five general strategies that can inform your current managerial role or your search as an investor.

1. *Draw a map of the territory.* Too many Web businesses rush forward to turn a technology into a product before mapping out the industry terrain. In the Internet security business, there are hundreds of point-product companies that built products to do one thing, such as encryption or antivirus protection, without a vision for how their technology would fit into the overall industry value system. To be a survivor in the endgame, managers need a map of the territory. This map will show how the company fits into a broader system of value creation. It will chart the flow of key inputs to the firm and how the firm's products and services create value for customers and customers' customers. As the flow of value inevitably changes, managers can update the map to reflect the changes.

2. *Chart a course.* Once they have drawn a map, managers must use it to think about how they can lead their industry. As we saw, leaders in the Internet security industry have realized that customers are now seeking integrated security solutions. And these industry leaders have responded to the challenge by finding ways to build integrated security suites—through either acquisition or internal development.

For investors, mapping out the territory and charting a course can also provide useful insights. By viewing industries from the perspective of managers, investors can more easily identify the companies with the greatest chance of long-term industry leadership.

3. *Think at the industry and company levels.* One of the critical skills that distinguishes the long-term survivors is their ability to think and act at both the industry and company levels. Winning firms develop a vision of how the industry must evolve in order for it to become profitable for the average participant. For Internet security firms, this vision has meant recognizing that the way to lower sales and marketing costs in a fragmented industry is to encourage consolidation of the industry. Consolidation leads to the emergence of a handful of recognized leaders with the financial, technical, and managerial resources to meet evolving customer security requirements.

4. *Invest in the industry leaders.* As industries evolve, their indicators of investment value change. Most Web industries are at such an early stage of evolution that their nonexistent profits are not a useful indicator of investment value. During this phase, a potentially useful measure of investment value is market leadership. At the early stage of industry evolution, investors should seek out the companies with the largest market share. If the industry is large and growing rapidly, it is generally reasonable to assume that the firm with market leadership stands the greatest chance of reaping the lion's share of the industry profits.

How the structure of the industry evolves will determine the return on capital of the average participant in the Internet security business. But profitability is not determined by the industry structure alone. To pick the firms that will be most profitable in the Internet security business, it is necessary to recognize the strategy that determines market leadership.

5. *Look for firms that are closing loops.* In Chapter One, we said that companies offering open-loop solutions tend to perform less well than firms offering closed-loop solutions. This pattern is at work in the Internet security business. As we have discussed, companies that offer point solutions are being acquired by companies that are seeking to offer integrated solutions. The providers of point solutions solved a piece of the security problem: they offered a good firewall product or a strong antivirus solution. But these companies could not grow with the industry because they lacked what customers were eager to purchase. Companies that could piece together products offering authentication, intrusion detection, firewalls, and encryption capabilities were the ones that got the big contracts because they could meet the real needs of corporate customers.

CASES

The following cases will show how two leading Internet security companies are building organizations that can deliver these closed-loop solutions. CheckPoint Software Technologies is an example of a profitable company that is leading the way in weaving a collection of point products into an integrated solution, primarily through internal development. Network Associates is an example of a company that is trying to build an integrated suite of networking products through acquisitions.

As we review the strategies of these firms, it will become clear that the ability to sustain superior performance in the medium term depends heavily on a firm's skill at building integrated product portfolios. Over the longer term, prevailing firms will be the ones who can reshape the structure of the Internet security industry to make the business more of a leverage point.

CheckPoint Software Technologies: Weaving an Integrated Web

In 1998 revenues, CheckPoint was a $142 million vendor of Internet security technologies. Co-headquartered in Israel and Redwood City, California, CheckPoint is the leader in the firewall market with an estimated 35 percent share, four times the share of its nearest competitor. With 1998 net income of $71 million, Check Point is solidly profitable.

When Deborah Rieman, former CEO of CheckPoint's U.S. operation, joined CheckPoint in 1995, the company founders realized that the Internet would be used more broadly. They realized that high-bandwidth Internet traffic would become much more prevalent. Companies would increasingly use e-commerce and full intranets to run major parts of their businesses. Expanded use of the Internet would create new security challenges.

CheckPoint's firewall was designed to protect such high-bandwidth communications. CheckPoint's founders applied the architectural ideas used in its firewall products to develop Internet security products that could protect Internet traffic among many applications and many users (Rieman, interview with the author, Aug. 1998).

CheckPoint's success at anticipating changes in technology is not shared by all its peers. The fate of Security Dynamics is a compelling example of how unanticipated change can quickly jeopardize a market leader in the Internet security business. A Massachusetts-based Internet security firm, Security Dynamics, is a leader in the market for authentication with 65 percent of the market. Within the course of a few months in 1998, Security Dynamics went from being profitable to being unprofitable.

The reason for this shift was that, unlike CheckPoint, Security Dynamics was unable to respond quickly enough to a fundamental change in technology. Security Dynamics controlled roughly 65 percent of the market for authentication software with its so-called Token technology. Tokens are credit-card-sized devices that generate new passwords every minute to gain access to a secured device; an individual types the password on the Token and a personal identification number (PIN) into the device's keypad. A separate machine called an authentication server verifies the password and the PIN.

Another technology called Digital Certificates (DCs) was much better suited to securing e-commerce applications. Over the course of three months, VeriSign, a leading proponent of DCs, grew very rapidly at Security Dynamics' expense. DCs grew faster than Tokens because they were less expensive and easier to use.

The irony of the situation is that VeriSign had been spun off from RSA Data Security, a company that Security Dynamics had acquired. Security Dynamics was intellectually aware of the change happening in the marketplace. However, Security Dynamics had been selling Token technology since the 1970s that made it very difficult for the company to adopt DCs. Although Security Dynamics has announced its intention to begin selling a DC product in the first half of 1999, the company was hurt by its slow reaction time (Rieman interview, Aug. 1998).

CheckPoint did not allow itself to be caught in this same trap. The company used its market leadership in firewall technology to build a strong position in enterprise network security management. While CheckPoint has made one acquisition, it has chosen to develop most of its technology in-house. CheckPoint also struck alliances with vendors of other products. The company and its alliance partners worked together to integrate their products meticulously and at a deep level. As a result of this intense collaboration, CheckPoint can offer a unique advantage to its customers: "clean" software code rather than code that is superficially stitched together after acquisitions.

Also, CheckPoint emphasizes a "policy-based management" approach to security that makes it easier to integrate products from other vendors. *Policy-based management* enables a network manager to allocate network resources to the most important applications and to establish and monitor security policies. These security policies determine such details as who in the company is authorized to view which pieces of corporate data and what procedures they must follow to gain access to the data. Policy-based management lets corporate managers establish and implement security policies at a higher level—that of the network—rather than at the lower level of devices, where point products generally operate (Boslet, 1998).

CheckPoint appears to have followed the strategic principle illustrated by companies like Cisco Systems: that of building exceptional market power through an operating system that permits interoperability. In 1996, CheckPoint introduced its Open Platform for Secure Enterprise Connectivity (OPSEC), an architecture designed to ensure that popular security products could work together. Less than six months later, more than eighty network security, internetworking, Internet, and intranet applications vendors had joined the OPSEC alliance. This helped to position OPSEC as a de facto industry standard (Harrison, 1997). By January 1999, OPSEC's membership had grown to 160.

Rieman believed that no one company would be able to provide a total, integrated solution, but she and her company also believed that firewalls would remain an important component. As companies connected to other organizations' networks, security would be an essential enabler of e-commerce, and the key to solving network security problems would be to see that CheckPoint's firewalls and others could fit within an integrated framework.

In addition to having tremendous foresight regarding how the market for Internet security would evolve, CheckPoint also made two important strategic choices that have differentiated the company. First, according to *Fortune*, CheckPoint developed a product that was fundamentally different from traditional firewalls. Traditional products were built by former government data security workers who custom-built complicated and obscure firewalls for corporate and government customers. By contrast, CheckPoint had developed an off-the-shelf product, called FireWall-1, to suit the needs of many customers (Warner, 1998). To further broaden the potential market for its products, CheckPoint built FireWall-1 to run on the two most prominent client-server operating system platforms.

Second, CheckPoint gained dominance of the ISP market, an increasingly strong channel for security products. Major ISPs such as

AT&T, MCI, UUNet, and US West offered to manage Internet and intranet services for their corporate customers using FireWall-1. Due to the low profits in basic Internet access services, ISPs are seeking new revenue sources. One such service is managing corporate network security. By helping ISPs deliver this new service, CheckPoint got a jump on its competitors who are selling solutions to non-ISPs.

But despite CheckPoint's strategy and performance, it is vulnerable to powerful new entrants. For example, Microsoft's Steve Ballmer announced in March 1998 that Microsoft would compete with Check-Point in the future. Instead of simply purchasing CheckPoint's firewall technology, Microsoft announced its intention to incorporate firewalls into its Windows NT operating system. Between March and July 1998, CheckPoint stock lost over 30 percent of its value (Warner, 1998). Other strong competitors include Cisco Systems and Computer Associates. CheckPoint's ability to continue to succeed depends on its ability to stay ahead of these new competitors.

To stay ahead of the rapid changes in the market, CheckPoint has adopted specific management techniques that have worked effectively. CheckPoint has a flexible, flat organization. In Rieman's view, the Internet security industry is changing too fast to allow time for the impeding effects of hierarchy. CheckPoint is also tightly connected to its end users and third-party partners. CheckPoint's strategy and products are driven by its ever-changing view of its customers.

Reiman cautions that a company cannot be led by its customers, because they may not understand the full potential of new technologies. CheckPoint understands and anticipates change on their behalf. Whereas in the past, companies were relatively slow to adapt new technology, companies are keeping much more current with Internet technology. To monitor their propensity to adopt new technology, CheckPoint watches closely to see where customers put their money. Its priorities evolve over a six- to twelve-month period, depending on constant conversations with customers and on close observation of where they spend.

CheckPoint views its most significant competitors as Cisco and, potentially, Microsoft. Rieman is trying to build its future strategy around a product area that Microsoft and Cisco will not be able to execute as well as CheckPoint. She believes that while firewalls could be absorbed into Cisco's router or Microsoft's Windows NT operating system, it will be very difficult for Cisco or Microsoft to do a good job at integrating products from multiple vendors. She wagers that Cisco and Microsoft are too dedicated to their proprietary architectures to build a piece of software that can secure a corporation's entire network, which may be made up of products from vendors other than Cisco and Microsoft (Rieman interview, Aug. 1998).

It remains to be seen whether CheckPoint will succeed in its policy-based networking. Although the stock market certainly punished its stock between March and September of 1998, CheckPoint's 90 percent earnings growth for the first nine months of 1998 helped drive its stock price from seventeen to fifty-five between the earnings announcement and early November. As change in the Internet security business accelerates, CheckPoint's business model will continue to be tested.

Network Associates: A Doubtful Strategy of Acquisitions

CheckPoint is a clearly profitable industry participant. By contrast, Network Associates is a much larger firm with sales of $700 million and a net loss of $193 million for the nine months ending September 30, 1998. It has been unprofitable due largely to $340 million in acquisition costs. Its case articulates some of the hidden costs associated with the strategy of piecing together a portfolio of security products through acquisition.

Formerly McAfee Associates, Network Associates is the world's leading maker of antivirus software, such as NetShield and Virus-Scan, and of the Sniffer family of software tools for monitoring and troubleshooting computer networks. Recent acquisitions have moved the company into hardware sales and encryption technology. Network Associates pioneered electronic software distribution (originally with antivirus shareware); the Internet is still a major sales channel. It also sells its products through a direct sales force and through resellers, distributors, and retailers. Network Associates focuses primarily on Windows NT-based corporate networks. Nearly 30 percent of its sales are outside North America ("Network Associates Company Background," 1998).

As its third-quarter 1998 financial statement suggests, the short-run costs of Network Associates' acquisition strategy have exceeded its benefits. During the latter half of 1998, Network Associates concentrated on completing and digesting acquisitions that it had announced in the first half of the year, instead of making new ones. The genesis of its current struggle to integrate its acquisitions is a set of principles that supposedly drove Network Associates' acquisition strategy. The principles appear flawed and the deals seem haphazard. We will explore these problems later in this discussion.

According to *Forbes*, in Network Associates' view, consolidation in the Internet security market takes place for the following reasons:

- The cost of marketing Internet security products is too high for a small firm to support profitably.

- Internet security customers are increasingly demanding an integrated suite of security products across the enterprise. Firms that lead in one product category are finding it more efficient to acquire the full portfolio of products.

- Acquisition is an effective means of expanding geographically.

According to *Forbes* (Foster with Pitta, 1998), throughout late 1997 and 1998, Network Associates attempted to build an Internet security software company by supposedly adhering to the following three principles:

1. *Expand the product line.* By itself, McAfee Associates (Network Associates' predecessor) initially sold an antivirus program that did not add much value on a stand-alone basis. As a result of thirteen acquisitions, Network Associates has built a full suite of products for managing and hacker-proofing a network of PCs. It offers such features as encryption, intrusion detection, firewalls, and software to run help desks.

2. *Bundle products to get higher returns.* Whereas once its clients purchased software for smaller amounts, Network Associates now has clients paying as much as $500,000 a year for bundled products.

3. *Market aggressively.* Network Associates' advertising budget to launch itself was $10 million, including a television advertisement that ran during the Super Bowl. In April 1998, Network Associates leased an eleven-story mirrored building near Silicon Valley's Highway 101 and put the Network Associates name on it. Network Associates has one thousand salespeople, including telemarketers who average seventy-five calls a day. Experienced salespeople are paid 50 percent salary and 50 percent commission (Foster with Pitta, 1998).

—⁓—

Several transactions exemplify Network Associates' consolidation principles but also reveal their flaws. The basic flaw is that the principles focus too heavily on product push rather than on a deep understanding of customer needs. The principles drive Network Associates to spend too much time doing deals and not enough time managing the integration of the products it has acquired. If the products are not tightly interwoven, customers may find a gap between the integrated security solution they need and the quilt of point products they get. Furthermore, acquiring to broaden the product line can slow down Network Associates' growth if the acquired company is in a line of business that grows slowly. Finally, as we will see in the discussion of the CyberMedia acquisition, Network Associates' deal fever can drive it to make acquisitions that violate even its flawed principles. We will explore the following three cases:

1. McAfee and Network General

2. Network Associates and Doctor Solomon's

3. Network Associates and CyberMedia

MCAFEE AND NETWORK GENERAL. Network Associates was the result of a merger between McAfee Associates of Santa Clara, California, and Network General of Menlo Park, California. The merger was consistent with the "expand the product line" principle mentioned earlier. According to a Network Associates press release, this deal was announced in October 1997 and took effect on December 1, 1997.

The two firms placed a value of $1.3 billion on the deal. McAfee reported gross annual sales of about $181 million in 1996 to Network General's $189 million, for a combined gross sales figure of $370 million. Analysts said that the merger made sense because there was not much overlap between product lines of the two firms. Whereas McAfee focused on antivirus software, Network General made fault, performance, and security management tools. Under the terms of the transaction, McAfee offered 0.4167 shares for each share of Network General stock. Bill Larson took over as chairman and CEO of Network Associates; Leslie Denend, the CEO of Network General, became president ("McAfee to Combine . . . ," 1997).

McAfee and Network General had very different corporate cultures. McAfee was a young, entrepreneurial company that had experienced a compound revenue growth rate of 116 percent over three years. In contrast, Network General was older and more established, with revenue growth over three years of a more sedate 28 percent. The merger also involved cutting jobs. In December 1997, 150 of Network Associates' 1,700 employees were fired.

The merger did expand Network Associates' product line. However, despite the clear sense that McAfee management ended up dominating the combined firms, the financial results a year later suggest that the growth rate of the combined firms slowed dramatically. Whereas McAfee had been growing at 116 percent, above the 100 percent industry average, the combined firms are now growing at 33 percent. This slowdown suggests that McAfee's entrepreneurial culture had been damped in the acquisition process.

NETWORK ASSOCIATES AND DR. SOLOMON'S. In June 1998, Network Associates announced its intention to purchase competitor Dr. Solomon's Software, based in Aylesbury, England ("Network Associates to Acquire . . .," 1998). The price was $640 million. The deal was consistent with the "market aggressively" principle, increasing Network Associates' installed base by 20 percent to 25 percent, or well over fifty million desktops. The desktop-installed bases provided a point of distribution for additional products that do authentication, sniffing, and network-performance monitoring.

Network Associates also planned to use the acquisition to build its European channel as it attempted to increase its European market share. In the United States, Network Associates sold most of its products directly to end users. The Dr. Solomon's merger introduced a new element to Network Associates' marketing strategy, namely, selling its products indirectly through a network of Value Added Resellers (VARs). VARs are systems integrators, like the ones we analyzed in Chapter Three, who at times recommend security software to their clients. Network Associates anticipated that an increase in its share of revenues from VARs would enhance corporate profits. By acquiring Dr. Solomon's U.S. VAR base, Network Associates hoped to increase the proportion of its sales through the VAR channel.

Network Associates planned for Dr. Solomon's name to continue to have a presence on retail shelves. Network Associates intended to absorb the Dr. Solomon's products into a suite due in early 1999. After the acquisition was completed, both companies' complete antivirus lines were expected to be included in the Network Associates suites. Network Associates expected that sometime in early 1999 it would begin shipping an upgrade that would incorporate both Network Associates and Dr. Solomon's.

Network Associates and Dr. Solomon's also anticipated that the new firm would have stronger research skills and a broader product portfolio. The acquisition, when combined with the VirusScan team from the McAfee Associates side of the business, doubled Network Associates' research and development team to over 150 people. Network Associates planned to launch Dr. Solomon's VirusScan 4.0 onto the U.K. market, the first product to combine the Dr. Solomon's virus-finding engine with McAfee's VirusScan user interface. This product was intended to be the desktop component of a suite of antivirus products to be called Dr. Solomon's Total Virus Defense. The engine, groupware products, and Internet gateways would continue to be developed in the United Kingdom, while desktop and NT file-server products and quality assurance would be handled at Network Associates' facility in Beaverton, Oregon.

The Dr. Solomon's acquisition raises questions about whether Network Associates will be able to earn a return on its $640 million investment. Network Associates must overcome significant challenges to manage the integration of a company based in a different country, with new channels of distribution and an unfamiliar set of products. The most optimistic analysis of the deal suggests that Network Associates will generate significant new European revenues for its other products and develop VAR marketing skills that it can import to the United States. A more pessimistic assessment is that the Dr. Solomon's acquisition was a knee-jerk reaction to Symantec's acquisition of IBM's antivirus product line, an effort that will founder as a result of integration problems.

NETWORK ASSOCIATES AND CYBERMEDIA. In July 1998, Network Associates made a friendly all-cash offer of $130 million to purchase CyberMedia. This offer represented a 25 percent premium over CyberMedia's closing price. CyberMedia, based in Santa Monica, California, was the creator of First Aid, the self-healing diagnostic software for Windows. Network Associates described the takeover as a tactical rather than strategic acquisition. To which acquisition principle this deal adhered is not clear.

Network Associates planned to merge the CyberMedia business into its McAfee software division, which was intended to sell to retail customers. Retail represented 10 percent of Network Associates' overall sales. But CyberMedia's second-quarter 1998 sales of $5.8 million were down dramatically from $20.4 million in the same period of 1997. Despite these bad results, Network Associates expected to use the CyberMedia acquisition as a way to increase its retail sales.

The logic behind the acquisition was that Network Associates would embed First Aid and UnInstall into its own Total Service Desk Suite. Network Associates would also gain greater market visibility via CyberMedia's well-known shrink-wrapped packages, such as Guard

Dog and Oil Change. It seems unlikely that an unprofitable company with only $25 million in annual sales would be able to earn back the purchase price of the deal.

CyberMedia had a troubled 1998, apparently due to mismanagement. As mentioned earlier, sales declined during 1998, and its stock price plunged 50 percent. CyberMedia's CFO and CEO resigned in February and March respectively, and CyberMedia brought former Novell executive Kanwal Rekhi out of retirement to serve as its troubleshooter. CyberMedia took a $28.1 million net loss in the first half of 1998 on revenues of $10.5 million.

In a press release in September 1998 ("Network Associates' Acquisition . . .," 1998), Network Associates announced that once the acquisition was complete, the CyberMedia products would be distributed in the United States through Network Associates' traditional retail channels. The product would also be sold through Network Associates' additional global sales outlets, including its direct sales force, VARs, and system integrators.

The CyberMedia acquisition reinforces the notion that Network Associates is making acquisitions because they are doable. Network Associates acquired a troubled company and a raft of lawsuits alleging violations of securities laws. It is not clear how the acquisition would add to Network Associates' profitability. It appears unlikely that the incremental profits from the new product will be sufficient to offset the purchase price. Perhaps Network Associates simply made the acquisition to eliminate a competitor.

IMPLICATIONS

The industry analysis and cases suggest a set of implications for investors and managers.

1. *Industry leadership depends on interoperability.* In order to meet its customers' needs for enterprise security, CheckPoint realized that it needed to deploy a platform that many other industry participants would be able to accept. By opening up its software to others in the industry, CheckPoint was trying to take advantage of network effects. If a sufficiently large proportion of the industry became dependent on CheckPoint's product, then that product would become the most convenient for the incremental user to adopt. Thus CheckPoint's leadership in market share would be reinforced.

2. *Internet security is a business in which acquiring new technology may be disadvantageous.* In other segments, such as network equipment,

acquiring new technologies has proven to be an effective approach. In the Internet security business, the hidden cost of acquiring technology is very high. This hidden cost is the time and talent that must be dedicated to making different point products work together effectively. In the case of Network Associates, it is not yet clear whether customers are actually getting integrated solutions from a single vendor.

Network managers want all their security products to work seamlessly with each other, regardless of their source. CheckPoint has been able to avoid high integration costs by developing most of its products internally—and its products actually do work together.

3. *In the Internet security business, targeting the right customers is as important as building the right products.* CheckPoint's decision to work with ISPs has helped it become proficient at helping clients develop new revenue sources. CheckPoint then uses this experience as a selling point with other companies.

4. *Invest in targets as well as leaders.* If firms such as Network Associates or Cisco Systems acquire smaller Internet security firms, it makes sense to invest in the likely targets for acquisition.

Industry leaders like CheckPoint have the potential to grow profitably at a rapid rate without acquisitions. Such firms could be attractive candidates for a "buy and hold" investment strategy.

CEOs of Internet security firms must decide whether they will seek industry leadership or whether they are positioning themselves to be acquired. If seeking industry leadership, they should identify the gap between what their customers want and what they can deliver. They should then decide whether to close the gap through acquisition or internal development. A firm that is seeking to be acquired should analyze the technology gaps of aspiring industry leaders and seek to be acquired by the firm that needs their technology the most.

THE NET PROFIT RETRIEVER'S ASSESSMENT OF THE INTERNET SECURITY SEGMENT

The Internet security industry does not satisfy the Net Profit Retriever's three tests. It lacks economic leverage, it is struggling to offer a closed-loop solution, and the management teams of industry participants vary in their ability to adapt to change.

1. *Economic leverage.* The Internet security industry is pushing hard to create real value for customers. Although there is likely to be

consolidation into a handful of industry leaders, there is the risk that Internet security may be absorbed into the network operating system industry controlled by Microsoft and others. If the Internet security business is absorbed, it will create specific risks and opportunities depending on how that absorption takes place.

2. *Closed-loop solution.* Internet security firms recognize the value to customers of an integrated suite of network security solutions. The challenge is that no firm in the industry has been able to emerge as the clearly dominant provider of those solutions.

3. *Adaptive management.* The Internet security industry includes management teams that have adapted fairly well to change and others that are more moribund. Network Associates' acquisition strategy reflects an effort to lead the industry, but the implementation of that strategy appears misguided. CheckPoint leads the firewall industry, and its approach to working with customers appears effective. If it succeeds in its policy-based network management initiative, it could emerge as the Internet security industry leader.

CHAPTER SIX

Web Portals: Walking Through Virtual Doors

~~~

Consider the following trading snippets from 1998. On June 1, Yahoo stock was trading at one hundred. By July 6, it was up to two hundred. On July 6, Lycos announced that it was splitting its stock. On the same day it added twenty points, a 25 percent one-day increase. On July 6, Zapata Corporation, a fish extract company founded by former president George Bush, announced that it would split into two companies, one a fish extract seller, the other a Web portal. Its stock doubled on the day of the announcement.

These trading results reflect investors' panic about missing a chance to get in on the ground floor of the next Microsoft. Four publicly traded companies are most commonly grouped together as the object of this trading frenzy: Yahoo, Lycos (which announced a merger with Barry Diller's USA Networks in February 1999), Excite (whose acquisition by At Home was announced in January 1999), and Infoseek. These four companies currently call themselves Web portals. Basically, a Web portal offers a visitor to the Web a starting point: a site from which to search and link outward to a very wide range of other Web sites, according to the visitor's interests. The companies' 1998 revenues totaled about $464 million, and their net loss was roughly $114 million. In February 1999, their collective market capitalization (total shares multiplied by the price per share) was about $25 billion.

WHAT DRIVES THE CURRENT HIGH VALUATION OF WEB PORTAL COMPANIES?

No other segment of the Web business has produced such feverish investor behavior. Investment analysts are consistently at a loss to offer "fundamental" (that is, based on future earnings) explanations for the valuations of these companies. In other words, if one were to judge their valuations as a multiple of their future earning power, the valuations are way too high. And although forecasting earnings for any company is fraught with uncertainty, the underlying assumptions on which to base a forecast of the earning power of Web portal companies are extremely tenuous.

Using fundamental analysis to understand the value of a Web portal company is difficult. Warren Buffet wryly noted at the 1998 Berkshire Hathaway annual meeting that he was going to give a final exam with one question: How much is an Internet company worth? Anyone who gave a quantitative answer to the question would be flunked. Buffet's quip points to an important truth. The assumptions that analysts use in their calculations of the value of Web portal companies are very speculative.

To understand the market value of Web portal companies, it is necessary to look at a more basic phenomenon: the supply and demand for the stock itself. The nontraditional but very useful "momentum theory" of stock valuation says that a stock whose price is rising quickly will attract new investment that will drive the stock price up even further.

The explanation partially fits the available evidence. The momentum theory is that a stock goes up because it is going up. As long as the supply of stock is fixed, this pattern fuels a dramatic upward rise in price.

The reason this theory is not totally ridiculous is that certain companies are particularly vulnerable to a stock market phenomenon called short-selling. A short seller looks for companies with high stock prices and no earnings, companies whose accounting methods are flawed, or companies that are likely to post disappointing earnings. He or she borrows stock in these companies from brokers to sell at a high price, betting that the stock price will go down. If the price does go down, the short seller can buy the stock back and pay off the stock loan (and keep the money left over).

Sometimes the short seller bets wrong, and the stock price starts to go above the level at which the short seller sold it (a phenomenon called a short squeeze). In this situation, formal market rules force the short seller to go into the market and buy the stock immediately to cover his or her position. If the short seller happens to have sold short a company that has very few shares traded, the limited supply of shares—coupled with the spike in demand induced by the short seller—will send the stock price skyrocketing.

Consider how this phenomenon affected an e-commerce stock, Amazon.com (AMZN). According to *MSNBC*, in twenty trading days between June 9 and July 7, 1998, AMZN more than tripled to $139.50 per share. During this period, the stock price increased at a rate of 30 percent and 40 percent per week. AMZN's run-up can be traced to a limited supply of stock that cannot keep up with the demand from individual investors. Although AMZN has 47.9 million shares outstanding, most of the stock is actually held by company insiders and other pre-IPO investors. Only about 7 million shares are publicly traded, of which only 4 percent to 5 percent are held by institutions. So the vast majority of the shares are held by individual investors (Byron, 1998). We will explore this phenomenon further in Chapter Thirteen.

Whereas in 1997 average daily trading volume in the stock was roughly 500,000 shares, daily trading volume reached 1.5 million shares during spring 1998. And as AMZN rose from $30 to $40 per share, professional short sellers began closing out their positions to limit their losses.

Into the breach created by the departure of the professional short sellers leaped less sophisticated individual short sellers who also thought that AMZN was overvalued. However, these individual short sellers did not understand the risks inherent in covering a short position with a small supply of actual stock. On June 9, 1998, another group of market players, day traders (who try to profit from tiny changes in a firm's stock price throughout the day) began to purchase AMZN, driving up trading volume to 3.2 million shares per day. The result was that AMZN's price went up 10.8 percent to $51.25 per share. By June 24, daily trading volume surged to 9.7 million shares, and AMZN's price had doubled to nearly $100. By July 7, the stock had risen even higher to $139.50, with 8 million shares—more than the 7 million float (meaning the total number of AMZN shares publicly traded)—sold short and not covered. Since short sellers can obtain credit from their brokers for up to ten times their equity, short sellers can end up borrowing more shares than are really available. In other words, there were a million more shares sold short than could be covered in the event of a short squeeze.

When more than 30 percent of a stock's float is sold short, professional short sellers typically become nervous and cover their positions. The 114 percent level of uncovered short positions in July 1998 far exceeded what professional short sellers considered safe. In order for that level to drop back, far more nonprofessional short sellers needed to close out their short positions. The momentum investors, who bought when they saw the stock price rise, expected to continue to profit from the spike in the stock price induced by this short covering. After the individual short sellers covered their positions, the momentum investors moved on to another stock (Byron, 1998). Between July 1998 and February 1999, Amazon's stock rose about 300 percent, so the drama continues.

Although these so-called technical factors play a role in the behavior of these stocks, there are also fundamental factors that investors can use to evaluate whether or not to invest in Web portal companies. The factor cited most often is the rapid growth of the Internet. For example, whereas it took thirty-eight years for the telephone to reach ten million customers, the Internet reached ten million customers in four years. Another less frequently cited factor is that many of the investors in the stock of Web portal companies actually use Web portals themselves. These investors are following Peter Lynch's maxim of investing in what they know. A third factor is that the mass media, particularly TV and newspapers, are devoting a great deal of attention to the Internet, mainly because they view the mass media as a potential threat or opportunity, depending on how they approach it. This media attention creates tremendous popular interest in the stocks.

There is also evidence that the media companies are interested in acquiring Internet companies. According to *USA Today,* on February 9, 1999, USA Networks announced its merger with Lycos. USA Networks, a media company with properties such as Home Shopping Network and Ticketmaster, generated 1998 revenues of $12 billion and net income of $77 million. Lycos, a web portal whose sites include Tripod (an online community) and HotWired (a well-known Internet brand), generated $56 million in 1998 revenues and a net loss of $97 million. The stock market's reaction to the deal was a 26 percent drop in Lycos stock price. The market's reaction was due in part to disappointment that Lycos had not merged with a better-known media firm such as Time-Warner or NBC (Kornblum, 1999). In June 1998, Disney swapped its Starwave business and $70 million in cash for a 43 percent stake in Infoseek and $165 million worth of services from Infoseek for various promotions until 2003. In June 1998, NBC paid $64 million for a 60 percent stake in CNET's Snap Web site directory. Therefore, the stock prices of the Web portal companies may reflect a takeover premium—the amount over the company's "normal" stock market value that an acquirer must pay to convince the target's management to cede control to the acquirer.

SEARCH ENGINES, PORTALS, AND MAKING MONEY

What are Web portals, and where did they come from? Most of the Web portal companies started out as search engines. Search engines are computer programs that let a user type in a keyword and then direct the user to a list of Web pages that match that keyword. Even when a person follows the directions precisely, search engines do not work that well. From the user's perspective, many of the sites listed by the search engines are irrelevant. Nevertheless, search engines are the best tools available for tapping into the huge amount of information on the Web in a relatively efficient way.

Yahoo, the leader in the Web portal business, started off using a slightly different type of search engine. The Yahoo search engine includes an index of Web sites. The index is organized around topics of common interest, such as business, finance, or sports. It is updated every day to reflect the rapid growth in the number of Web sites.

Search engines had a way to go before they would become Web portals. One important development was the emergence of firms, such as Media Metrix, that counted the number of people who visited a Web site in a month. Media Metrix reported that the search engines were among the most popular sites on the Web. When executives at the search engine companies realized that people were visiting their sites, they used data from Media Metrix to convince companies that they would be able to get wider exposure for products and services if they placed advertisements at the search engine sites.

The search engine companies realized that there were other services they could offer, which would achieve two objectives. The first objective was to attract more visitors. The second was to encourage those visitors to spend more time at the site. To achieve these twin objectives, the Web portal companies tried to create "communities." These communities were facilitated by a technology called chat, a means by which a group of people with common interests can type messages to each other. Chat posts the transcripts of messages so that all participants can see what others are typing. The business benefit of the chat technology was that it encouraged people to spend a great deal of time at the site. These chat functions were further enhanced by offers of free e-mail at the search engine sites. With these added features, the search engine companies had transformed themselves into Web portals.

In 1998, the Web portal companies all began to offer visitors the ability to personalize the service by creating their own individualized "start page" that included specific types of information they wanted, such as sports news, specific stock prices, and the local weather. The benefit of personalization to the Web portal companies was that visitors would spend more time at the sites if they could get information individually tailored by them.

The basic focus of this business model was much like that of a broadcaster. For example, a TV network comes up with programming that attracts a certain number of people. The network shows the statistics to companies, who then place advertisements that are seen by viewers. The network then tries to make money from the advertising revenues.

E-Commerce and the Power of Banners

Most of the current revenues in the Web portal business are generated by selling advertising. The advertising usually takes the form of *banners,* rectangular images that usually include a company and product name as well as a message to induce the visitor to click on the banner for more information. Web portal firms charge advertisers for placing the banners on their sites. In some cases, Web portal firms can charge higher advertising rates for placing the banners on Web pages that are more likely to be visited by target customers. For example, a retailer of mountain climbing equipment might pay a premium to have its banner on a Web page pertaining to mountain climbing vacations.

As we will see in the U.S. Cavalry case in Chapter Twelve, Web portals also charge advertisers for providing a link to those firms' Web sites when a visitor searches on a topic that is related to the advertisers' product. For example, if a Yahoo visitor was searching for mountain climbing vacations, the mountain climbing equipment vendor might pay Yahoo to link that visitor to the firm's Web site. Although this practice could be construed as undermining the objectivity of the Web portal, consumers might view the practice as helping them achieve the goal that drove them to do the search in the first place.

Web portal companies have realized that the Internet offers the potential for another source of revenue—e-commerce. If a visitor to the Web portal actually were to purchase a product as a direct result of the banner advertisement, then the Web portal company could attempt to charge a commission to the vendor of the product. This concept has yet to translate into cash flows for the Web portal companies, but the technology exists to make it possible to follow the visitor's path through the Web.

Here's an example. A visitor could be in the market for a dozen roses and therefore visit Yahoo to do a search for roses. The search might produce a list of fifty-five Web sites. On the same page as the listing of Web sites there might be an advertising banner for 1-800-THEROSE. The visitor might click on that banner advertisement, thus linking to the Web site for 1-800-THEROSE. After viewing pictures and prices for a number of different types of roses, the visitor could place an order for a dozen long-stemmed yellow roses. The visitor would place the order by typing credit card information and an address into a form on the Web site. Web tracking software would trace the source of the purchase to the banner advertisement on the Yahoo site, and Yahoo could collect a commission on the transaction.

The tracking software creates the potential for a new kind of advertising. Let's use the phrase *interactive advertising* to describe the sum of advertising on Web search tools and directories, Web content services, commercial online services, Web magazines, and Web e-mail services. Although interactive advertising makes up only a tiny portion of total advertising revenues, the market has been growing rapidly. According to *Merrill Lynch,* total interactive advertising grew from $181 million in 1996 to $551 million in 1997. Between 1998 and 2000, the interactive advertising market was expected to grow at a 100 percent compound annual rate from $1,266 million in 1998 to $2,902 million in 2000. The interactive advertising numbers remain very small as a percentage of the total advertising market, however, advancing from 0.3 percent to 1.3 percent of the total from 1997 to 2000

(Cohen, 1998). Although it is important to note that there is a wide variety of estimates of the size of this market, there seems to be universal agreement that its growth rate is very high.

Traditional TV or newspaper advertising pricing is based on "cost per thousand impressions." Think of it as paying for eyeballs. In the case of Web portals, the number of eyeballs has been growing rapidly. For example, in 1997 there were 45 million Web users in the United States; the number of households online was 23 million. This latter number was expected to grow to 28.3 million in 1998 and to more than double by 2002 to 61.7 million.

The question an advertiser on the Web needs to answer is whether it gets a payoff from simple viewing exposure of a banner to a certain number of potential customers. With traditional media, the equivalent question has been difficult to answer definitively. On the Internet, however, there arises a clear means to measure the payoff.

This new means is the "click-through." A visitor is counted as a click-through if he or she clicks on a banner advertisement. Clicking through transports the visitor to the advertiser's Web site, where a more intensive marketing process begins. Although most Internet advertising is still quoted based on cost per thousand impressions, the ability to count click-throughs could potentially form a new, more discriminating basis on which to develop advertising rates.

The recent evidence on click-through rates is not overly encouraging, however. *Upside* interviewed a developer who noted that click-through rates for regular banner ads are a mere 1 percent of banner advertisements placed. To improve its rates, in late November 1998 Amazon launched a new series of so-called rich media interactive Web ads to promote Tom Wolfe's book *A Man in Full.* The ads let visitors print excerpts from the book and play a Tom Wolfe trivia game without leaving the ad site. Procter & Gamble used the rich media technology in an online ad for Pampers and found that 22 percent of the ad's viewers interacted with the ad banner. Despite this somewhat encouraging result, there is a danger that the click-through rates could continue to be dismal (Harvey, 1998).

Although a click-through is more valuable to a Web advertiser than a non-click-through exposure to a banner, it is true that the click-through itself is still several steps away from an actual customer purchase. Supposing the visitor does click through, he or she may peruse the advertiser's Web site and decide not to purchase that advertiser's product. Or the visitor may decide to purchase the product but make the purchase in person at a store or over the telephone, instead of using the Web. Although these possible outcomes introduce a variety of measurement problems and uncertainties into the process of evaluating the payoff from Web advertising, the technology creates the potential for improvements in advertising effectiveness.

It should be noted that there are powerful forces suppressing the spread of this technology. Advertising agencies and corporate marketing departments have long enjoyed an environment of creative freedom that lets them escape the kind of financial scrutiny that faces managers who propose large capital expenditures. It has always been difficult to trace the benefit of advertising expenditures in a rigorous way. Many advertising agencies and corporate marketing departments could feel threatened by a technology that audits the linkage (or lack thereof) between spending on a banner advertisement and a subsequent purchase.

As more and more outcomes are measured, e-commerce itself also becomes increasingly attractive as another potential market that Web portals could exploit. How big is this potential market? Although there are wide variations in estimates of market size, the U.S. Department of Commerce (1998) estimates that the total value of e-commerce in the United States totaled $2.7 billion in 1996 and grew to $21.8 billion in 1997. This number reached an estimated $73.9 billion in 1998 and could reach $1.2 trillion by 2002.

Needless to say, the Web portal companies are not expecting all of these billions to flow into their coffers, but it is reasonable to assume that some fraction of the e-commerce transactions will flow through the Web portals. And Web portals may charge a small transaction fee, say 2 percent to 5 percent of the purchase price, for each transaction that originates from a banner on the Web portal. Thus e-commerce could represent a large source of future revenues for the Web portals.

Of course Web portals could decide that they are giving up too much profit by merely passing on leads to other firms. They could therefore decide to backward-integrate into selected e-commerce businesses. For example, many of the Web portals let visitors check stock prices, but they do not let their visitors trade stocks on their sites. The Web portals might decide they could earn higher returns by offering the ability to trade stocks. To do so, they would need to invest in the back-end systems to execute trades. In addition, they would need to work with a broker-dealer to clear trades through the payment and regulatory systems. In view of such costs, it may prove more profitable for the Web portal firms to backward-integrate only partially, for example, by offering a capability for visitors to trade stocks while outsourcing the trade processing. But Web portals will weigh the incremental costs and benefits of such a move before doing it.

Audience over Technology

In theory, the value of a company is related to its future cash flows. If the cash flows are negative, then the company should be paying the investor to take the company away. Considering that the Web portal companies are currently unprofitable, investors are implicitly expecting the present value of future profits to far offset the cumulative losses that the industry has experienced so far. As we saw earlier in this chapter, the four publicly traded Web portal companies generated $464 million in revenues and $114 million in net losses in 1998. When we analyze their income statements, we find that their sales and marketing expense is two to three times larger than any other expense item on the income statement.

This one number reveals an important insight about the nature of competition in the Web portal business. Just as competition among TV networks is not about who has the state-of-the-art broadcast technology, so competition among Web portals is not driven by technology considerations. The driving force behind the competition for eyeballs has to do with programming and promotion. Competition in the Web portal business, as it is in TV broadcasting, is based on the ability to produce the right content to attract and retain the largest audience.

The Web portal with the largest audience share can generate the highest advertising revenues and can also use its higher volume to negotiate better rates for Internet access. Lower costs then free up more cash to invest in enhancing the value of the brand. As advertisers renew their contracts with Web portals, they increasingly seek to place their banners on the most widely trafficked sites in order to get the best return on their investment. Through this process, the winners get bigger and the losers get acquired.

SOURCES OF FUTURE PROFITABILITY

The competition for visitors among Web portal companies is one of the most important forces driving down the profitability of the business. But other forces enhance the industry's profitability and are likely to be stronger than the forces that erode it.

Let's take a look at these pro-profit forces. They include the industry's rapid growth, the growing power of brands to block new entrants, the economies of scale in purchasing for market leaders, and the higher customer switching costs that result from personalization.

Growth

Along with the record of rapid growth for Web advertising and e-commerce, the actual revenue growth of industry participants has been extremely high. For example, Yahoo, Excite, Lycos, and Infoseek experienced revenue growth ranging between 40 percent and 207 percent between 1997 and 1998. Yahoo's 1998 revenue was 202 percent higher than its 1997 revenue. The rapid growth has a positive impact on the future profitability of the industry as long as the companies can manage that growth without losing control of their operations.

Brand Barriers to Entry

Brands are emerging as a powerful force shaping the profitability of the Web portal business. Firms that have powerful brand recognition, such as Yahoo, are able to build greater loyalty among visitors, advertisers, and investors. This loyalty creates the kind of virtuous cycle we described in Chapter Three, which makes it increasingly difficult for new entrants to break into the business. To the extent that a firm is able to increase its brand recognition, the barriers to entry rise, thereby lessening the threat of new entrants. If the threat of new entrants is diminished, incumbents have less need to resort to cutting prices as a means of deterring new entrants.

A by-product of the investor loyalty resulting from effective brand management is a high market capitalization. Several large media companies have cited these high valuations as a financial barrier to acquisition. For example, if Yahoo's market capitalization had not been so high, it is likely that Disney or NBC would have acquired it. Instead, Disney and NBC decided to pay less money to acquire brands that were less well established. Their reasoning may have been that they could use the money they saved by not spending billions on Yahoo to build up the brand of the less known firm. The effectiveness of this strategy has yet to be revealed.

Economies of Scale

Economies of scale in purchasing Internet access help maintain gross margins as Web portal companies grow. As a Web portal company buys a higher volume of bandwidth, the ISP is compelled to offer a discount. The ISP cannot pass up the economic advantages of locking in high-capacity use. For its part, the Web portal company is happy to maintain gross margins. In the case of Yahoo, these gross margins have actually increased from 84 percent to 87 percent in 1998. Connectivity purchase discounts make it more difficult for new entrants that have lower purchasing volumes and higher relative costs. Because these costs cannot be passed on to advertisers, new entrants must spend more of their revenues on connectivity, leaving less capital for building a brand. So economies of scale in purchasing not only help Web portal market leaders maintain high gross margins but also lower the threat of new entrants.

Switching Costs

Visitors to Web portals certainly have no obligation to be loyal. Unlike America Online and Microsoft Network, which charge monthly fees to subscribers, Yahoo, Excite, Lycos, and Infoseek have no contract between them and their visitors. Nevertheless, they invest substantially in creating content that will encourage visitors to come and stay at their sites. Web portals also raise switching costs by offering visitors the ability to personalize the site by picking news, stock quotes, and other information that is of particular interest to each individual.

Although switching costs cannot be quantified, one available measure of loyalty is the number of registered—albeit nonpaying—visitors. For example, the number of registered Yahoo users increased from twelve million to eighteen million between March and June 1998. This number represents a group of visitors who are more likely to stick with Yahoo because they are likely to personalize their experience of the portal's services.

—⁓—

We can see that the forces working in favor of the long-term profitability of the Web portal business are formidable. As the winning firms continue to extend their lead over their competitors, it becomes more likely that only a small number of firms will survive. After the industry shakeout has occurred, visitors and advertisers will be increasingly loyal to the Web portals with the strongest programming and promotion. The biggest firms will enjoy economies of scale in purchasing that will also give them cost advantages over new entrants.

FORCES AGAINST PROFITABILITY

In addition to the intense competition for brand leadership that we discussed earlier, there are two other powerful forces militating against future profits in the Web portal industry. The first is low mobility barriers; the second is a high threat of forward, backward, and downward integration into the Web portal business.

Easy Mobility

Up to this point, the mobility barriers have been very low. They are likely to continue to be low in the future, because the cost and time required for a firm to imitate a successful strategy will be very low. Of course the cost of copying a strategy is often higher than the cost incurred by the innovator. For example, all the Web portals offer free e-mail. Yahoo was first with its $92 million acquisition of Four11. Microsoft followed much more expensively with its estimated $400 million acquisition of Hotmail. These deals indicate that Web portal firms value the registration lists of these free e-mail firms. In addition to free e-mail, the Web portals are also copying each other by offering chat, sports scores, stock quotes, directories, and so on. The effect of all this copying is that firms tend to preserve their relative position without achieving the market leadership that one of them—Yahoo—has managed to sustain.

Integration

The more threatening force is the increased likelihood of forward, backward, and downward integration. It is important to distinguish between these different types of integration because it helps to focus attention on the relative strengths and weaknesses of different groups of potential entrants.

Forward integration is happening as ISPs attempt to differentiate themselves by transforming themselves from mere suppliers of Internet connectivity to destination sites. AT&T, MCI WorldCom, and

EarthLink are three ISPs that are forging deals intended to transform their services into destination sites. Backward integration came from firms like Netscape that used their desktop software (for example, Web browsers) to build additional links with visitors and thereby grab a piece of the advertising and commerce markets. Since Netscape's acquisition by AOL, it has become clear that the costs of this strategy were too high for Netscape to bear without help. Downward integration is coming from broadcast networks, such as NBC and ABC, who are making acquisitions to gain a foothold in what they perceive to be a parallel access channel to "their" audience.

The intensity of the threat to Web portal companies varies by potential entrant. The greatest threat is from the broadcast networks. Their power is greater than that of the ISPs and desktop software firms for two reasons. First, the broadcasters have demonstrated the ability to build brands. They can build and sustain the loyalty of viewers with a demographic profile that interests advertisers. Second, they have access to a substantial amount of capital.

The desktop software firms lack one or both of these sources of advantage. Netscape suffered from both a lack of capital and an absence of a compelling track record for building a media brand. Netscape's strategy appeared to be a last-gasp effort to reinvent itself after its software-based business model collapsed under pressure from Microsoft. And although Microsoft clearly has access to capital, it has not demonstrated its ability to build a powerful media brand with its Microsoft Network. So the threat from the backward integrators appears less severe.

The forward integrators are even less of a threat. The ISPs require tremendous capital investments to build out their networks fast enough to keep pace with growing demand for connectivity. In addition to their constant need for capital, the ISPs lack a compelling track record for building powerful media brands. Although some of the firms have started from a leading position in long-distance telecommunications (for example, AT&T and MCI WorldCom), their leadership may be related more to their skills in the regulatory and technology arenas than in brand building. AT&T, as the owner of TCI, a major shareholder of At Home, was clearly trying to bolster its branding skill when it approved At Home's acquisition of Excite. So the forward-integration strategies of the ISPs are an attempt to differentiate an unprofitable commodity without the capabilities to achieve that objective.

—⁓—

As mentioned earlier, the pro-profit forces in the Web portal industry are likely to be greater than the antiprofit forces. The victors in the battle for Web portal profits will be those firms with the greatest skill in building the largest audiences for advertising and e-commerce. Two critical components of that skill will be people and capital. As long as the capital barriers to entry remain high for the broadcasters, the leading Web portal firms are likely to sustain their leadership during the next phase of industry evolution, in which the number of Web portals will drop. If broadcasters ever perceive that the cost of acquiring a leading Web portal has dropped to a reasonable level, they will pounce. The people at Yahoo and NBC, combined with NBC's capital, would be a powerful force in the Web portal industry.

FOUR IDEAS FOR FUTURE PROFITS

The foregoing analysis of the future profitability of the Web portal industry suggests several important principles for managers and investors.

1. *At an industry's incipiency, it is most important to shape the industry in a way that favors the strengths of the firm.* If managers cannot shape the forces of the industry to favor the strengths of their firm, they should align their firm with another firm that can. In the Web portal business, firms that are relatively weak at branding their services should sell out to firms that are good at it. Firms that are good at branding should sacrifice short-term profitability to build the preeminent brand. Over the long run, this investment will pay off in terms of higher advertising and e-commerce revenues.

2. *Web portal managers must carefully weigh the benefits of partnerships with firms that are trying to compete with them.* As we saw earlier, a wide variety of firms are seeking entry into the Web portal business through partnerships with the Web portal companies. The potential entrants view these partnerships as an intermediate step to direct competition with the Web portal companies. The Web portal companies must structure these arrangements to accelerate the up-front benefits while deferring any long-term losses that may result from helping out a potential competitor. They need a clear understanding of the real

requirements for competitive success in the Web portal arena, and they need to find ways of working effectively with their partners while not turning those partners into effective competitors.

3. *Rivalry among direct competitors may have less impact on the long-term profitability of the Web portal business than competition from potential entrants.* The relative position of the various Web portal firms has not changed. Yahoo maintained the lead until they were acquired; Excite and Lycos trail behind, and Infoseek is even farther back. As we discussed, the mobility barriers among the firms are extremely low, so any strategic innovations are quickly copied. Web portal firms need to pay more attention to threats from the broadcast firms and to use deals with ISPs to lower their access costs.

4. *Investors should remember momentum and industry dynamics as they consider where to place their bets.* At the beginning of this chapter, we explored the dynamics of momentum investing that appear to be driving the stock prices of some of the Web portal companies. In addition, the threat of new entrants could dramatically change the market position of firms that are now leaders. As investors consider whether or not to place their bets in this business, they should evaluate the risks more carefully than the upside opportunities.

CASES

Having looked at the factors driving the profitability of the average participant in the Web portal business, we must ask, What factors separate the leaders from their peers? What do the winning firms do differently from their peers? What insights into competitive strategy can we glean from this comparison?

To address these questions, we look at case studies from two of the leading Web portal firms: Yahoo and Excite. As the Media Metrix report (1998) indicates, Yahoo's lead in terms of share of Web visitors from home and work has been formidable. For example, in May 1998, Yahoo attracted 43.3 percent of Web users from home (about 2 percent behind AOL) and 52.9 percent of Web users from work (giving Yahoo a 14 percent lead over the number two site, AOL). This means, for example, that during the month of May 1998, 43.3 percent of Web users from home visited Yahoo at least once. In that same month, Excite attracted 23.3 percent from home (ranked sixth) and 29.3 percent from work (ranked fifth).

These statistics demonstrate the wide gap between the two firms whose strategies we will examine. As we discussed earlier, the Web portal industry rewards the market leader disproportionately. Market leader Yahoo enjoys a much higher ratio of stock market valuation to sales than do its peers. And, as we will see, the strategies of the leader and its peers are different as well.

Yahoo: Tight Ship on Customer Service

With 1998 revenues of $203 million and a net profit of $26 million for that year, Yahoo is the leading Web portal. Yahoo's principal product is an advertising-supported Internet directory that links users to Web pages. Yahoo leads its field in traffic with 95 million pages viewed per day and is second to America Online in advertising revenues. Yahoo has targeted guides for geographic audiences, demographic audiences, special interest audiences, and community services.

Tim Koogle, Yahoo's CEO, takes nothing for granted. The company is paranoid about the competition. Over the last three years, the market structure has settled out among a short list of challengers: Infoseek, Lycos, and Excite. Yahoo has pulled ahead during those three years, but still Koogle views these three as scrappy competitors, and he maintains a sense of vigilance (Timothy Koogle, interview with the author, May 1998).

The sense of vigilance is reflected in Yahoo's January 1999 purchase of GeoCities for $5 billion. GeoCities is a Web-based community site that lets its members build free Web sites. With this acquisition, Yahoo added ten percentage points to its market share.

The biggest competitive threat is not from a start-up company. In Koogle's view, it is too late for a raw start-up to get into the Web portal business. A purely new entrant would need to overcome substantial barriers to entry, such as critical mass, distribution, and a database of customer consumption patterns. The most significant threat of new entry comes from the media companies.

There is also a real fear in Silicon Valley of Microsoft (Koogle refers to the company as "Redmond"). Yahoo has focused on a different business model than Redmond. Whereas Microsoft viewed the Web as a technology business, Yahoo focused on information and media delivery. Although technology was important to Yahoo's business from the beginning, the key to winning was ultimately not technology. Yahoo consistently focused on brand, distribution, and quality content. The firm sees competitors as less practical and more likely to focus on technology as the key source of advantage.

Yahoo's practicality extends to financial matters as well. The company is tightly managed. Everyone in the company pays attention to costs. Yahoo underhypes and overdelivers, and it builds a brand that resonates with advertisers and consumers.

Yahoo tries to create tight links with paying and nonpaying customers—the advertisers and the consumers, respectively. Yahoo views the best-run media businesses as its model for how to manage itself. Although consumers do not pay subscription fees, Yahoo's ability to attract merchant partners, sponsors, and advertisers depends on audience support.

Sustaining large audiences depends on managing the tension between editorial and advertising. Yahoo believes that audience loyalty depends on trust. Advertising revenues are the lifeblood of the company, but if editorial is compromised in order to take care of an advertiser, then a company gets a different reputation. For example, if a company tricks the audience into watching an infomercial, it loses its credibility and the trust and loyalty of the audience.

One way that Yahoo seeks to distinguish itself from the competition is by creating greater audience loyalty. Yahoo believes that the way to build loyalty is to personalize and streamline the content. Yahoo attempts to make it easy for users to express their individual preferences in terms of news and stock quotes, for example. Its site is designed to help audience members help themselves. The site includes the "killer applications" that have become popular, such as chat, communities, and e-mail. As we discussed earlier, Yahoo's competitors have replicated many of these services; however, Yahoo had a big head start over its competitors and has managed to maintain its lead, even as its new services have helped build switching costs with its ever-growing population of visitors.

Yahoo's site is designed to facilitate communication. Once a person begins giving out his or her e-mail address, it becomes difficult to undo that address if the service provider maintains a relatively low price. Yahoo is also involved in developing voice-enabled Internet telephony. The company provides message boards that let people with common interests exchange ideas in a time-shifted chat session. Through its acquisition of Four11, Yahoo has also developed a real-time chat facility linked to a pager through AT&T. When an individual logs onto the chat session, designated friends can be notified by pager. The individual can also be notified by the server whether or not the friends are currently online. If they are, the individual can communicate with them in real time over the Internet at the cost of a local connect charge. This service can reduce communications costs significantly, particularly when the parties are communicating internationally.

These strategies to maintain audience loyalty are valuable to advertisers. Advertisers like a big, loyal audience. Advertisers perceive that there is a self-perpetuating cycle in which the medium with the biggest audience stands the greatest chance of getting bigger. The loyal audience provides useful information in that Yahoo can follow its consumption patterns. The cumulative history log shows what sites people like to visit, and advertisers can target their big offerings to people who are most likely to take advantage of them. In addition, through the registration process, visitors declare their preferences, whereupon advertisers may target individuals whose preferences match the profile of their target customers.

This targeting has a benefit for Yahoo as well: Yahoo can charge a higher rate for helping an advertiser target a promotion. When an advertisement about a specific product or service is placed in a content area that is more likely to contain potential buyers of that product or service, the value to the advertiser is enhanced. For example, Isuzu can place an advertisement for its Pathfinder sports utility vehicle in an outdoor entertainment content area, and without anyone's knowing anything about the individuals who are visiting the site, an audience more amenable to purchasing the Pathfinder is self-selected.

Web advertising has a closed-loop quality that differs from other media. For example, direct mail has a low hit rate and a delay between the mailing and the receipt of an order. With Web advertising, it is technically possible to follow the path of an individual from the banner advertisement to the purchase of the advertised good.

One example of this closed-loop solution is an automotive sweepstakes that could be advertised on Yahoo. This sweepstakes gives an individual a chance to win a car just by registering at Yahoo. The online registration process causes the registrant to receive a coupon. If the registrant goes to the dealer with the coupon and test-drives a less expensive car, he or she can then enter a sweepstakes to win a more expensive car by dropping the coupon in a box at the dealer.

In general, this type of promotion illustrates the potential that a well-done piece of creative work can generate for an advertiser if it is coupled with an attractive offer and a call to action. The payoff from these promotions indicates that they are cost-effective for advertisers, and the ability to measure the outcomes of these promotions stimulates the advertiser to try many other ideas.

The line between competitor and partner in the Web portal business is thinly drawn in some cases. Yahoo has struck many partnership arrangements with media companies. The media companies appear to have mixed views on the Web portal business. The partnership deals give them a chance to see how consumers and advertisers behave on the Web. Media companies are attracted to the growing audience that the Web portals are drawing, but they are concerned about their lack of knowledge about how to win in the Web portal business. They also are afraid that the Web could cannibalize their base business. So Yahoo has observed vacillating behavior from the media companies rather than clear strategic intent.

As we noted earlier in the chapter, investor response to Yahoo's strategy and performance has been very positive. Yahoo even has surveyed its investors to find out why they invest in its stock. The answer is that Yahoo has the characteristics of an Internet company in which investors are comfortable placing a bet. It is going after a big market that is likely to get bigger. It has a business model that can be leveraged in several ways; Yahoo can remain profitable as it grows quickly and can add products and services that contribute to its long-term goal of building loyal audiences and advertisers, as the GeoCities deal illustrates. Investors also like Yahoo because it is the leader in its market.

Investors correctly perceive Yahoo as being well managed. One important aspect of its good management is its stinginess. The company was started in a rented one-bedroom apartment. As the small staff increased, the company tried to fit as many people as possible into the space. Yahoo tries to make each dollar go far. This means not spending money on things that do not contribute to company productivity. And at Yahoo, all employees have stock options. They know that being tight with expenses translates into greater personal wealth.

Yahoo has always exercised traditional budgeting disciplines, even when it had only twelve employees. The company creates an operating plan that sets sales quotas. The expense levels in the plan must be lower than the anticipated revenues. Yahoo consistently provides conservative guidance to Wall Street analysts regarding its quarterly financial performance. Management keeps tight control over the business through weekly flash reports that present key metrics, such as revenues and expenses for the different business units. Tim Koogle was influenced in his thinking about management by his father, who was a mechanic. This influence extends to Koogle's view of Yahoo's management reports: he thinks of them as gauges on a dashboard, helping him to control the course of the company.

Yahoo is a low-ego company. Executives are encouraged to hire people who are smarter than they are. Koogle sets an example by hiring people who are smarter than he is in their functional areas to run sales, software development, and the other areas of the company. In addition to hiring smart people, Yahoo pushes decisions down to them rather than forcing all the decisions to be made at the top. The role of top executives is to stay available to functional managers if they feel that they are getting in trouble. By distributing decisions, Yahoo is planting the seeds for the next generation of management. To maintain the flow of ideas between executives and management, Yahoo has replaced Hewlett-Packard's management by walking around, in which managers visit employees on the plant floor, with what Yahoo calls open e-mail. Yahoo people worldwide use e-mail to stay in constant touch with each other (Koogle interview, May 1998).

The Yahoo case offers important insights into how to make money in the Web portal business. First, maintain a constant sense of vigilance, because competitors are fighting to dethrone the market leader. Second, gain the trust and loyalty of a mass audience by making it easy for them to get value from the Web portal experience. Third, create a closed-loop solution for advertisers so that they get a great return on their advertising. Fourth, maintain tight financial discipline to create the flexibility needed to exceed shareholder expectations. Finally, hire smart people and get them to make the decisions so that they can grow into the next generation of management.

Excite: Controller of Its Destiny

Excite is an example of how rapidly the Web portal business is evolving from Brandware to Powerware. With its January 1999 acquisition by At Home, Excite's CEO, George Bell, picked a partner with whom he was most comfortable. The companies announced that, according to *Red Herring,* At Home paid $6.7 billion for Excite's Web portal content. Kleiner Perkins, which owned stakes in both companies, encouraged the deal. Excite's content would help At Home secure a bigger share of 60 million potential subscribers (Henig, 1999c). With 1998 revenues of $154 million and a net loss of $37 million for that year, Excite is one of the leading Web portals. Through much of its brief history, Excite clearly recognized that its ability to survive as an independent company would depend on its ability to increase the number of eyes that viewed its site. For example, in April 1998, Excite announced an agreement to pay Netscape $70 million over two years to be its portal's premier search partner. The reason behind this move was to get access to the tremendous number of eyes that are focused on Netscape's Web site as a result of the high market share for its browser (outperforming Excite, netscape.com had a 25.6 percent market share from the home and a 37.4 percent market share from work). Because most people who use Netscape Navigator do not change the default setting, their first stop when they connect to the Internet is Netcenter, Netscape's Web site.

In the view of George Bell, CEO of Excite, the role of the Web portal is to organize the Web user's experience of access to some three hundred million to five hundred million Web pages. From Excite's perspective, the Web portal is not valuable to advertisers if it is simply part of indiscriminate Web surfing. To be valuable both to visitors and advertisers, the Web portal must be a mechanism for targeting groups of people with common interests. Just as ESPN attracts people interested in sports, so the Web portal must attract people with common interests and must display these interests to advertisers through the sites that the visitor peruses while on the Web portal (George Bell, interview with the author, Apr. 1998). AOL's subsequent acquisition of Netscape in November 1998 decisively undermined the potential value of this Netscape-Excite alliance. In fact, the AOL-Netscape deal accelerated Excite's decision to take control of its endgame.

To a great extent, Excite is a packager of content developed by others. Excite does not offer the indexing of Web sites that Yahoo offers. Instead, as we will see later, Excite can analyze a visitor's previous purchase experience to recommend additional items that might interest that visitor. This service was intended to help Excite overcome the inability of content-focused sites to attract a number of viewers sufficient for a portal to attain market leadership. It is not practical for Excite to accumulate critical mass by using content to add up large numbers of small segments of visitors with common interests. This approach takes too much time, and the cost of developing high-quality content is too high.

Instead of trying to build market share through content aggregation, Excite chose to build its growth strategy around the media industry's primary source of leverage—distribution. Cable companies gained this insight in the mid-1970s. Such companies as CNN, TCI, and Time/Warner realized that their control of the distribution channel gave them an opportunity to charge heavy hostage fees to get through the gateway.

The implication for Web portal firms is that to get an advantage it is crucial to attract visitors and to provide the technology and value-added activities that make visitors want to stay. Although the majority of people enter a Web portal through navigation, Bell believes that people will stay at a Web portal that gives them freedom from clutter and confusion. Ultimately, visitors will stay at a Web portal if it provides an easier way to conduct e-commerce. Excite perceived an analogy between e-commerce-driven strategy and the ability of the major TV networks to maintain the largest audiences. Even though the major TV networks are not the best at any one content area, they offer a broad variety of content that attracts the largest audiences. Because the major networks are so large, it becomes difficult for the more targeted services, such as CNN in continuous news or ESPN in sports, to knock the major networks out of their market share leadership.

In Bell's view, if Yahoo, Excite, and Lycos were the NBC, ABC, and CBS of the Web world, then the market valuations of the Web portal firms were related to the perceived value of getting in at the beginning of a new and rapidly growing industry. The value of the strategies of the Web portal firms is reflected in who is imitating them. For example, CNET, ESPN, and i-Village are all beginning to add search, directory, free e-mail, buddy lists, and other services to try to create a sense of community on their Web sites as well.

The first phase in the evolution of Web portals was search, the second was browsing. The third phase is e-commerce. Although firms such as Amazon are grabbing a large part of the e-commerce traffic in books and CDs, there is still tremendous value for the e-commerce firms to buy access to a steady flow of traffic from the Web portals. For an e-commerce company, the visitors to a Web portal are similar to people strolling a mall. Once a Web portal gets the person to the mall, Amazon can take care of moving him or her into the bookstore.

Excite intended to adapt its business model to this third phase, providing a compelling place for visitors to do e-commerce and taking a piece of the cash that flows in the process.

As we discussed earlier, one of the distinctive elements of Excite's business model was its effort to use database technology to track users' experiences, including their e-commerce purchases. This database marketing capability, which Excite added by acquiring a company called Matchlogic, had the potential to help Excite raise the rates it charged advertisers, who can better target their promotions to specific segments of customers that are more likely to buy that advertiser's products (Bell interview, Apr. 1998). In light of its acquisition by At Home, it is clear that the database marketing strategy did not yield sufficient additional revenues to support Excite's long-term survival as an independent company.

Excite was a follower in an industry that puts a very high premium on undisputed leadership, and it scrambled hard to stay in the game. Ultimately, Excite realized that it could not survive as an independent firm, so it decided to take control of its destiny, agreeing to be acquired by a firm with much deeper pockets and a management team with which Excite felt comfortable. Nevertheless, its efforts to simplify the user's experience of the Web and to provide target marketing capabilities to advertisers were valuable contributions to the thinking about how to succeed in the Web portal industry.

IMPLICATIONS

The Web portal business is among the most closely watched segments of the Web industry. Although it is currently unprofitable, it is likely to become profitable in the future. But this future profitability depends on changes in the structure of the industry, namely consolidation into a small number of leaders who can exercise leverage over advertisers and visitors. The most profitable of these survivors need strategies that will enable them to continue to build their share. Only through sustained growth in market capitalization can the Web portal firms make themselves unappetizing to potential acquirers.

What are the implications of the analysis in this chapter for managers, investors, and advertisers?

1. *Recognize that the endgame is rapidly approaching.* Firms that are running out of cash and market capitalization cannot spend the money

needed to sustain their position in the programming and promotion game. The smaller firms will need to seek partnerships.

2. *Investors will be rewarded by betting correctly on the survivors of the consolidation process.* But investors should expect some volatility as a result of the presence of momentum investors who are trying to deal with the limited number of shares available to cover short positions.

3. *Advertisers need to keep themselves from being swept up in the Web euphoria.* Ultimately, they need to weigh the benefits and costs of advertising on Web portals. It is important for advertisers to devote a portion of their marketing budget to the Web so that they can learn what works, if anything, and what is a waste of money. On the one hand, at some point the advertising rates may get so high that the Web will not be the most worthwhile medium for promotion. On the other hand, if the closed-loop solutions such as the one we saw with Yahoo's Isuzu promotion are actually put in place, the return on advertising could be exceptional.

THE NET PROFIT RETRIEVER'S ASSESSMENT OF THE WEB PORTAL SEGMENT

The Web portal segment, as exemplified by Yahoo, does not make the Net Profit Retriever bark three times. Although industry consolidation is likely to confer economic leverage on the long-term survivors, the Web portal industry currently lacks this leverage. Yahoo offers some of the elements of a closed-loop solution, but not all. Yahoo's management has adapted effectively to rapid change.

1. *Economic leverage.* Consolidation in the industry may ultimately give Web portals the economic leverage they lack. This consolidation is occurring rapidly, allowing a small number of firms to control most of the market. Once this consolidation takes place, it is likely that the big survivors will be able to force advertisers to pay high rates to get access to their visitors. Nevertheless, the threat of entry from the major TV networks, ISPs and other media companies could keep economic leverage out of reach for the Web portal industry.

2. *Closed-loop solution.* Firms like Yahoo and Excite are trying to offer closed-loop solutions. The essence of their strategy is to segment customers and deliver an advertising platform that can trace a Web advertisement to the purchase of the product. Now this closed-loop solution is more of a concept than an economic reality.

3. *Adaptive management.* Yahoo and other firms in the industry have adapted effectively to change. Yahoo's founders brought in experienced executives who have helped the company evolve from an indexer of Web pages to a media and e-commerce firm. Furthermore, Tim Koogle has hired a talented group of executives to help manage Yahoo's growth. Although Web portals have yet to achieve economic leverage, Yahoo's adaptive management team could ultimately achieve that objective. George Bell's decision to control Excite's destiny by picking At Home as its partner may also prove to have been a wise move.

CHAPTER SEVEN

Electronic Commerce: Profitless Prosperity?

~~~~~

E lectronic commerce (e-commerce)—the conducting of business over the Web—has received more attention than any Web business segment. Visions of business done virtually, rather than in the physical world of bricks and mortar, seem to excite the media and politicians. E-commerce so excites the media that stories about it appear on the nightly news. Its political importance is such that vice president Al Gore has claimed paternity for the Internet to boost his 2000 presidential prospects.

There could be a connection between Gore's rhetoric and campaign contributions from Silicon Valley's public policy coalition, Technology Network (TechNet). TechNet, led by John Doerr of Kleiner Perkins, holds "educational seminars" for Congress on issues that are important to Silicon Valley. TechNet's members also raise money for political campaigns, including Gore's. According to the Center for Responsive Politics (1998), Doerr himself has given money to Gore directly and to the Democratic National Committee. According to *Upside* (O'Brien, 1998b), politicians who support TechNet issues seem to benefit from TechNet's financial largesse. So it may be that Gore's support of the Internet and other issues that are of concern to

Silicon Valley could be related to Silicon Valley's fund-raising efforts on Gore's behalf.

The reasons for all this attention are complex. The media see e-commerce as a potential threat to its dwindling share of advertising revenues—threatened already by the growing power of cable TV. At the same time, with exploratory investments in the Internet via such joint ventures as MSNBC, the media may be trying to grab a piece of what could become an important business opportunity. Politicians see e-commerce as a way to create jobs and potential tax revenue. E-commerce spurs growth while keeping inflation low. The payoff for politicians is that e-commerce helps keep the stock market growing and public approval ratings high.

The purpose of this chapter is to help answer some questions facing managers and investors: What happens in an e-commerce transaction? How attractive is e-commerce as a business opportunity? Who makes money in e-commerce? How do they do it? What are the principles that separate the winners from the losers? What should managers and investors do to take advantage of the opportunities?

OVERVIEW OF THE E-COMMERCE MARKET

A typical e-commerce transaction involves three broad steps. First, a person uses the Web to collect information to decide which product or service to purchase. Second, the person transmits payment information (such as a credit card number) to the vendor over the Web. Third, the vendor processes the payment information and delivers the product or service to the customer.

One debate in measuring e-commerce is how to count a transaction in which the purchaser uses the Web to gather information but places the order over a different channel. As a practical matter, there are many consumers who will continue to use the Web to get information yet place orders over the telephone or by visiting a store. These transactions are not counted as e-commerce even though they should count as Web-facilitated transactions.

Estimates of the size and growth rate of e-commerce vary widely, but all the sources agree that the market is big and forecast to grow very rapidly. As we noted in Chapter Six, for example, the U.S. Department of Commerce (1998) has estimated that the e-commerce market totaled $2.7 billion in 1996 and grew to $21.8 billion in 1997. This number more than tripled to $73.9 billion in 1998 and could reach $1.2 trillion by 2002.

As these and following statistics will indicate, there is no lack of enthusiasm for the magnitude and growth of the e-commerce business opportunity. This enthusiasm is a manifestation of the Heisenberg uncertainty principle as it applies to business. Heisenberg was a physicist who observed that the act of measuring a phenomenon will alter the state of the phenomenon being measured. In the case of e-commerce, the statistics pertaining to its size and growth rate are causing investors to pour money into companies that otherwise would be shunned as too small and too unprofitable to offer an attractive return. However, the deluge of investment brings with it the possibility that some subset of the companies that receive the money will figure out a way to build a profitable business.

Despite its size and growth, e-commerce is not a profitable business now. As Jeff Bezos, founder of Amazon.com, realized, the key to e-commerce is choosing to compete in the right industry. And to compete in the right industry, it is essential to understand the key trends that drive profitability.

TWO CHANNELS: BUSINESS-TO-CONSUMER AND BUSINESS-TO-BUSINESS

Conceptually, e-commerce splits into two different channels. Business-to-consumer (b-to-c) transactions are the most widely publicized. The b-to-c channel sells books, CDs, news and information, airline tickets, golf clubs, ostrich meat, office supplies, computers, stocks and mutual funds, and countless other consumer goods and services. According to *Time* (Krantz, 1998), by the year 2000, online consumer sales are expected to reach $20 billion, 233 percent more than the $6.1 billion estimated for 1998. As Figure 7.1 illustrates, with estimated 1998 online revenues of $2 billion and $1.8 billion, respectively, travel and PC hardware are the two most popular items sold through the b-to-c channel.

Business-to-business (b-to-b) is a channel for businesses to sell and pay for goods and services among themselves. B-to-b is used for selling networking hardware, automobile parts, computer servers, and other business products and services. In 1998, the b-to-b channel was expected to reach $15.6 billion in sales. By the year 2000, sales should be eleven times that size, or $175 billion (Krantz, 1998).

By further analyzing the structure of the e-commerce channels, we can discern principles that will help managers and investors choose the

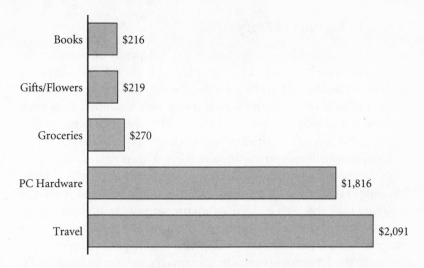

**Figure 7.1.   Estimated Online Revenues by Industry, 1998
(in Millions of Dollars).**
Source: Jupiter Communications, 1998.
[http://www.pathfinder.com/time/magazine/1998/dom/980720/cover4.html].

most attractive arenas and shun the least attractive ones. In order to get started with such an analysis, we need to recognize that there are fundamental differences in the inherent profit potential of various e-commerce market segments. In the future, b-to-b is likely to be inherently more attractive than b-to-c. However, within b-to-b and b-to-c, the market structure is likely to vary depending on the specific product or service being sold through the channel. So managers and investors should understand the specific profit drivers of the e-commerce channel and industry in which they are competing or investing.

In general, b-to-b is more structurally attractive than b-to-c. For b-to-b, the barriers to entry are moderate, the switching costs are high, and the intensity of rivalry between incumbents and new entrants is modest. B-to-c has very low barriers to getting started but has very high costs to build a brand. Although the high cost of building a brand can potentially become a high barrier to new entrants, it is a drain on b-to-c profitability while the brand is being built. In addition, rivalry between incumbents and Internet-only new entrants is extremely intense, and switching costs are relatively low. We look at each of these structural forces in more detail in the sections that follow.

Barriers to Entry

In both b-to-b and b-to-c, the cost of entry depends on whether the firm is an incumbent or an Internet-only new entrant. For a large incumbent, the cost of building a Web site may be a much lower percentage of total capital than for an Internet-only new entrant. In both the b-to-b and b-to-c channels, there is a big difference between getting into the business and becoming a dominant participant.

To become a dominant participant, the cost of entry is actually quite high. In the b-to-b channel, the most significant cost derives from building systems that create seamless integration between the act of ordering over the Web and the company's supply chain. For a large firm, the cost of seamless integration can exceed $20 million in systems integration fees. Seamless integration also may require changes in the way different departments work together, a change that demands training and new ways of measuring and rewarding the performance of people in the company.

Nevertheless, incumbents in b-to-b have substantial initial advantages that can keep out Internet-only new entrants. Perhaps the most important of these is the network of business relationships that the b-to-b incumbents have developed over time with their customers. These relationships and the value that flows from them make it very difficult for Internet-only new entrants to emerge in the b-to-b segment. The effect of this barrier to entry is that compared to b-to-c, the cost of building a strong b-to-b channel is relatively low for an incumbent.

To become a dominant participant in the b-to-c channel, the major cost derives from creating a brand that is perceived as the best in the category. The cost of creating the dominant b-to-c brand is probably higher than the cost of creating seamless integration in the b-to-b channel. To create a dominant b-to-c brand, a firm must manage perceptions across several groups simultaneously. These groups include the popular, financial, and technical TV, print, and online media; investment and industry analysts; mutual fund managers; corporate advertisers; and consumers. Creating the perception of dominance requires heavy investment in marketing and sales. Thus, as mentioned earlier, although branding raises the cost of entry, it also has a negative impact on the profitability of the b-to-c channel while firms are investing to create the brand.

One way to measure the effectiveness of the brand-building effort is to compare the incremental marketing expenses that a company incurs in a quarter to the number of new subscribers to the service during that time. If the cost per new subscriber goes down over time, then the investment in brand building is paying off. In theory, this drop in the cost of adding new subscribers reflects a growing proportion of word-of-mouth advertising that brings in new subscribers for free.

By this measure, some of the leading participants in the b-to-c channel are still investing in brand building in anticipation of generating a return. According to *Microsoft Investor,* in the first quarter of 1998, Amazon spent $19.5 million and added 750,000 customers, a cost of $26 per new customer. In the second quarter of 1998, Amazon added 880,000 customers for its $26.5 million in marketing expense, a cost of about $30.11 a customer. The trend clearly indicates that Amazon is still building its brand (Jubak, 1998).

The trend for E-Trade Group, the online stock trader, is of even greater concern. In the first quarter of 1998, E-Trade spent $10.6 million on selling and marketing and added eighty thousand new accounts. The cost per new account in the first quarter came to $132.50. In the second quarter, E-Trade increased its selling and marketing spending slightly to $11.6 million but added only fifty-six thousand new accounts in the process, yielding a cost per new account of about $207. (Keep in mind, however, that because an E-Trade customer makes stock trades *and* leaves assets with the firm, each E-Trade customer is more valuable than an Amazon customer, who simply buys books.) So adding an account at E-Trade got almost $75 more expensive in the course of a quarter (Jubak, 1998).

This 50 percent increase in the cost of adding a new E-Trade customer reflects the intense increase in rivalry coming from such discount brokers as Charles Schwab and Fidelity. It also exemplifies the rising costs that firms must face as they struggle to build a powerful brand in the b-to-c channel—a struggle that has yet to yield an attractive return on investment for E-Trade or Amazon.

Rivalry Within the Channels

Although rivalry is intense for both the b-to-c and b-to-b channels, the rivalry within the b-to-c channel cuts deeper into industry profitability. B-to-c channels spur expensive marketing wars and even acquisitions designed to control product supply to rivals. In the discussion of online trading, we quantified the rising costs of the marketing wars among participants in the b-to-c channel.

The b-to-c rivalry rose to a new level—that of making acquisitions to gain control over a competitor's supply lines—in the online book-selling business. According to *Reuters,* in November 1998, Barnes & Noble (B&N) announced the $600 million acquisition of Ingram Book Group, one of the largest wholesale book distributors in the United States, which supplies over 50 percent of Amazon's books (Intindola, 1998). This acquisition could threaten Amazon's ability to fill its customers' orders on a timely basis. Considering that one of the reasons Amazon located itself in Seattle was to be near Ingram, it is likely that the B&N acquisition could disrupt Amazon's operation. Although it is possible that Amazon will end up finding alternative suppliers, it remains unclear whether the new suppliers will be able to match or improve on the terms that Amazon received from Ingram prior to the B&N acquisition.

As the online trading and book selling examples indicate, the key to rivalry among firms in both channels is the different motivations and capabilities of incumbents and the Internet-only new entrants. Although rivalry certainly exists among the Internet-only new en-trants, the more important rivalry is between the leading Internet-only new entrants and the incumbent non-Web purveyors.

The latter form of rivalry is more important because the Internet-only rivals are gaining market share at a much more rapid clip than the traditional bricks-and-mortar firms. For example, before Ama-zon got into the business, B&N had figured out how to maintain its market dominance over Borders in the world of bookstore retailing. However, in the course of a few years, Amazon was able to grow very rapidly. Most irksome to incumbents, Amazon built a market capital-ization greater than that of B&N and Borders combined.

In the b-to-b channel, there are also two levels of rivalry. Rivalry is moderate between incumbents and Internet-only new entrants. An example is the rivalry in distribution of electronics components. Here there are two groups of competitors: traditional distributors and the new entrants. The traditional distributors purchase electronics com-ponents from their manufacturers and resell them to firms that use the components to build systems such as computers. The new entrants are purchasing cooperatives that use the Web to cumulate purchases from smaller computer makers and thereby achieve volume discounts. The traditional distributors enjoy an advantage over the new entrants because of their long-standing relationships with suppliers and cus-tomers. In the b-to-b world, these relationships constitute a significant switching cost. Nevertheless, newly formed online purchasing cooperatives offer compelling advantages by streamlining administrative processes and accelerating order fulfillment. Ultimately, incumbents may respond by Webifying their own operations rather than by engaging in costly marketing wars.

Oddly, in the b-to-b channel, the other level of rivalry is within an incumbent firm itself. This internal rivalry occurs between the incumbent's traditional and Internet distribution channels. For example, Office Depot, a vendor of office supplies to business, developed a Web site for placing and filling orders. Prior to building this Web site, Office Depot reached its customers through its retail stores, via a sales force, and over the phone. So the Internet site was perceived as a potential threat by the other groups within the company. Office Depot was able to address and resolve the issues associated with the perceived threat. Nevertheless, firms seeking to add Internet b-to-b capability to a set of existing sales channels should not discount internal rivalry.

Rivalry between incumbents and Internet-only new entrants in the b-to-b channel, although quite real, is often easier to manage than such rivalry in the b-to-c channel. We saw an example of the intense rivalry in the b-to-c channel in the online stock trading business. E-Trade Group, a "pure play" (whose sole business is online stock trading) new entrant into the online stock trading business, is finding it more and more expensive to add new customers. One of the reasons for this rising expense is that well-financed incumbents, such as Charles Schwab and Fidelity, are spending heavily on advertising. These two incumbents have substantially greater resources to spend on advertising; and although they would never admit this intent, they could be hoping that a continued barrage of ad spending will force E-Trade to spend so much money just to keep up that it will eventually run out of cash.

Switching Costs

Although b-to-b and b-to-c channels are somewhat similar in terms of barriers to entry, they differ greatly in the relative prevalence of switching costs.

The b-to-b channel is much more likely than b-to-c to create high switching costs. As mentioned in Chapter One, the reason for this is that companies do not find it profitable to evaluate vendors every time they want to purchase a good or service. Companies want to find the "best" vendor for a specific product or service and then develop an efficient process for doing business with that vendor for as long as the vendor remains the best. Such a process requires systems for placing orders, tracking orders through the product supply process, getting installation and maintenance service, and making payments. Once these systems are in place, it becomes quite expensive to yank them out and start all over again with a different vendor.

The same process does not take place in the b-to-c channel. In b-to-c, consumers are more likely to seek out the best deal on each transaction. The Web empowers consumers with information about where to find the best price on specific items. According to *Time*, for example, a consumer who wants to buy a $900 suit for $150 can do so via countryroadfashions.com. Because the company is in Thailand, purchasers must take their own measurements (Krantz, 1998). The best deal in the world may be available in Thailand this month, but there may be a better one in Hong Kong next month. The Web enables consumers to find that deal. With consumers using the Web to tilt the balance of bargaining power in their favor, it is difficult for b-to-c firms to build switching costs.

Nevertheless, some b-to-c firms are investing to raise switching costs. It remains to be demonstrated whether these costs will become high enough to get consumers to pay a price premium that offsets the investments. For example, Amazon keeps a record of its customer purchases. These records are used to send e-mail to individuals when another book or CD becomes available from the same author or artist. E-mail notifications may also be sent when a new book or CD is released on a topic that interests the individual. The effect of these e-mails is to encourage a fairly high level of repeat purchases.

Although Amazon gives consumers a reason to make multiple purchases from the company, it is difficult to consider this facility as a real switching cost. For example, there are Web sites that let consumers find the least expensive source of a book anywhere. Some consumers may take the information about a new book that they receive from an Amazon e-mail and use the Web to find an even less expensive source for the book.

FIVE STRUCTURAL PRINCIPLES

The foregoing analysis highlights the importance of understanding the profit drivers of the e-commerce channel you are about to invest in or manage. Because this kind of analysis is so important and so frequently neglected by investors and managers, we will look at five key principles of the structural analysis of e-commerce channels.

1. *Identify where the business fits within the value system (the chain of activities that link suppliers to ultimate consumers).* This advice applies whether you are considering an investment or are about to take over management of an e-commerce business. One of the most important considerations is the extent of the business' vertical integration. Does the business merely create a destination for placing orders, or is it fully integrated—from attracting eyeballs to delivering and servicing products? Knowing which activities the firm will perform itself and which activities it will outsource can help determine which forces will influence the firm's profitability.

2. *Assess the barriers to entry and to sustaining market leadership.* Although it may appear obvious that the cost of entry into e-commerce is low, the key issue that managers and investors should assess is the cost of building a leadership position. Consumers, advertisers, and investors confer a disproportionately high premium on market dominance. Potential entrants should consider whether they have the will and the resources to hurdle the barriers to market leadership. If so, they must also consider how much their current and potential rivals are willing to invest to occupy that leadership position. If the firm still has the will and the resources to sustain a long-term battle for market leadership, then it makes sense to attack.

3. *Evaluate whether it is possible to build robust switching costs.* Managers and investors must also assess how durable the bonds are between the e-commerce firm and its customers. As we have seen, the switching costs between a b-to-b firm and its customers are inherently more robust than those in the b-to-c channel. There are likely to be exceptions to this conclusion, however. Therefore, managers and investors should test the level of these switching costs. One way to do this is to track the level of repeat orders from existing customers over time. An even better way is to talk to consumers and advertisers to understand their actual switching behavior and the factors that drive that behavior. Regardless of the research technique they use, managers and investors *must* gain a fact-based understanding of the level of switching costs if they hope to assess the profit potential of an e-commerce segment.

4. *Assess the level of rivalry from incumbents and Internet-only new entrants.* In general, sources of rivalry include incumbent firms within the vertical segment, other Internet-only new entrants, and even

other divisions or channels within the firm itself. Having identified the sources of rivalry, managers and investors need insight into the rivals' competitive arsenals and their readiness to use these weapons. More specifically, they need to assess the rivals' capital resources and capabilities as well as their willingness to use these weapons to gain market share.

5. *Model competitive scenarios and quantify the costs of staying in the game.* If managers and investors understand the entry barriers, switching costs, and level of rivalry expected from various groups of competitors, they can examine different scenarios. The benefit of this process is that it will force decision makers to think through various internally consistent scenarios of how competition will evolve. After thinking through these issues in a rigorous way, decision makers can consider strategic alternatives and ultimately decide whether it makes sense to invest or compete in the specific e-commerce arena. And by quantifying these strategic alternatives, managers and investors can assess how likely it is that the returns generated will be sufficient to offset the cost of the investments required to implement these strategic alternatives. In short, gamelike scenarios can help temper the enthusiasm of managers and investors by providing a more analytic perspective on possible e-commerce business outcomes.

CASES

The choice of industry in which the e-commerce firm competes is a crucial determinant of that firm's profitability. After choosing the right industry, choosing how to compete is also important. To highlight the principles underlying the strategies of leading e-commerce firms, we will explore two examples. The first example is E-Trade Group, an online trading firm that has decided to sacrifice short-term profitability to build a dominant brand. The second is a highly profitable b-to-b Web site used by Cisco Systems, called Cisco Connection Online (CCO). For each case, we look at the history of the business, how the Web site works, the evidence of its profitability, the reasons for its success, and its prospects for the future.

E-Trade Group: Business-to-Consumer

E-Trade provides online investing services for investors who prefer to make their own investment decisions rather than seek the advice of a broker. E-Trade offers automated placement of orders for stock, options, and mutual funds at low commission rates. The company also provides portfolio tracking, Java-based charting and quote applications, real-time market commentary and analysis, news, and other information services. For the fiscal year ending September 1998, E-Trade generated revenues of $245 million and a net loss of $2 million.

E-TRADE HISTORY. According to *Fortune,* E-Trade was founded as TradePlus in 1982 by Bill Porter. Porter liked to trade stocks for his own account. He could trade commodities for under $30, but he paid his discount broker $100 for stock transactions. At the time, PCs were just becoming available, and Porter envisioned a world in which people could trade stocks on their PC at much less than $100 a trade. Although it was ten years premature, Porter designed an electronic version of the process of checking a stock price and placing an order. Online services caught on slowly, and after the 1987 crash, trading volume dried up (Wyatt, 1997).

By 1992, trading volume had picked up, and online trading services had started to catch on. E-Trade began to offer retail investing through CompuServe and AOL. E-Trade also offered the ability to trade via a direct modem connection. As the company began to take off, Porter hired Christos Cotsakos, an executive who had helped manage the rapid growth at Federal Express, as CEO. In August 1996, E-Trade went public at a split-adjusted $15.50 a share; in March 1999, the stock was trading at $55.

Since going public in 1996, E-Trade has added a number of additional trading channels. Now customers can also access E-Trade at its Web site, through WebTV, via Prodigy, AT&T Worldnet, Microsoft Investor, personal digital assistant, and the TELE*MASTER interactive telephone system. To use these trading channels, individuals must file an application and send a check for $1,000 to E-Trade to cover the minimum balance. After E-Trade provides the individual with a password, trading can begin.

E-Trade's initial source of advantage was its much lower commission rates. For example, in an August 1997 survey (printed in E-Trade marketing literature), E-Trade's commission for a telephone trade of eight hundred listed shares at $20 per share was $14.95. This compared quite favorably with eSchwab and Schwab, which both charged $117.36 for the same trade, and even more favorably with Merrill Lynch, whose commission was $324. For PC trading over the Web, E-Trade's advantage was also high. In the same August 1997 survey, E-Trade's commission was $19.95 to trade eight hundred NASDAQ shares at $20 per share compared to $29.95 for eSchwab and $104.32

for Schwab. Merrill Lynch did not offer Web-based trading as of the date of that survey.

E-TRADE RESULTS. E-Trade's strategy has produced strong growth. In fiscal 1998, E-Trade generated revenues of $245 million, 56 percent higher than in 1997. While most of E-Trade's revenues come from commissions, 23 percent come from interest on the balances that subscribers must deposit with E-Trade. Interest on these balances gives E-Trade a source of profit that other b-to-c vendors cannot tap.

Beyond E-Trade's strong revenue growth, it has also won big in the currency that makes the market assign such high values to leading Web portals; that is, E-Trade enjoys high market share and rapid growth in visitor traffic and trading volume. For example, measured by traffic, in July 1998 E-Trade was one of the top three financial services destination sites on the Internet and one of the top ten financial destination sites (Media Metrix, 1998). In the quarter ending September 1998, the average value of securities traded electronically through E-Trade per week averaged more than $1.7 billion, up 13 percent from $1.5 billion per week in the third quarter. Transactions reached an all-time high of 1,952,000 for the quarter, up 27 percent from 1,542,000 in the fourth quarter of 1997. For fourth-quarter 1998, E-Trade's Web sites hosted 28 million visits, up 24 percent from 22.6 million visits during the third quarter. Total page views equaled 171 million, up 22 percent over 140 million page views in the third quarter.

Despite this impressive string of numbers, E-Trade had its problems. Due largely to a decision to spend $100 million on marketing and technology in its fourth quarter, E-Trade was unprofitable for fiscal 1998. This decision represented a competitive response to a problem that emerged in fall 1997. At that time, E-Trade dominated the online trading market. However, its cut-throat pricing strategy actually backfired when start-up firms such as Ameritrade and Suretrade entered the market. These new entrants drove commissions down to as low as $10 a trade.

E-Trade was facing competition not only from new entrants but from incumbents as well. According to the *Industry Standard*, Charles Schwab was by far the largest player in the online trading market with 32 percent of the market in the first quarter of 1998, up from 30 percent in the last quarter of 1997. During this same period, E-Trade's share of online trading dropped from 14 percent to 12 percent (Kelleher, 1998).

E-TRADE'S CUSTOMER SATISFACTION. Although E-Trade's share of online trading had dropped off, its ranking in terms of customer value was quite strong in the third quarter of 1998. Gomez Advisors (1998) ranked E-Trade first in terms of its overall score compared to nineteen of its competitors. It is interesting to note that there does not appear to be much correlation between the Gomez rankings and relative market share. For example, Schwab was ranked tenth out of twenty on the Gomez list. The key for Schwab is that it starts from such a large base of loyal discount brokerage customers that it can afford to stumble in some of the Gomez metrics.

Gomez Advisors scores the online brokers in terms of five variables that customers care about. Gomez derives the scores on these measures from its assessment of the online brokers themselves, from direct examination of their Web sites, from questionnaires, and from conversations with the online firms' brokers and customer service staff. The five variables are ease of use, customer confidence, on-site resources, relationship services, and overall cost. Using these measures, E-Trade came out first in ease of use, fifth in customer confidence (Waterhouse was first), third in on-site resources (DLJDirect was first), second in relationship services (AMEX was first), and fifteenth in overall cost (Lindner FarSight was first) (Gomez Advisors, 1998).

Schwab scored poorly on ease of use and overall costs but came out near the top on what appear to be the two most important Gomez measures: customer confidence and on-site resources. Emphasis on these measures should be expected considering that customers are entrusting the custodianship of financial assets to the online broker.

E-TRADE'S MARKET SHARE RECOVERY STRATEGY In summer 1998, E-Trade developed a strategy to regain its lost market share. The company based the strategy on important insights into changes in customer purchase behavior and financed it through a sudden shift in E-Trade's ownership structure. A key element of this new strategy was to create a public financial destination site (that anyone would be able to access for free) to complement the subscriber-only site that E-Trade had already built.

E-Trade's public financial destination site was intended to include free content and financial tools for the general public. According to *Gomezwire*, E-Trade had carefully rolled out and tested the destination site among its 459,000 customers. The site was launched to the public in September 1998. E-Trade expected to receive three benefits

from the financial destination site. First, it anticipated adding substantial revenues by letting advertisers place banners on the site. Second, it anticipated that the public destination site would attract new
subscribers by offering a demonstration of the advanced functional-
ity of its subscriber-only site. The goal was to demonstrate the value
of E-Trade to more people by using the public site to bring in visitors.
E-Trade anticipated that many visitors to the public site would be
so impressed with it that they would subscribe to the subscriber-only
site to take advantage of its value-added services. Third, the company
hoped to lower its costs by running an unencrypted destination site
that would be less expensive for E-Trade to operate (Robb, 1998). By
adding customers who cost E-Trade less to serve, the unencrypted site
would lower the firm's average cost per customer.

There were other components of the E-Trade growth strategy, one
of which has to do with the Web portal segment of the Internet industry. Research suggests that the Web portals (examined in Chapter Six)
enjoy a market share and market valuation advantage over the vertical
b-to-c Web sites, such as E-Trade. Despite the advantages that the vertical sites enjoy for executing financial transactions, it is the Web portals that draw the biggest market share of individuals with an interest
in finance. According to the *Industry Standard*, a July 1998 report called
Cybercitizen Finance revealed that 32 percent of online investment site
visitors polled use AOL's Personal Finance resources, 13.5 percent use
Quicken.com, and 10.8 percent use Yahoo Finance. A mere 6.1 percent
use Charles Schwab's site. We should note also that as of mid-1998, the
online discount brokerages such as DLJDirect, E-Trade, Waterhouse
Securities, and Ameritrade were paying substantial fees to AOL for a
share of AOL's Personal Finance home page (Barnett, 1998).

This evidence reinforced the notion at E-Trade that marketing
arrangements with the Web portals would be a valuable way to build
traffic and transaction volumes. One question E-Trade must continue
to address is how to generate this additional revenue cost-effectively.
But addressing this question became easier when Softbank decided to
make a $400 million investment in E-Trade for a 27.2 percent share of
the company on July 10, 1998. Because Softbank already owned 31
percent of Yahoo and 71 percent of Ziff-Davis, the rapid formation of
this Internet "keiretsu" (see Chapter Four) presented some intriguing
cross-marketing opportunities.

Less than a month later, according to *PR Newswire*, these cross-
marketing possibilities were crystallized when E-Trade announced

deals with Yahoo and ZDNet, a Web site focused on high-tech content. E-Trade trumpeted an agreement that would increase its visibility on Yahoo's Personal Finance site and also make E-Trade the prime provider of online investing tools to ZDNet's customers. For E-Trade, the strategic intent was to attract the nine-million-plus individual investors who were using the Web for investment research but had not yet opened Internet investing accounts. The deals were part of E-Trade's overall strategy to increase its account growth while highlighting the capabilities of its public destination site ("E*Trade Expands . . .," 1998).

As the E-Trade case demonstrates, things change quickly in b-to-c e-commerce. The case highlights some key issues on which investors and managers need to focus when they evaluate participants in the e-commerce industry.

1. *Does the company have the financial resources to compete?* E-Trade will probably need to spend so much money on marketing that it will remain unprofitable as it deploys its new strategy. E-Trade is probably betting that the stock market will reward its pursuit of market share at the expense of profitability by giving E-Trade a higher stock price. If the stock price goes up, the company can begin to use its stock as currency for financing future profitable growth. This assumption has worked well for Amazon, for example, which has grown rapidly while sacrificing profits.

2. *Is the company creative in finding cost-effective ways to increase revenues?* E-Trade's deals with Yahoo and ZDNet may be structured cost-effectively because of Softbank's ownership stake in the three companies. But it remains to be seen how much its ongoing marketing campaign will produce positive returns. This is a huge dilemma for all b-to-c e-commerce companies because as long as competitors have sufficient resources to keep spending to build brand awareness, it remains difficult to stand out from the crowd.

3. *How well is the company diversifying its sources of earnings?* The most profitable Web businesses will continue to find ways of diversifying their sources of earnings. E-Trade has more diverse earnings sources than many b-to-c e-commerce companies. As we noted earlier, E-Trade gets over 20 percent of its revenue from interest on customer balances. Once its financial destination site becomes established,

the company is likely to be able to add advertising revenues as a source of earnings. So E-Trade is an example of a firm that is making a bet on an increasingly diversified set of revenue sources.

4. *How well does the company understand its customers' needs, and how well can it deliver on its commitment to meet these needs?* As its trading volume has grown, E-Trade has had some problems in meeting customer needs to make trades. E-Trade's problems with trade execution led to many customer complaints on trading bulletin boards. E-Trade has responded effectively to these complaints, and the level of customer confidence in the firm has improved. As E-Trade grows, this process is likely to recur. The b-to-c e-commerce firms that succeed in the long run will be those that can respond to complaints in a similar fashion. Because the Web provides a means of rapid and intense feedback to Web vendors, the ability to respond well to the feedback is an essential factor in determining which firms will come out on top.

5. *Can the company deploy strategies built on its competitive advantages relative to powerful incumbents and other competitors?* E-Trade has grown rapidly in the face of some very well financed and well managed incumbents, such as Schwab and Fidelity. By investing in its financial destination site and through partnerships with Web portals, E-Trade is trying to leverage market share out of its primary source of advantage relative to the incumbents. Nevertheless, E-Trade's online trading market share remains less than half that of Charles Schwab's. And the strategic dilemma facing E-Trade is replicated over and over again as "pure play" b-to-c e-commerce companies attempt to compete with incumbents. Whether E-Trade's strengths in marketing and technology will become decisive advantages over incumbent firms remains to be seen. The result hinges on whether the majority of customers consider Schwab's ability to offer a wide variety of innovative financial services to be more important than E-Trade's ease of use and lower commissions. The principle here is that to gain meaningful insight into the outcome of the rivalry between incumbents and "pure play" firms, managers and investors must analyze the strengths and weaknesses of both groups relative to the needs of the largest customer segments.

6. *Can the company partner effectively with firms with which it may be competing now or in the future?* Because of the limited resources and tremendous uncertainty about how the market will evolve,

e-commerce firms find themselves needing to form partnerships. No e-commerce firm has the capital or the capabilities needed to compete successfully on its own. E-Trade has formed partnerships to increase its subscriber base. It remains unclear whether the cost of these partnerships is offset by the incremental profits earned by new customers. The analysis we did earlier suggests that in the case of E-Trade, the cost of adding subscribers is growing ominously. The general principle is that managers and investors should seek ways to quantify whether the value of partnerships offsets their cost. This evaluation should include the cash costs as well as the strategic costs. Strategic costs might be incurred if the partner suddenly became a competitor who used the insights gained from the partnership as a competitive weapon.

Cisco Connection Online (CCO): Business-to-Business

Although the profit potential for b-to-b e-commerce appears greater than that of the b-to-c channel, there are no publicly traded Internet-only firms in this segment. Our exploration of profitable b-to-b sites must therefore be based on less rigorous financial reporting. One of the most profitable b-to-b e-commerce sites is Cisco Systems' Cisco Connection Online (CCO). In examining the CCO case, we will explore the reason CCO was created, how it works, what results it has produced, and where it may be going in the future. From this case will come some principles that may be helpful for companies trying to implement b-to-b e-commerce sites.

Cisco Systems' 1998 revenues totaled $8.46 billion. Roughly $5.7 billion (67 percent) of these sales were generated over CCO. According to Donna Hoffman (1998) of Vanderbilt University, in 1998 CCO had eighty thousand registered users and thirty-five million hits a day. As we noted in Chapter Two, Cisco has estimated that CCO added $500 million to its profits.

CCO HISTORY. Cisco began the development of the Web site in 1993, when it also formed a team of three to four people to identify ways to enhance productivity in technical support. Cisco had heard of a browser tool called Mosaic, from the University of Illinois. In 1994, Cisco began to use the Mosaic browser and an Apache Web server. At the time, companies tended not to do b-to-b commerce over the Net.

The Net was considered for government only. Cisco called the Web site cio.cisco.com (*cio* stood for Customer Information Online) (Pete Solvik, interview with the author, May 1997).

Cisco used cio.cisco.com to put its technical information on the Web. Using the same system, customers asked questions, which were analyzed by the system and then linked to a likely response. The system also allowed customers to download software. Within eighteen months, 70 percent of technical support questions could be handled with the system. Using this system, Cisco Systems was rated the best in the industry in customer satisfaction while tightly managing the cost of its support operation.

In 1995, Cisco connected its partners, customers, and resellers to the system, thus creating the networked model of conducting business. This business model change led cio.cisco.com to evolve into CCO. Cisco also decided to expand b-to-b e-commerce to include giving customers information on the status of their order. In August 1995, Cisco introduced the first version of this "window into the company" and evaluated its effectiveness, revising the system every three months. Subsequently Cisco introduced several e-commerce tools that the company revised every six months based on feedback from users. This system became the largest e-commerce application in the world. In 1996 CCO's annual revenues were $1 billion, in 1997 $2 billion, and in 1998 $5.7 billion.

The success of CCO was based on three initiatives:(1) Cisco developed the technology needed to fulfill the requirements of the application; (2) Cisco created an equal partnership between the information technology (IT) department and the business; and (3) Cisco focused on customer wants. In fact, Cisco's IT department created a subunit called E-Commerce Ambassador, whose job it is to go out to resellers and large direct customers and find out how Cisco can do a better job of doing business electronically.

Cisco's IT department has been able to do more than others for several reasons. First, many other IT departments are caught up with operating or replacing legacy back-end systems, working on the Year 2000 problem, or installing SAP. These initiatives consume so much time that IT departments do not have time to look for breakthroughs. Because Cisco did not have legacy systems, it could build CCO unimpeded from scratch.

Second, CCO was not an IT initiative. In most companies, there is a big gap between IT, business functions, and executive management.

At Cisco, there is a high degree of alignment toward building tools to solve customer problems. Cisco's IT department talks to European resellers, British Telecom, and other large customers. Because Cisco is aligned, it has fast cycle times. Cisco's IT department can release a version of the system in sixty days, try it for thirty days, and refine it based on that feedback. Cisco is a fast-turnaround, fast-feedback corporation (Solvik interview, May 1997).

According to *Internet Computing*, in September 1998 CCO allowed Cisco's forty-five thousand customers around the world to gain real-time information on price, availability, configuration requirements, ordering, invoice status and validation, and shipments of complex internetworking products (Pang, 1998).

Cisco customers can forward procurement information to their own employees for modification and approval via CCO's e-mail features. Customers can also access product specifications, join discussion forums, receive bug alerts, and download software patches and tools.

Cisco estimates that it now takes fifteen to sixty minutes for a buyer to enter a clean order through CCO and for Cisco to complete the process by directing it into its back-end system for production. This compares favorably with a process that took days or weeks in the past when Cisco's own sales force and support staff and the purchasing managers of its customers were tied up in paperwork to process an invoice that was often full of errors.

According to Susan Aragon-Stemel, manager of networked commerce information systems at Cisco, rather than sending Cisco customers CDs or documentation, CCO implemented a download feature for software kits and tools that as of February 1998 was estimated to have saved Cisco $80 million a year (Pang, 1998).

Whereas the benefits of CCO to Cisco are clear, the reaction from customers is not overly enthusiastic. Some Cisco customers view placing and checking orders electronically as a natural progression regardless of any prodding from Cisco. Digex, an ISP based in Beltsville, Maryland, has ordered millions of dollars worth of Cisco equipment each quarter. Christopher McCleary, the former CEO of Digex, felt that Cisco was pushing its customers and getting them to adopt online ordering primarily to lower Cisco's costs. (Pang, 1998).

Despite being generally supportive of CCO and Cisco's e-commerce strategy, some customers are hard-pressed to determine the exact benefits of ordering products from the vendor via the Internet versus faxing in a purchase order or using electronic data interchange (EDI).

Another Cisco customer, Boeing, points out that although Cisco is reducing its overhead by streamlining its order fulfillment process, it is likely that CCO would help improve Cisco's profitability more than Boeing's. Although Boeing placed an order for $124 million worth of routers and switches for its worldwide corporate network in 1998, the company could not assess how much using CCO would reduce Boeing's overhead (Pang, 1998).

Cisco distributors, such as NCR, appreciate CCO because it gives salespeople more current information. Efficiency has improved because CCO streamlines the process of getting information from account managers to NCR. NCR perceives that CCO has helped free up Cisco account managers to spend more time closing deals. In NCR's view, its regular business relationship with Cisco continues to depend not on the details in CCO but on the network of interpersonal relationships between the two companies (Pang, 1998).

In 1998, Cisco began to roll out an offer to its top customers, such as Alcatel, NCR, and NEC. This offer consisted of a set of messaging tools that allow Cisco's customers to connect their sales force automation and purchasing systems through CCO into Cisco's database and enterprise resource planning (ERP) systems. Customers submit the valid orders to Cisco with the right configuration and pricing information. Then the resellers immediately go back to their customers and validate the orders. Cisco's objective is to place an order with a valid configuration from the start and get that order scheduled and built (Pang, 1998).

———

Clearly CCO is an important example of b-to-b e-commerce. And Cisco shows an important difference between the b-to-c and b-to-b segments. There are many examples of "pure play" b-to-c applications that create important rivalry dynamics between incumbents and new entrants. In the b-to-b segment, such dynamics are virtually absent. Why?

The barriers to entry for an incumbent in b-to-b e-commerce are virtually insurmountable. It would be difficult, if not impossible, to convince a business executive to allow an independent e-commerce firm to get in between the company and its customers. When it comes to such fundamental activities as placing orders, fulfilling orders, and providing service to customers, most business executives will continue to choose to do most of these activities, with the exception of customer service, themselves.

Of course there are compelling reasons why systems like CCO are so rare. As we noted early in this chapter, the Web can represent a parallel channel for reaching customers. As such, in most companies, it may threaten the managers of the other parallel channels. The manager of a direct sales force, an indirect sales force, or a telephone sales force will feel uncomfortable when a new channel gets introduced.

Because the Web is most effective when it encourages functions to work together, a b-to-b e-commerce initiative creates unique management challenges. Not all companies are managed with the same philosophy that Cisco follows. At Cisco, a large percentage of employee compensation is tied to improvements in corporate scores received on independent assessments of customer satisfaction. This compensation arrangement reflects a corporate emphasis on teamwork and industry leadership that few companies can match. Therefore, whereas it might be natural for Cisco's IT and customer service departments to work together to benefit the customer, this sense of teamwork may be difficult for other companies to achieve, thus inhibiting these firms' ability to obtain the most benefit from b-to-b e-commerce.

IMPLICATIONS

Although the e-commerce segment will not pass the Net Profit Retriever's Assessment in the next section, the CCO case suggests that e-commerce can substantially benefit the operations of many firms. Here are some things that executives can do to realize that benefit, especially in b-to-b transactions.

1. *Go online.* If executives in a company have not yet learned how to use the Internet, this should be the first step. The company's chief information officer should arrange for the CEO to gain access to the Internet with a high-speed connection. This connection should enable the CEO to discover for himself or herself some of the benefits of the Internet. Such benefits could include using e-mail to communicate with colleagues worldwide, following investments, purchasing airline tickets, and purchasing books. Once CEOs have found personal value in using the Web, they will be more inclined to see how it can help the company.

2. *Start with strategy.* The Internet can change the way a company works. For example, it could be an alternative sales channel or could leverage the customer service operation. The important point is that

the Internet creates the opportunity to change the business so that customers will get a better value proposition. Using the Internet simply to publish an existing set of product brochures does not capture its full potential to enhance the firm's competitive position.

3. *Set an objective.* CEOs should pick a measurable objective and a deadline by which to achieve it. The goal might be a 20 percent reduction in the cost of handling a customer service transaction, to be achieved within twelve months. Or the goal might be to generate 20 percent of corporate sales over the Web within two years. Without a destination, any road is equally ineffective.

4. *Get different functions to work together.* Harnessing the power of the Web involves making fundamental changes in the way the company works. The change can happen only if the CEO drives the different functions to work together to achieve the objective. These internal partnerships should include a close working relationship between the IT department and the business managers. CEOs should make it clear that compensation will be linked to achieving the goal.

5. *Experiment and learn.* Looking at how other companies are using the Web is often a good way to get ideas. It is also essential that a company look at its new Web site from the perspective of customers. One large company developed a site that was organized around the company's organizational structure. The problem was that customers did not know how the company was organized, so the site was difficult to navigate. The only way to learn all the lessons is to experiment and to get feedback.

THE NET PROFIT RETRIEVER'S ASSESSMENT OF THE E-COMMERCE SEGMENT

The e-commerce segment does not pass the Net Profit Retriever's three tests. Its industry lacks economic leverage. In many cases, however, it does offer its customers a closed-loop solution, and its management has adapted fairly well to rapid change.

1. *Economic leverage.* Most b-to-c e-commerce firms lack economic leverage. As we saw with Amazon, the book business has low margins and is extremely price competitive. Because Amazon has been spending heavily to build its brand, the only source of capital to finance its operating losses is the firm's huge stock market value. If that were to evaporate, Amazon would be in a difficult position.

As we noted in Chapter One, the Web can decisively tilt the bargaining power of an industry in favor of the customer. B-to-c e-commerce is a zero-sum game. Greater customer information diminishes the economic leverage of b-to-c e-commerce providers. It is possible that b-to-b e-commerce firms may come to enjoy greater economic leverage because of the potential to build switching costs. Nevertheless, e-commerce is plagued by structural problems, such as enhanced customer bargaining power, that diminish margins.

2. *Closed-loop solution.* Many e-commerce firms do offer their customers an excellent closed-loop solution. For example, Amazon takes the order online and delivers the books to the customer's doorstep. In fact, it is the quality of the e-commerce closed-loop solution that may account for the popularity of many of the services.

3. *Adaptive management.* The management teams of the e-commerce firms vary in how effectively they adapt to change. Amazon's management team was quite visionary in creating its business. By adding CDs to its selection of products, Amazon is trying to use its platform to build a profitable portfolio of products. As this book goes to press, it remains to be seen how Amazon will adapt to B&N's acquisition of its book supplier. While its stock price rose substantially in early 1999, E-Trade appeared in some danger of succumbing to competition from Schwab and the many others in its space. Overall, there is some evidence that e-commerce firms can adapt to change, but profitability remains elusive.

CHAPTER EIGHT

Web Content:
Let's Talk About Us

here is an entire industry devoted to gathering and disseminating information about the Web. Reporters collect the information; once collected, the information is broadcast through a range of information distribution channels. These channels include TV, radio, print, trade shows, and the Web itself. To the extent that information about the Web is broadcast over the Web, *res ipsa loquitur:* the thing speaks for itself.

By *Web content* we mean information about the Web, regardless of what medium may be used to spread it. There is an emerging market for it. The level of interest in Internet industry events is such that an entire industry segment of media companies is focused on the Web. For example, the *Industry Standard* and *Network World* are print and Internet-based publications that focus on Web industry activities. CNET offers television programs that focus on the Web. Forrester Research and Gartner Group are consulting firms that provide information and advice to purchasers of technology in general and Web technology in particular.

OVERVIEW OF THE WEB CONTENT INDUSTRY

There are four kinds of Web content companies: general media, Internet-only media, general consulting, and Internet-only consulting.

Figure 8.1 shows how the four types can be viewed in terms of the way they deliver their content and the breadth of that content. *Delivery method* refers to whether the content is delivered via an inanimate channel or primarily through personal consulting. If the content is delivered via an inanimate channel, such as TV, radio, newspaper, magazine, or the Internet, then the company falls in the media category. If the content is delivered primarily by a person, with the help of a report or presentation, then the company falls in the consulting category.

Breadth of content refers to the scope of the information. If the firm distributes information about technology in general, including the Internet, then we call it a general technology source. If the firm distributes information about the Internet only, we call it Internet-only.

Some media companies attempt to charge subscriptions and sell advertising, whereas others give away the information to build up an audience, hoping to make up the opportunity cost of not charging for

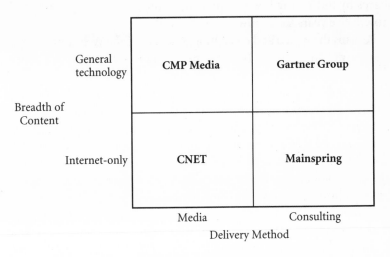

Figure 8.1.   Web Content Categories, with Examples.

the content by getting a bigger audience that will yield higher future advertising revenues. Within the media category, there are general technology media companies, such as CMP Media and Ziff-Davis; there are also Internet-only firms, such as CNET and Mecklermedia (which was acquired in October 1998 by a trade show firm called Penton Media).

The consulting firms depend on subscriptions and professional fees for their revenues. Web content consulting is dominated by general technology consulting firms, such as Gartner Group, Forrester Research, and International Data Corporation. Although there are technology consulting firms that focus exclusively on Internet-only content, such as Mainspring, the general technology consulting firms are much larger. Companies hire the general technology consultants to help them buy the right new technologies. The client companies pay for these services through annual subscription fees, supplemented by proprietary consulting fees.

The consulting firms also produce forecasts of growth for various technology markets. The forecasts find their way into the prospectuses for technology companies that are making their initial public offerings (IPOs), so the consulting firms play an important role in the business of new venture creation that we explored in Chapter Three. Their forecasts of revenues typically bolster the investment case for the firm's shares by indicating low revenues now and, say, exceptionally high growth five years from now.

Perhaps the media and consulting branches of the Web content business are not so different. Both are perceived as providers of relatively objective analysis of technology and are paid for their ability to provide vendors of the technology with access to consumers of the analysis. The delicate task that both groups face is separating the editorial and advertising sides of the business with the appropriate degree of independence. If the editorial side devotes too much space to attacking the advertisers, this could harm the business. If the advertising side forces the editorial side to devote too much effort to praising advertisers, then the reputation for objective analysis will be undermined.

But what is the inherent profit potential of the Web content business? What trends are likely to shape its future profitability? And what are the key capabilities required to succeed in this business? The following analysis will focus on the three main groups: Internet-only media, general media, and general consulting. We will skip the Internet-only consultants because that part of the industry is so small.

PROFITABILITY OF WEB CONTENT SUBSEGMENTS

The Internet-only media firms have a mixed profit performance. For example, 1997 losses for CNET were $25 million on revenues of $34 million. CNET improved in 1998, posting $56 million in revenues and over $2 million in profit. By contrast, Mecklermedia earned a profit of $4 million on revenues of $55 million in 1997.

The general technology media firms performed somewhat better. The publicly traded media companies, Ziff-Davis and CMP Media, generated 1998 revenues of $1.6 billion with a net loss of $68 million. Between 1997 and 1998, revenues fell flat and there was a transition from a small profit to a net loss.

The general technology consulting firms were the profit winners of the Web content business. The publicly traded consulting firms—Gartner Group, Meta Group, Forrester Research, and Giga Information—generated $816 million in reported revenues in 1998, and net income of $86 million. This net income figure includes a $19 million loss by Giga Information. The consulting firms earned average net margins of 11 percent.

The recent financial performance of these three strategic groups reflects differences in the inherent attractiveness of their business models. For example, the Internet-only media companies, CNET and Mecklermedia, have created businesses whose form is patterned after more traditional media companies, such as NBC. Although their delivery methods are similar to firms like NBC, the content is specifically focused on what is happening with the Internet. This focus is a two-edged sword. Focus on the Internet creates the potential for a competitive advantage in developing Internet-specific content. This potential advantage results from deploying reporters to build a better network of contacts in the Internet business and developing a better understanding of Internet technology and markets. But the narrow focus also makes the firms dependent on a market that may not be big enough at the moment to support a profitable operation. Whether the market they are targeting ultimately will become big enough is uncertain. In fact, it may be this uncertainty that was behind Mecklermedia's decision to sell out to Penton Media late in 1998. By contrast, CNET's 1998 results suggest that the market reached sufficient scale to support at least its profitable operation.

The general technology media companies, such as CMP Media and Ziff-Davis, have developed a large number of media properties (such as magazines and Web sites) that cover a range of technologies. As technologies fade, these firms tend to repackage magazines that covered the fading technologies to cover new emerging ones. The key source of advantage for these firms is a broad set of relationships with readers and viewers who buy the technologies. As the technologies change, readers need information on which to base their purchase decisions. The key to long-term profitability for these firms is their ability to keep up with changing technology. Therefore, as the Internet changes in importance, these general high-tech media firms will need to evolve as well.

The general technology consultants constitute the most profitable Web content branch. As mentioned earlier, these firms rely primarily on their ability to forge direct relationships with technology decision makers. Building on these relationships, the technology consultants sell subscriptions to reports on specific technologies and broader trends. Their ability to charge relatively high subscription rates depends on their ability to sustain a reputation for producing excellent research based on solid evidence.

The general technology consultants' high profitability is related to the inherent economic leverage of their business model. They provide information that helps executives mitigate some of the risk associated with very high stakes investment decisions regarding the purchase and installation of technology. In effect, through the subscription fee, the technology consultants receive an annuity that represents a small percentage of their client's investment. Although this cash flow has the advantages of an insurance premium for the technology consultant, it does not come with a concomitant obligation to assume the financial risk of the technology's failure. And the technology consultant can charge much more for its services than it needs to pay its people. Therefore, its profit margins are attractive.

The forces that shape the inherent profitability of the Web content industry are likely to evolve differently for the three different types of firms. The Internet-only media firms are likely to be merged into the general technology media companies. The general technology media companies are likely to remain moderately profitable due to the maturity of the industry structure. The inherent profitability of the general technology consultants is likely to increase as the less profitable firms are merged out of existence. Let's examine more closely the forces that are likely to shape the inherent profitability of each segment.

INTERNET-ONLY MEDIA FIRMS

Firms that focus solely on Web content, such as CNET, may not be able to continue to exist independently and therefore could be acquired, as has already occurred with Mecklermedia. However, CNET's transition to e-commerce could help it survive. One contributing factor is the inherent low profitability of their segment: the bargaining power of customers is likely to remain strong; the intensity of the rivalry among competitors is likely to be very high; and the barriers to entry, including mobility barriers, are likely to remain low.

Bargaining Power of Customers

Just as with the Web portal business, the Internet-only media Web content firms are targeting two segments of customers. The nonpaying customers are the people who visit the Web sites, watch the TV programs, or read the magazines. The paying customers are the advertisers. Both groups of customers must get larger if the firms are to grow.

However, the bargaining power of both sets of customers is high and likely to remain so. The nonpaying customers have thousands of different media that they can visit. And because they are not paying for subscriptions in most cases, there is no compelling reason for them to return to a site. Even if these customers do develop the habit of visiting a particular site because of its content, it is difficult to demonstrate that these visits result in much economic activity beyond the gathering of information. In the foreseeable future, there is not likely to be any reduction in the bargaining power of the nonpaying customers.

Advertisers, the paying customers, do not spend significant amounts on Web advertising to the nonpaying customers. Many advertisers view Web advertising as experimental. They do not know whether there can be any payoff from the placement of Web banners. As of this writing, there were still few compelling demonstrations of the ability of the Web banners to lead to closed-loop solutions in which the advertisements actually caused more purchases to take place.

Furthermore, the Web-specific content does not attract a large enough audience, relative to Yahoo for example, to create a compelling case for high advertising rates. In short, for the Internet-only media Web content firms, the bargaining power of both paying and nonpaying customers is likely to remain high. In 1999 and beyond, the strength of this force could diminish if CNET is able to increase its market share.

Rivalry Among Current Competitors

The firms in the Internet-only media Web content segment are competing against each other with great intensity, and this intensity is likely to continue. The fundamental reason for this high level of rivalry is that the firms are building capacity in anticipation of the development of huge demand. In particular, the investment in TV facilities, Web sites, and the related marketing, selling, and administrative overheads is being made to establish a strong market presence. The firms are betting that advertisers will spend so much money using these distribution channels that the firms will be profitable.

So far, however, the firms are not getting the level of demand that they had anticipated and are therefore competing intensely through marketing and price competition. This rivalry has depleted the financial resources of such firms as CNET. Its 1998 deal to sell its Snap portal along with 4.99 percent of its common equity to NBC reflects this tapping out of financial resources.

Barriers to Entry

Mobility barriers—barriers that prevent firms in a related industry from entering—are likely to remain low. The CNET-NBC transaction foreshadows the future of the segment. For larger firms like NBC, the Internet-only Web content providers represent an excellent beachhead into what appears to be a promising industry. By investing at a time when the Internet-only media firms are about to run out of cash, these big firms are able to acquire assets cheaply. And once they have acquired these assets, such firms as NBC can leverage their leadership in TV to provide valuable marketing resources to promote the brand.

NBC's entry reflects the beginning of a trend that is likely to continue. Internet-only firms do the heavy lifting of building up the initial asset base required to create a presence in the Web content business. Then larger firms with substantial capital and marketing resources hurdle the relatively low barriers to entry by acquiring the depleted firms at very low prices.

As the major TV networks see their growth stunted by cable, they are likely to view entry into the Web content business as a way to recoup the losses. Whether or not this assumption proves to be accurate, the networks can take advantage of the financial vulnerability of the Internet-only media firms to acquire Internet properties at low prices if they strike at the right time.

Whether the big media have the skills required to build profitable Web content businesses remains to be seen. It may be that Web content can never be a profitable business, regardless of how much money and marketing skill is applied to it.

Barriers to entry also will remain low for smaller entrants to the Internet-only segment. The key requirement for entry in the business is an individual with experience working for one of the more established media firms who carries away a network of contacts with advertisers. Such an individual with strong sales skills can convince venture capital firms to invest, and he or she can use the venture capital to attract the talent required to produce useful content. As long as no clear leader emerges in the Internet-only media category, the barriers to entry are likely to remain low.

GENERAL TECHNOLOGY MEDIA FIRMS

Such firms as CMP Media and Ziff-Davis approach the Web content business from a very different perspective. The general technology media firms are relatively mature businesses with low to moderate profitability. The biggest challenges they face relate to the struggle to renew what are fundamentally slow-growing businesses that have substantial overheads. The general technology media firms view Internet-specific content as potentially attracting a whole new group of advertisers, the size of which is likely to grow much faster than the number of the traditional high-technology clients from which they have received advertising in the past.

Structurally, the general technology media business is a more attractive business than the Internet-only media business. Barriers to entry are higher, and the bargaining power of advertisers is more moderate. Nevertheless, the rivalry in setting advertising rates with such vendors as Sun Microsystems and Hewlett-Packard is fairly high among existing market participants. The firms therefore depend on growth to offset the revenue losses due to lower rates. Whereas CMP grew by acquiring McGraw-Hill's technology publications in 1998, Ziff-Davis actually experienced double-digit percentage shrinkage in revenues.

Barriers to Entry

To create a general technology media firm requires substantial resources, including a staff of reporters, a network of relationships with advertisers, a printing operation, and a distribution capability. Although some of these resources can be rented, the cost of performing these activities still constitutes a substantial, though not insurmountable, barrier to entry. As we noted earlier, with the right people and venture capital, a new entrant can be created.

However, there is an additional barrier: the presence of a handful of already well established firms. CMP Media and Ziff-Davis control significant market share, as illustrated in Figure 8.2.

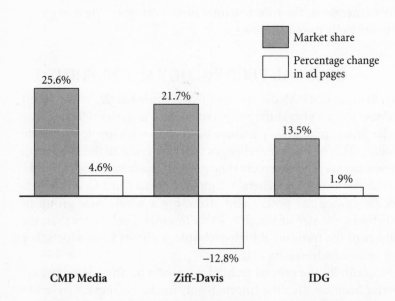

Figure 8.2.   U.S. Advertising Market Share and Annual Percentage Change in Advertising Pages: CMP Media, Ziff-Davis, and IDG, as of June 30, 1998.
Source: "CMP Media Leads . . .," 1998.

It is difficult to persuade an advertiser with a limited budget to spend money on a new publication with a limited audience when the market is dominated by such large players. As is true also in the Internet infrastructure segment, the dominance of a few participants is an additional barrier to entry that supports the profitability of this portion of the Web content segment.

Bargaining Power of Customers

In the middle of 1998, three general high-tech media companies controlled 61 percent of the advertising revenues. This relatively high market share serves to mute somewhat the bargaining power of buyers of advertising. If an advertiser to the high-tech audience is seeking access to the greatest number of potential buyers, there are few choices, especially since CMP Media's acquisition of McGraw-Hill's high-tech publications. The general high-tech media companies can thus use their concentrated access to potential buyers to exact economic rents.

Rivalry Among Current Competitors

One problem with the structure of the industry is a slowing of growth. The total number of technology ad pages grew by 25 percent to 165,000 between 1992 and 1997. However, between 1997 and 1998, growth was virtually nil. As Figure 8.2 indicates, Ziff-Davis actually lost advertising pages, and IDG's advertising pages barely budged.

If a firm wants to grow, there are three options. One possibility is to acquire smaller titles that are losing money. This option is attractive, particularly if the seller is sufficiently motivated to sell at a low price. A second option is to start a new title that attracts a new set of advertisers. Many firms are starting Web-related publications with the hope of achieving that end. A third option is to grab market share by cutting advertising rates, particularly with the larger advertisers.

The first option may tend to raise the profitability of the industry by removing overhead, but the other options tend to lower the profitability of the business. Obviously, direct price competition is the option that most imperils industry profits. All in all, the slow growth rate is a two-edged sword for an investor. With a large, established firm comes a diversity of earnings sources from more mature magazines targeted at more slowly growing markets. The diverse earnings sources make the general technology media companies much less dependent on one technology. However, the maturity also makes it very difficult to jump-start growth to the triple-digit rates that drive the extremely high ratios of stock price to sales experienced by firms like Yahoo and Amazon.com.

GENERAL TECHNOLOGY CONSULTANTS

Of the three segments that we are examining in this chapter, the general technology consultants enjoy the most inherently attractive industry structure. Although barriers to entry are low, the bargaining power of customers is also quite low, and the level of rivalry among existing participants is moderate. The key to the attractiveness of this segment is that there are two groups of customers, both of whom are quite vulnerable to the power of the general technology content consultants.

Bargaining Power of Customers

The bargaining power of buyers is particularly low for customers of the most prominent technology consultants, such as Gartner Group, International Data Corporation, Meta Group, and Forrester Research. These firms enjoy power over the companies that buy the research for insight into which technologies to purchase. Perhaps more important, these firms have the power to decide which technology suppliers within a category are perceived as the market leaders. And as we saw in Chapter Two, the firm that is perceived as the de facto industry standard often ends up being the one firm left standing after the initial shakeout.

One technique that the leading technology consultants use to exercise their power is to write critical reports on vendors that are not clients. Often the vendor who was the subject of the critical report complains to the author of the report. On occasion, the author comments that there was not sufficient information available to write a more favorable report. If the vendor wants to provide the information needed to create a more balanced report, they must purchase the services of the technology consultant.

Another insidious reflection of the power of technology consultants is an iron triangle at work in the industry. According to *Upside*, technology reporters need to write about new high-tech markets, but the reporters are not in the habit of doing original research. More often they seek quotes from a handful of analysts in the employ of the small coterie of leading technology consultants. The vendors who are paying the technology consultants for their services are the ones most likely to be mentioned favorably by the analysts. Therefore, if a vendor wants a favorable press mention, the vendor must hire the analysts whom the reporters are most likely to use as sources (Franson, 1997a).

Perhaps the ultimate power of these general technology consultants is their ability to confer vast wealth on the executives and venture capitalists in small technology firms. An analyst's favorable report on a small venture, coupled with a forecast of rapid market growth, can play an important role in the success of an IPO. Conversely, a negative report can make it much more difficult to complete such an offering.

The general technology consultants exert tremendous economic leverage over their customers. This power increases as the market share of the technology firm grows. The fundamental reason for this power is that so much wealth hangs in the balance.

Barriers to Entry

In theory, the barriers to entry into the technology consulting business are very low. A technology analyst with a computer, telephone, fax, and a good Rolodex can get started in the business with very little capital. As a practical matter, the one formidable barrier to entry is this last item: the Rolodex. More specifically, to succeed as a technology consultant, an analyst needs to develop a network of influential decision makers in large organizations. These decision makers must believe that the analyst will continue to produce objective, fact-based research that helps them make the right technology investments and thus keep their jobs.

This barrier to entry limits potentially formidable new competitors to those who were consultants at the most prominent firms. For example, Meta Group was founded by Dale Kutnick, an analyst from Gartner Group; Giga Information was started by one of the founders of Gartner Group, Gideon Gartner, after he left Gartner Group in 1993. The reputation of these analysts certainly helped them start their own firms. For example, Kutnick was known as highly opinionated and outspoken. Gartner was known as an erudite student of technology. Both firms focus on clients who purchase technology.

The effect of the reputation barrier to entry is to limit the power of price competition as a means of gaining market share. Star technology analysts are in much greater demand than other analysts.

Charging a lower price to gain market share may in fact have the unintended consequence of signaling lower quality and may thus cause buyers to shy away from the firm that lowers its prices. Limited price competition mutes the power of new entrants to erode the inherent profitability of the general technology consultants' industry segment.

Rivalry Among Current Competitors

The rivalry among general technology consultants is moderate. Given the rapid growth in demand for services, these firms have tended to compete on reputation. This competition translates into higher spending on marketing and sales, which manifests itself in the form of industry conferences sponsored by the technology firms. At these conferences, major buyers and sellers of technology convene to attend speeches and presentations by the analysts at the technology firm. The intent of the conferences is to make existing clients feel good about renewing their subscriptions. The sessions are also intended to put pressure on new vendors and customers to sign up for the first time.

Rivalry among existing competitors centers around each firm sending signals of the high relative value of the analysis provided by that firm. Firms appear unwilling to undermine the signals of value by cutting price to gain market share. The strategic logic of this approach is sound, as long as all market participants have a tacit agreement not to cut price.

The reputation-based rivalry will most likely continue. Technology is likely to continue to change even as its potential to add value for customers increases. Firms are likely to continue to need the kind of insightful, fact-based analysis that the leading technology consulting firms can provide, and the industry should continue to experience strong growth.

CASES

The firms we will examine here are CNET and Mecklermedia in Internet-only media, CMP Media and International Data Group in general technology media, and Gartner Group in general technology consulting. Through this analysis, we will develop specific principles that determine the relative position of each firm within its branch of the Web content business.

CNET and Mecklermedia: One Independent, One Sold

A comparison of CNET and Mecklermedia demonstrates that different strategies within the same industry can produce different results. CNET is profitable and remains independent, and Mecklermedia was profitable prior to its acquisition.

CNET. CNET has three lines of business: Television, CNET Online, and Snap. Television produces shows about the Web. CNET Online publishes articles on technology and sells advertisements to firms that want the business of CNET Online readers. Snap is a Web portal that competes with Yahoo and Lycos.

An analysis of CNET's income statement indicates that the firm has one break-even business and one profitable business. According to *PR Newswire*, for the year ending December 1998, CNET had revenues of $56 million. Of this period's revenues, 87 percent were from CNET Online, 13 percent were from Television. CNET generated an operating profit during the period with Television just breaking even and CNET Online earning a gross profit of $26 million. CNET's sale of 60 percent of Snap staunched a significant cash drain. In the prior year, on revenues of under $1 million, Snap had generated an operating loss of almost $2.8 million. Television earned a scant $250,000 operating profit on revenues of $7.1 million, for a 4 percent gross margin. CNET Online earned a substantial 47 percent gross margin, with $23.3 million in gross profit on $49.4 million in revenue ("CNET, Inc. Reports . . .," 1999).

The financial analysis tells the story. CNET management highlighted nonfinancial measures in order to explain its profitable performance. For example, in the fourth quarter of 1998, traffic on CNET Online sites increased from 20 percent from the previous quarter to 8.2 million average daily page views. In December 1998, CNET's shopping services averaged an increase to 90,000 leads per day, 30 percent over the September 1998 level. CNET also noted that it had generated $80 million in sales to seventy merchants in the fourth quarter of 1998 ("CNET, Inc. Reports . . .," 1999).

What emerges from this case is a story of a dramatic improvement. CNET's community of visitors is interested in the Internet. CNET is building an e-commerce business in which vendors of computers and software pay CNET for access to that community. As the size of this community grows, CNET should be well positioned to profit from the e-commerce opportunities.

MECKLERMEDIA. By contrast, Mecklermedia, while profitable, decided to sell itself in October 1998. An analysis of a mid-1998 income statement shows why. According to *Business Wire* ("Mecklermedia . . .," 1998), for the nine months ending June 30, 1998, Mecklermedia generated almost $50 million in revenue. Of this, 72 percent was from trade shows, 19 percent from print publishing, and the balance from Web sites and "other." It is also interesting to note differences in growth rates by source. For example, Mecklermedia's trade show revenues grew 35 percent compared to the same nine-month period in 1997, while its print publishing actually declined by 35 percent.

Operating profit figures by line of business are not available for Mecklermedia. However, an analysis of gross profit margins provides some indication of which businesses were most profitable for the firm. For the first nine months of fiscal 1998, Mecklermedia earned $23.6 million in gross profit. Of this amount, $20 million, or 85 percent, came from trade shows. Mecklermedia's trade show business earned 55 percent gross margins; its Web site's gross margin was 45 percent, and its print publishing business gross margin was 15 percent. Of course, all these gross margin figures exclude indirect expenses, the largest of which is advertising and promotion. It is likely that a significant percentage of that expense went to the Web site ("Mecklermedia . . .," 1998).

Thus we see that Mecklermedia earned most of its profits from its substantial trade show business. Ironically, trade shows are by nature a relatively low-technology medium. But people are willing to pay high prices to attend trade shows because these shows meet a real need. They provide a way for people to find out what is going on in their industry and to make and reinforce their network of business contacts. The shows generate most of their profit from the fees that technology vendors pay to display their products to the trade show attendees.

Mecklermedia invested its resources to build on its source of advantage by expanding in its most profitable line. For example, during the third fiscal quarter of 1998, Mecklermedia acquired the ISPCON trade shows and announced the launch of future Internet World shows in Egypt, Turkey, Spain, Hong Kong, and Singapore, where Mecklermedia has a 51 percent majority interest, as well as ISPCON events in

Australia and the United Kingdom that are wholly owned subsidiaries. Mecklermedia acquired a 51 percent interest in an existing Internet show in Ireland. It also acquired the remaining interest in its Internet World France event ("Mecklermedia . . .," 1998).

—⁓—

The comparison of CNET and Mecklermedia reflects the interplay between fundamental economic reality and the aspirations of executives who are trying to build successful Web business models. Although aspirations help build companies that attract investor interest, it is fundamental economic reality that ultimately determines who survives and who does not. CNET's business model evolved into a successful e-commerce portal for selling technology products to people interested in technology whom it attracts through its content.

Mecklermedia has found a low-tech channel for purveying Internet content that has inherent profit potential. Mecklermedia's leading trade shows attract a critical mass of attendees and vendors that are willing to pay up for the benefits of being able to see customers, competitors, and partners together at one place and time. Although Mecklermedia supplements this business with print media and a Web site, these other lines are satellites orbiting the "profit sun" of the trade show business.

The comparison demonstrates an important principle that has been mentioned throughout this book: *technology for its own sake is not enough to make a profitable business.* Technology can only help drive a profitable business if it helps support an inherently attractive industry structure. CNET appears to be investing in technology for its inherent appeal. Mecklermedia views the technology as a subject of great interest to trade show attendees and vendors. The latter business strategy is more likely to survive.

CMP Media and International Data Group: Centralized Versus Decentralized

CMP Media (CMP) and International Data Group (IDG) are general technology media firms that started with private financing decades ago. CMP went public a few years ago. IDG has remained a private company for thirty-five years. Although the two companies have similar strategies, their differences provide some interesting insights.

CMP MEDIA. CMP, with $478 million in 1998 sales and $10 million in net income, is a medium-size technology media company. Its customers include the builders, sellers, and users of technology. CMP has published magazines and newspapers about technology since 1971. Despite its moderate revenues, CMP leads the technology publishing market in terms of total print advertising pages, with over 25 percent share (CMP, 1998 Form 10-K).

An important element of CMP's strategy is its inclusion of the builders, sellers, and users of technology. This broad coverage of customer segments is unique in the industry. CMP defines the builders of technology to include manufacturers, engineers, designers, and purchasers of high-technology products. The sellers include a wide variety of channels ranging from value-added resellers to consumer electronics retailers and mail-order sellers. The users include the end-users of information systems, personal computers, software, the Internet, and related products and services.

Each of CMP's print publications is designed for a distinct audience among the builders, sellers, and users of technology. CMP serves the builders of technology through its "original equipment manufacturer" publications. It serves the sellers of technology through its "channel" publications. And it serves the users of technology through its "technology buyers" publications. Because CMP is able to offer its advertisers access to this targeted subscriber base, it is able to sell advertising space at rates that are higher than the average rates charged by publications focused on a more general audience.

In 1994, CMP expanded its business onto the Internet with its launch of TechWeb. In addition, the firm has deployed other Internet-based services, including the Electronics Design and Technology News Network (EDTN Network), an Internet service that provides electronics engineers with design information and decision-support tools. Another service is ChannelWeb, an Internet service available by subscription only, which provides users with a customized news feed from CMP's channel publications and provides areas for vendors and resellers to exchange information, receive channel research, and learn more about industry issues, products, and technologies. Except for EDTN and ChannelWeb, whose revenues come primarily from subscriptions, CMP's Internet services generate revenues primarily from the sale of advertising space on their sites.

CMP's business model depends heavily on generating print advertising. Its ability to charge premium advertising rates depends on its heretofore successful efforts to develop magazines that target readers who are attractive to specific advertisers. Although Internet content is of growing interest to specific segments, it is not a significant part of CMP's business. Furthermore, CMP's use of the Web seems primarily designed to reinforce audience loyalty to its publications. In short, the Web helps reinforce the success of CMP's business model; the Web has not caused CMP to completely reinvent its business.

INTERNATIONAL DATA GROUP (IDG). Let's turn now to International Data Group (IDG), a global publisher whose foundation is hundreds of independent operating units. According to the *Boston Globe*, Patrick McGovern started IDG in 1964 and owns 75 percent of the privately held firm. IDG claims that its 1997 revenues exceeded $2 billion. It has nine thousand employees producing 290 technology magazines and newsletters. IDG's publishing network spans seventy-five countries (Schoenberger, 1998).

Two elements of IDG's strategy are essential to its success. First, IDG hires entrepreneurial managers and encourages them to make their own business decisions. This entrepreneurial culture has resulted in the IPO of some of the operating units. For example, in July 1998, 23 percent of the book unit, IDG Books Worldwide, was spun out to public shareholders. A similar spinout was planned for IDG's $150 million (estimated 1997 revenue) consulting arm, International Data Corporation (IDC).

The second critical element of IDG's strategy is its global presence. McGovern has used the insights he gains from the evolution of technology in the United States to predict the way that technology will evolve in other countries, such as Korea or China. The ability to make reasonable predictions about how technology will evolve outside the United States creates tremendous value for these other countries. And IDC plans to continue to expand into new countries. When a country begins spending at least $80 to $100 million on computers, McGovern is likely to open a new magazine there (Schoenberger, 1998).

IDG is 75 percent owned by a talented entrepreneur who has built a stable of small units that are patterned after his own vision. The success of the firm depends to a certain extent on its ability to continue to find new markets that its entrepreneurial employees can take advantage of. Unlike CMP, whose strategy appears to be directed centrally, IDG has spawned hundreds of small companies within the corporate umbrella that are encouraged to pursue their own destinies.

Gartner Group: Upstart Consulting

With $642 million in revenue and $88 million in net profit in 1998, Gartner Group is a leading general technology consultant. Gartner has 330 different products and services, ten distinct product lines, six research centers, eleven thousand clients, 3,300 employees worldwide, 750 analysts, and more than seven hundred sales executives.

Founded by Gideon Gartner in 1979, Gartner Group made its mark telling IBM customers what was going on at IBM. Gartner gained its excellent reputation by focusing on how IT managers viewed IBM and its plans, not just on IBM itself (Franson, 1997b).

In the process, Gartner, both the company and the man, made IBM angry and its customers grateful. The company provided customers its knowledge and its opinions about IBM's management, actions, products, and services. IBM's management was diligent in attempting to keep information away from Gartner Group. However, the company was still able to obtain the information for its clients.

Over time, however, IBM shrank from being practically the only important computer company to simply being one of many. It also opened up to the outside world, eliminating the need for such single-minded focus on its activities. Gartner Group changed accordingly and now covers the worldwide information market.

Despite its size, Gartner keeps growing profitably. Between 1997 and 1998, its revenues increased 26 percent while its net income increased 21 percent. The key to Gartner's success is its ability to deliver products and services that IT decision makers value. That ability to deliver depends on Gartner Group's knowledge of IT issues, its client-specific research, the breadth of its product line, and the technology and business expertise of its analysts (Gartner Group, 1998, Form 10-K).

Gartner Group continues to develop its product line to enable its clients to customize Gartner's research to support clients' specific decision-making processes. In the third quarter of 1998, Gartner Group launched GartnerOne, a Web-based product for clients who want access to broader IT issues. GartnerOne offers simplified pricing, flexible inquiry, and the opportunity for clients to create customized research. Earlier, the company introduced Decision Drivers, a software tool that lets clients use Gartner research content, allowing clients to weight the importance of their own criteria when making vendor or product selections.

Gartner retains its user orientation. Excluding Dataquest—its vendor-oriented consulting unit—roughly 80 percent of Gartner's revenues come from corporations and other organizations that use computers. However, most vendors subscribe as well, partially to know what the firm is saying about them and their competitors, and partially to maintain access and interest among Gartner's analysts.

Manny Fernandez, former CEO of Gartner, had previously run Dataquest. Although formerly criticized by Dataquest's alumni and employees, Fernandez enhanced Gartner's revenue growth and profits. He also helped prepare Gartner for the impact of the Internet on information needs and delivery.

Because of its user orientation, Gartner has a reputation for independence from vendors. In the past, that independence sometimes bordered on arrogance and abuse, especially in after-hours grilling of vendors who visited to update the company on their businesses. That attitude was also reflected in press quotes. As the company grew and moved more toward the mainstream of industry, however, its attitude has become more humble (Franson, 1997b).

Gartner Group's success is a result of two strategic decisions made by its founder. The company is in an industry segment that has economic leverage over two key groups of customers. Technology buyers rely on Gartner Group to provide insightful, fact-based analysis of technology to support large investment decisions. Technology vendors depend on Gartner Group for favorable research reports that can help support IPOs, or at least encourage customers to purchase the products. So Gartner's profitability depends in part on its decision to be in the "right" industry.

But Gartner's leadership of the industry is a result of the firm's second decision. Gartner Group competes by offering a closed-loop solution. Through its people and services, Gartner is able to package insights and analysis in a unique way for each customer. Companies who use Gartner Group to help make technology purchase decisions are able to get the information they need, when they need it, and in the form that they need it. The result is that companies look at Gartner Group as the de facto market leader. Therefore, as contracts come up for renewal, existing customers are likely to renew with Gartner, and noncustomers are increasingly likely to shift their contracts to Gartner.

IMPLICATIONS

What can investors and managers learn from this analysis of the Web content firms? What principles emerge from this analysis that can help them make investment and strategic decisions? Here are six:

1. *The Web can help reinforce a business model that works.* Web content firms whose business models offer economic leverage with customers and suppliers, such as Gartner Group, should not reinvent themselves because of the Web. The Web will affect their businesses in two ways: it represents a new "story" to cover for their analysts and reporters, and it may offer new ways to deliver content. Nevertheless, the Web should not replace everything else about the business. It should be introduced as a complementary force that adds to profits.

2. *Web content firms must resist arguments that it is useful to give away content just because it can be delivered over the Web.* Web culture reinforces the notion that information should be free, and Web technology makes it easy to give away that information. The proponents of these values, however, were trained in a world where the government paid the bills. In a world where business pays the bills, the cost of producing insightful information must be more than compensated for through subscriptions, advertising, or both.

3. *Content matters more than multiple channels.* In many technology businesses, managers are carried away by the ingenuity of their inventions. Although such enthusiasm can be contagious, it does not provide the basis for a profitable business. A profitable Web content business does not depend on the ability to provide a wide array of channels through which to distribute information. Firms that initially invest in creating several parallel channels—TV, radio, print, Internet, cable—may be splurging on capabilities that can never yield more than competitive parity.

The key to building a profitable Web content business is superior content. On the margin, a manager will get a better return by hiring the best reporters or analysts than by building a new information distribution channel. Particularly in the early stages of industry development, it is much more valuable to create exceptionally insightful and well-researched content. Managers should invest in this content, and investors should put their capital in companies whose content excels.

4. *Don't bet on just one technology.* There is a substantial appetite for information about the Web. For new entrants, filling this appetite is a good way to get started. Today's incumbents got started by jumping onto the mainframe, minicomputer, and PC bandwagons at their incipiency. The incumbents have learned over time that in order to survive they needed to use their reportorial skills to uncover useful information about prominent new technologies. At the same time, they needed the discipline to cut coverage of topics that were no longer so relevant. In short, there is economic value inherent in content where technological advances and audience interests intersect.

5. *Companies can earn profits by producing analysis that helps executives make big, risky investment decisions.* As companies build huge systems based on Web technology, there will be an opportunity to help executives evaluate the systems integrators and the technology providers in whom the investment is to be made.

As we have seen with the technology consultants, the most valuable role in the Web content business is providing critical information to support high-stakes investment decisions. Corporate technology decisions are always risky and complex to analyze. A consulting firm with an excellent reputation for providing insightful, fact-based analysis of such decisions will be able to charge a high price. Decision makers will perceive that price as being low relative to the cost of the technology being purchased. Over time, firms that recommend technology investment decisions which turn out to be right will be able to achieve high renewal rates with their existing customers and so yield high economic returns.

By contrast, the more distant relationships that exist between a media firm and its audience are not as valuable to advertisers. Subscribers may be mostly midlevel staffers without the authority to make major investment decisions. The potential payoff of both the advertising investment and the content is further diminished by the content's lack of customization to the specific needs of either the audience members or the advertisers. Technology certainly can provide a means of mass customization, but this is clearly not what creates higher profit margins for the Web content purveyors.

6. *Give customers closed-loop solutions.* Our Net Profit Retriever is always handy. Corporate customers ultimately care about getting a return on their investment. Customers of media firms hope that their advertising spending will spur incremental sales. Customers of

consulting firms hope that customized advice will help steer them into technology investments that generate higher revenues or lower costs.

The best way for Web content firms to deliver this value is to provide closed-loop solutions: they must help customers trace the flow of value from the decision to spend money on their services to the incremental revenue that these services are intended to generate. For example, a closed-loop solution for a corporate advertiser would trace the path from the specific advertisement to a new customer inquiry to a closed product sale. Web technology can help implement such a closed-loop solution and enable the advertiser to measure whether the incremental benefit of the advertising exceeds its cost.

THE NET PROFIT RETRIEVER'S ASSESSMENT OF THE WEB CONTENT SEGMENT

One type of Web content business satisfies the Net Profit Retriever's three tests; the other two do not. The general technology consulting firms enjoy economic leverage, offer closed-loop solutions, and adapt effectively to change. Other Web content categories, such as general and Internet-only media, lack economic leverage, do not offer closed-loop solutions, and adapt to change somewhat sluggishly.

1. *Economic leverage.* The general technology consulting segment enjoys economic leverage. A few firms, such as Gartner Group, Forrester Research, IDC, and others, enjoy a reputation for excellent work that makes their service crucial to technology buyers, vendors, and investors. Despite the fairly consolidated nature of their market, the general and Internet-only media have only limited economic leverage because their product has less influence on the decision-making processes of powerful people.

2. *Closed-loop solution.* The general technology consultants offer closed-loop solutions for technology buyers. They evaluate vendors and products on behalf of technology buyers and recommend the ones that best meet client requirements. General and Internet-specific media do not offer such customized solutions.

3. *Adaptive management.* The managers of Web content firms are somewhat sluggish in their response to change. General technology consultants were quicker to adopt the Web as both a topic for analysis and a means of delivering their services. General and Internet-only media were slower to adapt.

CHAPTER NINE

Internet Service Providers: Oceans of Red Ink

━∿∿━ T his chapter analyzes the current and potential profitability of the Internet service provider (ISP) market. It focuses on the drivers of industry profitability and forecasts how these drivers are likely to change in the future. This chapter also presents case studies of leading firms in the consumer and business ISP segments. The chapter concludes with some implications that ISP managers and investors should consider as they look to the future.

REASONS FOR CURRENT UNPROFITABILITY

ISPs connect individuals and organizations to the Internet. The ISP industry is currently unprofitable. The barriers to entry are quite low for an ISP seeking to serve customers in a local market, and there are now an estimated forty-five hundred ISPs. ISP revenue growth has not kept pace with the demand for connection to the Internet backbone. To meet this demand, ISPs have invested in additional capacity. Because ISPs are operating at a loss, the capital for this capacity expansion has come from the public equity markets, which are willing to bet that the additional capacity in which the ISPs are investing will eventually generate high profits. However, the large number of competitors places a ceiling on price increases that might offer ISPs the additional revenue needed to generate those profits. Customers who have problems with customer service can easily switch to a new ISP.

Low Barriers to Entry

It does not cost much to get into the ISP market at a local level. The high proportion of very small organizations in the ISP business testifies to the low cost of entry. In a *Web Week* survey of five hundred ISPs (Nesdore, 1997), more than half of the ISPs surveyed operated locally; regional ISPs accounted for about a quarter of those responding. Roughly another quarter had national operations. The median-size company employed only six workers, and 60 percent of the ISPs surveyed had fewer than ten employees. Roughly half had 1997 revenues under $500,000.

The low barriers to entry are likely to continue to encourage new entrants; however, only a small number of firms have reached the size necessary to be attractive to investors.

Telecommunications firms are also getting into the ISP market, although in light of the relatively large capital resources that telecommunications firms command, it is generally quicker and cheaper for them to hurdle the entry barriers into the ISP business through acquisition.

Rivalry Among Current Competitors

The ISP market is intensely rivalrous. The good news is that the market is large and growing. According to *InformationWeek,* industry revenue was $3.1 billion in 1996 and was expected to grow to $13.3 billion in 2001. However, revenues have not grown in proportion to the costs of meeting the new demand plus necessary margins. For example, some ISPs have reported that demand for access has been growing as fast as 10 percent per month, or 120 percent per year, whereas revenues are forecast to grow at a relatively tepid 34 percent annual rate (Dalton, 1997).

In theory, one obvious way for an ISP to work its way out of the profit squeeze is to increase prices to offset its increased costs. The evidence suggests that this is not happening. Internet access charges do increase with bandwidth, but vendors indicate that the cost of providing the higher bandwidth rises accordingly. Even though the prices are higher, the spread between prices and costs remains slim. So competition leaves little room for profit.

One result of this profit squeeze has been consolidation. Three kinds of companies have made ISP acquisitions so far, each for different reasons. Long-distance telecommunications companies are making the largest acquisitions because they perceive ISPs as a large and growing source of demand for long-distance connectivity. Stand-alone ISPs are making acquisitions to increase the number of subscribers. ISP consolidation firms are making acquisitions because they see the potential to cut costs by achieving economies of scale in purchasing access to the Internet backbone.

As we discussed earlier, long-distance telecommunications firms prefer acquisition as the method of entry into the ISP market. For example, in May 1997, GTE paid $616 million for BBN, one of the Internet's first networking companies. In September 1997, WorldCom agreed to pay $1.38 billion for the extensive infrastructures of Compu-Serve Networking Service and America Online's networking arm, ANS Communications. U.S. Sprint entered the ISP market in February 1998 by purchasing 30 percent of EarthLink Network.

Stand-alone ISPs, such as MindSpring and RCN, have been involved in the consolidation process as well. In 1997, for example, MindSpring made over twenty acquisitions and in early 1998 continued this trend by purchasing an ISP called WebBullet. In 1998, RCN purchased Erol's Internet and Ultranet.

The ISP consolidation firms have raised capital with the specific intention of collecting ISPs in an "industry roll-up." One such company is Verio, a nationwide ISP for businesses, which as of April 1998 had stakes in more than nineteen ISPs. In July 1998, Verio announced its intention to acquire Hiway Technologies, an ISP with a large customer base of Web site hosts, for cash and stock valued at approximately $355 million.

There is little doubt that consolidation in the ISP business will continue. It appears that ISPs below a certain size can survive without finding partners. However, when ISPs exceed that size, they run out of resources. For example, according to *Red Herring*, firms with fewer than thirty thousand customers may be able to survive as long as they choose not to expand. Once firms exceed three hundred thousand customers, they can begin to achieve some economies of scale in purchasing access,

182   NET PROFIT

building access infrastructure, and marketing. The result of this consolidation trend is that the number of ISPs is likely to drop from forty-five hundred in 1997 to five hundred by 2002 (Borland, 1998).

Yet taking out competitors is not likely to diminish the rivalry in this industry. The reason for the continued competitive intensity is that the acquirers will use their acquired resources to grab more market share. And in grabbing market share, they will also compete by spending money on marketing and adding new services. Because prices are so low already, firms are not likely to use price as a competitive weapon. They are unlikely to raise the price ceiling, however. As long as ISPs must continue to incur the cost of meeting demand that is growing much faster than revenues, the intensity of rivalry among existing competitors is likely to make it very difficult to earn a profit.

Switching Costs and Bargaining Power of Buyers

The bargaining power of buyers puts downward pressure on ISP profit margins. Although consumers are not in a position to negotiate individual access deals with ISPs, they switch vendors when the quality of service declines. And this ease of switching vendors keeps pressure on ISPs to keep prices competitive and to keep service quality high.

Nevertheless, ISPs can take advantage of the natural inertia that consumers feel once they have signed up for an ISP. For example, in 1997, America Online experienced severe service disruptions. Consumers were billed for their AOL subscriptions but were unable to connect. This service outage created tremendous consumer dissatisfaction. Nevertheless, the majority of AOL subscribers stuck with the firm, and AOL's subscriber base continues to grow.

Organizations do have greater potential bargaining power with ISPs. However, if an ISP can meet a company's need for near 100 percent uptime, security, and speed of access, the switching costs go up. Once an organization begins to rely on an ISP that consistently meets high standards of service, it will find switching to another ISP more difficult. As the switching costs rise, the ISP may be able to build a family of services for the organization that ultimately makes the ISP profitable.

Given the low barriers to entry, new entrants will be willing to cut price to encourage profitable organizational customers to switch from the incumbents. Thus horizontal bargaining leverage goes on in the commercial ISP business. If an ISP is able to meet an organization's service standards, it is likely that a new entrant will go after that customer to present an even more compelling value proposition. The new entrant will keep pressing until the benefits of switching to the new entrant outweigh the costs of leaving the incumbent.

Threat of Substitute Services

Another force that lowers the profitability of the ISP business is the threat of substitute services. Many technologies in the market could threaten current ISPs by offering superior performance at a comparable price. Well-known substitutes include cable TV, WebTV, digital subscriber line (DSL) services from local telephone companies, and satellite networks. Other powerful substitutes may be waiting in the wings.

Cable TV companies are already offering consumers PC Internet access at speeds hundreds of times faster than the 28.8 Kbps access that is typical of many consumer ISPs. The cable TV companies are charging their cable TV subscribers a $99 one-time installation fee and $40 a month for this high-speed link via their PCs. The dramatic improvement in Web access performance that cable TV offers makes cable a significant competitive threat to incumbent ISPs.

Whereas other Internet access technologies require a PC to gain access to the Web, Microsoft, through its purchase of WebTV, has a technology that makes it easy for consumers to access the Internet via their TV sets. Only 45 percent of U.S. homes own PCs, but about 99 percent own TVs.

According to *Fortune,* by purchasing a modem priced at $299, viewers can watch TV and access the Web simultaneously. The WebTV receiver works exclusively with the Internet service supplied by WebTV Networks. The WebTV receiver uses a 56 Kbps modem and a 1.1GB hard drive to speed up browsing and to store program listings that are downloaded nightly. It also has picture-in-picture capability for watching television and Web images simultaneously (Speiss, 1998).

WebTV's big threat to incumbent ISPs lies in its ability to penetrate the "other 50 percent"—the U.S. homes that do not have PCs. The extent to which these non-PC homes purchase the WebTV service remains to be seen.

Local telephone companies also represent a substitute threat to the ISPs through the so-called digital subscriber line (DSL) technology that they have been developing. According to the *Los Angeles Times,*

DSL technologies enable copper telephone wires to access the Internet at much higher than 28.8 Kbps, in some cases 30 to 250 faster. DSL operates over standard phone lines, carrying voice and data simultaneously. Lucent Technologies' WildFire, a DSL variant, uses a DSL modem to make home rewiring unnecessary, thus cutting installation costs. US West has introduced an asymmetric DSL (ADSL) service for $40 to $80 monthly, on top of $20 monthly for an Internet account (Komando, 1998).

Although the capital investment that the telephone companies face to install DSL is high, it is still much lower than the investment that the cable companies must make. For cable companies, installing high-speed Internet access involves digging up and replacing underground cables.

Nevertheless, the telephone companies are not expected to deploy DSL as quickly as the cable companies are deploying cable modem service. According to *PC Week,* after losing money on Integrated Service Digital Network (ISDN), the phone companies are leery of making the investment required for DSL, which includes the cost of setting up the ATM backbone networks and central office support equipment. The investment can only be justified if the returns are high enough. With consumers being somewhat reluctant to pay more than $20 a month for basic Internet access, it remains to be seen how many consumers are willing to pay a premium for higher-speed Web access (Surkan, 1998).

Finally, there is a potential threat from a number of low earth orbiting (LEO) satellite networks being developed to provide high-speed Internet access. For example, Teledesic is a 288 LEO satellite network under development, with such backers as Bill Gates, Craig McCaw (of McCaw Cellular), and Boeing. These ventures are investing several billion dollars to build satellite networks that can provide consumers and businesses with high-speed, low-cost Internet access. Although it may be years before these satellite networks are actually working, they represent an additional substitution threat for incumbent ISPs.

Although these substitute technologies are likely to gain market share at different rates, their cumulative effect is to push down ISP margins. Keenly aware of the threat of substitute services, ISPs feel pressured to invest in improving their technology in order to keep from losing their existing customers. This pressure results in parallel strategic initiatives: ISPs spend on researching new technologies; they may make acquisitions of particularly promising technologies; they may spend to develop value-added services; and they may keep a tight lid on price increases.

REASONS FOR FUTURE UNPROFITABILITY

We have seen that the current structure of the ISP industry makes it inherently unprofitable. But how is the structure likely to evolve? The most likely scenario is that the ISP industry will remain inherently unprofitable. Despite continued consolidation, it is likely that there will be many well-financed survivors who will continue to compete with each other for increased market share. One underpinning of that competition is likely to be the low monthly price for Internet access.

The fundamental reason for the future inability to raise prices is that customers will continue to expect low prices. Consumers and businesses are increasingly conditioned to shop for lower prices. Although the switching costs for consumers are likely to be lower than for businesses, the bargaining power of customers is likely to remain high for both segments. As a result, it is unlikely that ISPs will be able to pass cost increases on to their customers. Under these conditions, ISPs could be profitable only if they could operate fully depreciated access networks with costs per customer per month that were very low.

However, as long as the level of rivalry remains intense, firms will be able to survive only if they continue to invest in new network access equipment and new value-added services. There is no question that some ISPs are searching for ways to counteract these profit-constricting forces. One way is to forward-integrate into the Web portal business. Unfortunately, the Web portal business is full of competitors pursuing "me too" strategies, and ISPs may need to add people with consumer marketing expertise just to achieve competitive parity in the Web portal business. Thus it is difficult to see how ISPs will escape their profit paradox through forward integration.

CASES

Given the limited profit potential of the ISP business for the average participant, it may be worth examining how some ISPs are grappling with their business challenges. As we look at these cases, we will analyze the firms' strategies and identify principles that are likely to distinguish the long-term survivors from the other ISPs. We will be looking at America Online (AOL), MindSpring, and EarthLink.

America Online: Consumer Marketing Powerhouse

With fiscal 1998 revenues of $2.6 billion and net income of $92 million, America Online (AOL) is a profitable ISP. According to the *Wall Street Journal*, AOL's fourteen million subscribers make it the leading provider of online services. AOL's 1998 acquisition of CompuServe (now subsidiary CompuServe Interactive Services), which has two million subscribers, boosted the combined services' market share to 60 percent. AOL appeals to those seeking entertainment, but CompuServe is geared toward professionals and owners of small businesses. Flat-rate pricing and growing competition in providing Internet access have led AOL to look beyond subscriber fees for revenues. It is working to sell advertising on its Web site and is forging marketing agreements with other companies whereby AOL collects fees on sales to its subscribers. As we will explore here and in Chapter Ten, AOL announced the acquisition of rival Netscape in November 1998 ("America Online Briefing Book," 1998).

AOL HISTORY. Controversy has accompanied AOL's success. In the mid-1990s, AOL bombarded households with diskettes that were designed to encourage consumers to sign up for its service. The cost of the marketing programs was accounted for in a way that the SEC ultimately deemed improper. As a result, AOL changed its accounting procedures, writing off $385 million in October 1996. AOL also experienced severe service outages after it began offering flat-rate pricing of $19.95 per month in winter 1996–97. AOL was proud that its service was so popular that most customers stuck with AOL as it added infrastructure to solve its problem. From the point of view of many in Silicon Valley, the worst part of AOL is that it lacks technical sophistication. AOL is criticized for having a proprietary architecture, written in its own language instead of a Web lingua franca, such as HTML and Java. AOL's service also seems too simple to appeal to the tastes of the high-tech cognoscenti.

AOL'S SOURCE OF MARKETING EXPERTISE. AOL's consumer marketing expertise comes in large part from its current president Bob Pittman.

Pittman was one of the founders of MTV, earning him the distinction of *Time* magazine Man of the Year in 1984. He subsequently led the Six Flags theme park and ran Century 21. Pittman joined AOL in October 1996 to help Steve Case manage the organization. Since he started with AOL, AOL's stock price rose 3,025 percent from a split-adjusted $4 to $125 on March 26, 1999. AOL's revenues more than doubled from about $1 billion in 1996 to $2.6 billion in 1998 (Keegan, 1998).

Pittman's success in helping to build AOL is largely attributable to his keen insights into what drives mass-market behavior. Pittman believes that consumers buy brands, that they value convenience, and that their technological literacy is increasing. Pittman points out that although Coca-Cola loses in taste tests to Pepsi, consumers buy Coke because it is a brand that they are comfortable buying. While tacitly acknowledging that AOL may not be technically preeminent, Pittman suggests that its blitzkrieg of free sign-up disks spared consumers the need to do a scientific analysis of each ISP.

Pittman's second rule about consumers is that they place a high value on convenience. Pittman points out that a conventional oven cooks better than a microwave oven, yet consumers prefer the microwave because it works faster. In Pittman's view, AOL is just like the microwave oven—it takes things that people do in real life and saves them time by performing these activities online. Pittman points out that Americans like to spend time socializing. Because this is not convenient for people to do offline, it comes as no surprise to Pittman that chat and e-mail make up more than 40 percent of the use of AOL. Other activities, such as shopping, entertainment planning, and research, are also more convenient on the Web. AOL enables subscribers to buy clothes from J. Crew, plan an evening out using Digital City, and research a project with the *New York Times* and *Scientific American.*

Pittman's third point, that people are becoming more technologically literate, helps AOL because people are losing their fear and ignorance about the online universe. Pittman comments that Yahoo and Excite have trouble getting visitors to spend more than ten minutes a day on their portals. As we will explore further in Chapter Thirteen, AOL's acquisition of ICQ, a service that lets members chat and send instant messages, increases the time that visitors spend at AOL to sixty minutes a day. Although average Americans are wary about buying online, AOL believes that they are beginning to see how much quicker and more convenient online shopping can be. Pittman suggests that although AOL did a mere $329 million in e-commerce sales in 1997, AOL reminds him of the early days of cable networks. Pittman conveys to investors a sense that building a brand and managing a fast-growing business in a competitive arena with no road maps is a game with which he is quite familiar (Keegan, 1998).

AOL'S ACQUISITION OF NETSCAPE. AOL's acquisition of Netscape in November 1998 suggests that Pittman is quite comfortable charting new territory. In paying $4.21 billion for Netscape, AOL was actually buying three distinct businesses—a Web portal, Web browser software, and b-to-b e-commerce software. The most attractive asset from AOL's point of view is Netscape's Web portal. As we will explore further in Chapter Ten, Netscape's Web portal was created as a result of one of its other two businesses—Web browser software. Because of the way Netscape programmed its Web browser, its users were automatically connected to the Netscape Web portal when they logged onto the Internet. Although users can change this default setting, most do not. At the time of the acquisition by AOL, Netscape's Web portal, Netcenter, was attracting sixteen million visitors per month.

How is AOL likely to generate a return on its investment in Netscape? As we noted in Chapter Six, the Web portal business is about attracting eyeballs. According to *MSNBC*, between AOL's fourteen million subscribers and Netscape's sixteen million monthly users, the combined entity will reach 61.2 percent of the online work audience and 58.4 percent of the online home audience. AOL is thus a "must-buy" for advertisers and has drawn $450 million out of the industry's $1.3 billion in estimated 1998 advertising revenue (Weaver, 1998).

Its dominant share will give AOL the all-important economic leverage with advertisers to negotiate multiyear advertising commitments worth hundreds of millions of dollars. The big incremental growth in AOL's share of online advertising will make AOL the de facto industry standard. As competitors lose relative position, advertisers will shy away from the smaller players and create even greater momentum for AOL.

AOL is difficult to categorize. It is not a Web portal, because its system is built in an AOL-proprietary programming language, not in one of the open Web-based languages. Yet it is not an ISP that provides just the commodity service of connecting people to the Internet. Above all, AOL's experience demonstrates that building a consumer brand is the key to success in the ISP and Web portal businesses.

MindSpring: Attention to Costs and Customer Service

MindSpring is a national ISP based in Atlanta, Georgia. One of the only ISPs earning a profit, MindSpring generated $115 million in revenues and $11 million in net income in 1998. MindSpring subscribers can access the Web, send e-mail, participate in online chats, and access twenty thousand newsgroups. MindSpring offers local Internet service in 375 locations throughout the United States. It also offers Web hosting services on which small businesses operate Web sites.

MindSpring has added members at a rapid rate. According to *Business Wire*, MindSpring's membership grew over 15 percent between the first and second quarter of 1998. Membership grew at a compound annual growth rate of 115 percent between 1997 and 1998. Membership grew from 183,000 in the second quarter of 1997 to 341,000 in the first quarter of 1998 to 393,000 as of June 3, 1998. Included in the totals were Web hosting customers, whose number grew from 7,000 to 12,000 to 15,000 during the same periods ("MindSpring Announces . . . ," 1998).

SOURCES OF REVENUE. MindSpring gets most of its revenue from monthly subscriptions and start-up fees from individuals for dial-up access to the Internet. Customers have a choice of two flat-rate plans and two usage-sensitive plans. Consistent with other ISPs, MindSpring's average monthly recurring revenue per dial-up subscriber is about $20 (MindSpring Enterprises, Form 10-Q, Aug. 13, 1998, p. 2).

Start-up fees for new subscribers vary depending on the promotional method used to acquire the subscriber, ranging up to $25. MindSpring's subscriber start-up fees cover the costs of direct materials, mailing expenses, and licensing fees associated with new subscribers. Most individual subscribers pay their MindSpring fees by preauthorized monthly charges to the subscriber's credit card.

MindSpring also earns revenue by providing services to small businesses that are using MindSpring as the infrastructure for their Web sites. MindSpring generates revenues by providing these businesses a range of services, including Web hosting, domain registration and Web page design services, Web-server colocation, and full-time dedicated access connections to the Internet. MindSpring currently offers three price plans for Web hosting subscribers, ranging from $19.95 to $99.95 per month.

COSTS. Let us turn now to a close look at MindSpring's costs, particularly its direct cost of revenues. In broad terms, MindSpring has three general categories of costs: costs of revenue vary with the number of subscribers; selling, general, and administrative costs vary more generally with the number of MindSpring employees; and depreciation and amortization costs are related to the size of MindSpring's network and the deferred costs associated with acquired customer bases. MindSpring manages all these cost categories very tightly.

GROWTH THROUGH ACQUISITIONS. As we noted early in this chapter, some of MindSpring's growth has come through acquisitions. In the first nine months of 1998 alone, for example, MindSpring made seven ISP acquisitions, six of which were private companies for which no information about the purchase price or the number of subscribers was made available. MindSpring actually has a person whose title is director of acquisitions. Clearly, evaluating and doing ISP acquisitions is a full-time job.

An analysis of the one acquisition for which MindSpring did disclose information is instructive. According to *Reuters*, in September 1998, MindSpring announced that it would purchase America Online's SpryNet subscriber base and assets for $35–$40 million in cash. SpryNet had about 180,000 individual Internet access customers in the United States and Canada. MindSpring's SpryNet acquisition also included the cost of assets used in serving those customers, including customer support and network operations facilities in Seattle. AOL had acquired SpryNet in February 1998 when it took over CompuServe Interactive Services ("MindSpring Says to Buy . . .," 1998).

Assuming that SpryNet's 180,000 customers end up paying $240 per year to MindSpring, it appears that these customers will generate revenues that exceed the purchase price within a year. However, the SpryNet deal also represents a cost of $222 for each new subscriber. That is three times the $74 cost per new subscriber that MindSpring incurred in sales expense to increase its subscriber base by fifty-two thousand between the first and second quarters of 1998. Although this analysis excludes some of the costs associated with the internal generation of new clients, it does suggest that MindSpring is willing to pay a premium to acquire a large block of new customers at one time.

CUSTOMER LOYALTY. MindSpring's success is due in part to the value the company places on customer loyalty. Although the concept of customer loyalty is hardly original, it is relatively rare to find the concept working in the ISP business. Most ISPs are run by people with a better sense of technology than of how to motivate people. MindSpring's behavior toward its stakeholders makes it stand out in the minds of customers.

MindSpring is now in the process of installing a package called Web Speed, which will enable incoming calls to be routed based on information in the company's accounting database. For example, if a customer dials into MindSpring customer service, Web Speed software will look up information about that customer—for example, how long the customer has been with MindSpring, what type of operating system and system configuration they have, and how many times they have called customer service—and display it to the customer service representative. Thus if a customer who had been with MindSpring for only six weeks was calling for the fourth time, the Web Speed software would know to route the customer service call to a more advanced technician.

MindSpring's high degree of customer loyalty is based on a golden triangle that includes its employees, customers, and shareholders. MindSpring hires customer service people who enjoy helping other people, and it creates an environment that rewards excellent customer service—thus ensuring that MindSpring employees genuinely want to deliver great customer service.

The great customer service makes customers happy with MindSpring. Southern Appeal (southernappeal.com), an online golf retailer, uses MindSpring's Web hosting service to sell golf equipment and accessories over the Internet. According to Al Pink, cofounder and president of Southern Appeal, MindSpring is an excellent ISP. Pink particularly appreciates MindSpring's responsive attitude toward customer service. For example, as with many companies, MindSpring offers service hours twenty-four hours per day, seven days a week. However, MindSpring differentiates itself with the attitude of its customer service staff. In Pink's view, MindSpring's customer service staff is always willing to take responsibility for solving problems rather than passing them on to the vendor or another party (Al Pink, interview with the author, Jan. 1998).

Speaking more broadly, Pink believes that the behavior of MindSpring people is consistent with its corporate values of service and respect for the individual. MindSpring is also responsive to market trends without being prompted. For example, when MindSpring saw that competitors were lowering their prices for Internet access, the company preemptively contacted Pink and offered him a lower price for his Web space so as to keep competitors from taking Southern Appeal away from MindSpring.

Finally, Pink has never experienced any downtime problems with MindSpring, in contrast to reports he has heard about the reliability of other ISPs. Even as MindSpring has grown through acquisitions, Pink has never perceived the problems with slow e-mail or downtime that often accompany acquisitions.

The connection between loyal customers and shareholder value also works to MindSpring's benefit. By creating loyal customers, Mind-Spring spends less time getting new customers and more time selling additional services to its loyal customer base, which in turn enables the firm to earn profits. The profits help increase the stock price. For example, between January 1, 1998, and March 26, 1999, MindSpring's stock price rose 820 percent from $10 to $92.

Another result of this golden triangle is that MindSpring has received numerous awards from the industry press. For example, in the second quarter of 1998, MindSpring's dial-up service received *PC World* magazine's World Class Award for the best ISP and *Smart Money* magazine's Best Buy recommendation. MindSpring's Web hosting service also received a Best Buy recommendation from *Home Office Computing* magazine ("MindSpring Announces . . .," 1998).

EarthLink: Tele-Bedfellows

According to *Red Herring,* Sky Dayton, the twenty-six-year-old founder of EarthLink, started the company because he was having difficulty connecting his computer to the Internet. Dayton was deeply concerned that other people might be denied access to the Web as a result of similar difficulties. Concluding that people would pay for excellent technical support while getting connected, Dayton founded EarthLink in 1994. Like MindSpring, EarthLink has distinguished itself from such competitors as AOL by focusing on being friendly to users. As of August 1998, EarthLink, with seven hundred thousand customers, ranked as the fourth-largest ISP in the United States (McGarvey, 1998). By March 1999, that number had reached 815,000.

EarthLink is growing rapidly but remains unprofitable. In 1998, the company posted $176 million in revenues and lost $60 million. During the period, EarthLink increased its revenues 122 percent and, despite this growth, was able to reduce the rate of customer churn from 4 percent to 3.3 percent—much lower than AOL's estimated 10 percent churn rate (Earthlink, 1998, Form 10-K).

STRATEGIC CHOICES. EarthLink's rapid growth is attributable to a handful of key strategic choices. According to *Red Herring*, to avoid the expense of the backbone structure necessary to run an ISP, Dayton rented some capacity from UUNet Technologies and PSINet. EarthLink invested its own resources in marketing and intensive customer service. The portion of the network that EarthLink does operate has been expanded to allow for future growth, and the company's subscriber base has been keeping pace (Stubbs, 1998).

To raise capital for market share growth, in February 1998 EarthLink struck a key deal with Sprint. To see how that deal came about, we need to review some earlier history of the company.

PARTNERSHIP WITH GARRY BETTY. In the midst of EarthLink's initial growth, Dayton realized that he was "in over his head." Early in 1996, he recognized that the company had grown beyond his ability to manage it. So he brought in Garry Betty, an experienced high-tech executive, to run day-to-day operations. Betty had worked at Hayes Microcomputer Products and IBM.

While acknowledging the difficulty of giving up control, Dayton chose to delegate everything except a few key areas. The areas that Dayton kept for himself include setting strategic direction, forming big partnerships, and designing the overall product. Dayton views his main job as holding onto his original vision born of his frustration with trying to connect to the Internet.

Although Betty came to Dayton with the endorsement of two board members, Dayton made the final decision to hire Betty after a driving incident during a ski trip. Dayton had invited Betty to go skiing; on their way to Big Bear, a Southern California ski resort, it began to snow. Dayton had not packed chains for his BMW M5 and had never driven in snow. The situation turned grim. Betty and Dayton were trapped on a hill behind an overturned Twinkie truck. The BMW's wheels were spinning out, and the car was turning in circles. Betty stepped in with advice and tips to get the pair safely off the mountain. Betty's ability to remain calm and offer advice impressed Dayton. Dayton has turned over the day-to-day running of the company to Betty; the two have established a clear division of responsibilities that works effectively (McGarvey, 1998).

According to the *Industry Standard,* when Betty joined EarthLink in 1996, the company had thirty thousand subscribers and was growing at a rate of 15 to 20 percent a week. Despite Dayton's best efforts, the rapid growth was being achieved in the complete absence of financial controls. According to Betty, EarthLink lacked counts of its cash position, its cash requirements, and how much it owed (Rafter, 1998).

Over the following six months, Betty installed basic accounting systems to track the sources and uses of cash. He set up the accounting and financial systems that he had used to manage larger, public companies, such as Hayes Microcomputer. After EarthLink installed these systems, the company was in a position to raise the capital it needed to fuel its growth.

CUSTOMER SERVICE OPERATIONS. To keep up with its growing customer base, EarthLink has invested more than $23 million in a ten-thousand-square-foot data center at its year-old Pasadena headquarters. This data center can handle the needs of up to three million subscribers. EarthLink's customer support department hires people constantly. As of May 1998, EarthLink's customer service department accounted for six hundred of the company's one thousand employees (Rafter, 1998).

RAISING CAPITAL TO BUILD MARKET SHARE. Subsequently, Betty has played a crucial role in raising capital to fuel EarthLink's growth. He helped put together many of the deals that have kept the company going.

Before Betty's arrival, EarthLink had raised $4.4 million from existing and new investors to promote its national status after signing a deal with UUNET. In the UUNET deal, EarthLink leased national access to the Internet backbone at wholesale rates. EarthLink spent the $4.4 million in a five-month marketing campaign.

In subsequent private placements, EarthLink raised $22.7 million, including investments from George Soros, before its $26 million public offering in January 1997. In September 1997, EarthLink raised another $15.4 million in a private placement, with $5 million coming from Soros's investment arm, Soros Fund Management.

To continue its expansion, however, EarthLink needed more funding. Betty and Dayton spent the first half of 1997 talking to the local exchange carriers (the so-called Baby Bells) about marketing partnerships, but came away without capital. Then, in September 1997, EarthLink director Sidney Azeez asked his friend Carl Peterson, president and general manager of the Kansas City Chiefs, to inform Peterson's colleague William Esrey, chairman of Sprint, that EarthLink was seeking to raise capital.

PARTNERSHIP WITH SPRINT. Esrey liked the idea of working with Earth-Link. He set up a meeting between top EarthLink and Sprint executives at Sprint's headquarters in Kansas City, Missouri. Within a month, Esrey and top Sprint Internet managers were in Dayton's office finalizing negotiations. The deal was announced February 11, 1998.

Sprint had built Internet Passport, an ISP that had been plagued with problems. According to *PC Week,* even with a mere 130,000 customers, Sprint's service was unresponsive to consumer needs. For example, the Sprint service had consumer access connections that did not work. More important, Sprint lacked the culture of consumer responsiveness that successful ISPs such as EarthLink clearly had mastered (Rendleman, 1998).

Sprint saw EarthLink as a way to jump-start its Internet strategy. In Sprint's view, EarthLink had the scale that Sprint was seeking. Furthermore, Sprint's strategy and direction ran parallel to those of EarthLink. Sprint believed that its customers would be happy because they would get a better product than that provided by Sprint at the time of the deal. Sprint thought that EarthLink's product equaled the one that Sprint was trying to develop and that Sprint had anticipated would have taken twelve to eighteen months to introduce into the marketplace.

As part of the deal, Sprint paid $4.2 million for 10 percent of Earth-Link stock; extended to EarthLink a three-year, low-interest $100 million credit line; and became EarthLink's third access provider. Sprint also handed off to EarthLink its 130,000 Sprint Internet Passport customers. Sprint promised to deliver another 750,000 customers from 1998 to 2003 through a joint marketing program.

The deal also gave EarthLink access to Sprint's two-thousand-person telemarketing staff. Both parties had anticipated that Sprint's telemarketing staff would be able to sell EarthLink-Sprint Internet access to long-distance customers and prospects.

In exchange, Sprint also received 4.2 million restricted, nonvoting shares (in addition to EarthLink common shares), giving it an aggregate 30 percent stake in the ISP, as well as two seats on EarthLink's board, to be filled by Esrey and Patti Manuel, head of the company's $14.8 billion consumer long-distance division.

CONCERNS ABOUT EARTHLINK-SPRINT. But questions remain about the future of the EarthLink-Sprint deal. Sprint may prove more of a hindrance than a help to EarthLink. Sprint came late to the consumer dial-up business, and Internet Passport had floundered while Sprint invested in other areas.

Another source of potential difficulty is that executives at both companies will not rule out the possibility that Sprint could buy EarthLink after the three-year hands-off period spelled out in their deal. Sprint included this clause in the transaction to avoid fueling the growth of a large ISP that could ultimately become a competitor that Sprint could not control. EarthLink interprets the option merely as Sprint's right to present an offer for the 70 percent of EarthLink that Sprint does not already own. So the issue of ownership remains an open one that is likely to cause disagreements in the future (Rafter, 1998).

POTENTIAL SOURCES OF REVENUE. Despite its growth and its success at raising capital, EarthLink still faces the challenge of earning a profit. Betty sees three sources of incremental revenue over and above the $20 monthly subscription fees. The first source of incremental revenues is a premier partnership package that gives a cluster of sponsors an opportunity to promote their products and services on EarthLink's site. Premier partners include American Greetings, Surfwatch, Netopia, Datek, and Sprint. Betty anticipates that these premier partnership packages could generate incremental revenues of $50,000 to $200,000 per quarter (Garry Betty, interview with the author, May 1998).

EarthLink's other sources of incremental revenues include providing access for other people's content. For example, EarthLink provides a platform for companies that offer small business services. An example is the Nolo Press Self Help Law Center, which provides information that can help small business people deal with common legal problems, such as landlord-tenant law. For these partners, EarthLink provides search and navigation capabilities from Hotbot and the Mining Company, respectively, in exchange for an up-front fee. EarthLink will also continue to sell traditional banner advertising priced on the basis of the number of impressions per quarter.

Looking to the future, Betty sees e-commerce as a wildcard. Earth-Link envisions a business model in which its site includes an online shopping mall of e-commerce, from which EarthLink would take a royalty percentage of each transaction. Through its Hotbot and Mining Company technology, EarthLink would monitor and characterize the volume and source of traffic, thereby assessing the cost-effectiveness of advertising. Although this technology has the potential to make customer profile data available through so-called cookies (an audit trail of each Web site that a user visits) on Web browsers, EarthLink does not use the technology for this purpose because it believes that it has a responsibility to protect the privacy of its customer profiles.

It is difficult to predict whether EarthLink's efforts to become profitable will succeed. Given its 30 percent ownership by the deep-pocketed Sprint, the most likely scenario is that EarthLink will be acquired when the hands-off clause expires. In light of the differences in culture between EarthLink and Sprint, it is possible that some of the efforts at cross-marketing will be hindered by internal barriers. To make cross-selling work involves changing how performance is measured and rewarded. Cross-selling also involves cross-training the people who are doing the selling. What is clear is that the Sprint deal did provide EarthLink with cash that it needed to continue on.

IMPLICATIONS

We began this chapter by pointing out that the ISP business is a very difficult one in which to earn profits. So on the face of it, the ISP business would appear to be a good one to stay away from, both for managers and investors. There are plenty of managers and investors who have seen their stakes in these companies increase tremendously in value, but over the long term, it is likely that many ISPs will simply run out of cash.

So what is an investor or manager to do? The most likely strategy for making money is to take advantage of the consolidation trend. For investors, this means trying to identify those firms that are likely targets. In general, acquirers pay a premium to take control of a company. Investors can try taking stakes in public and privately held ISPs. Although it is generally easier to take a stake in a publicly traded ISP, it is also more likely that much of the potential returns from an acquisition will already be reflected in the stock price.

Taking a stake in a privately held ISP that is likely to be acquired requires more effort and involves more risk, but it also could generate higher returns. Well-heeled investors (angels) may be able to identify privately held ISPs that could be attractive acquisition candidates for some of the publicly traded, acquisition-hungry ISPs. One way to identify such opportunities is to study the acquisition histories of firms like MindSpring, AOL, Verio, and others. This analysis can help pinpoint the characteristics of firms that would make attractive acquisition candidates. Having identified such candidates, angels seek out introductions to board members or CEOs and explore their interest in an investment.

For ISP managers, the strategic options depend on where the firm is positioned. For medium-size firms, one option is to use limited capital and human resources to build up the number of subscribers. A focus on customer service, coupled with carefully considered geographic expansion, appears to be a viable approach, as it has been for MindSpring. Small firms should find ways to serve the customers in their local area with enough paying services to exceed their operating costs. The largest firms will seek to expand through acquisition.

Ultimately, consolidation appears to be an insurmountable trend in the ISP industry. So even though all these groups of ISPs may find it useful to pursue independent strategies, it is likely that many of the firms will be merged into larger ones due to the inherent inability of the ISP industry to support adequate profitability for the average participant.

The case studies, particularly that of MindSpring, suggest that it may be possible to turn an inherently unattractive industry into a potentially profitable one. Following are seven principles for making that transition.

1. *Good customer service may have the potential to turn a commodity into a profitable business.* Internet access is a commodity. MindSpring offers Internet access for the standard price. But through its culture, MindSpring is able to earn higher than average customer loyalty. And this loyalty may translate into better financial performance and a higher stock price. Whether MindSpring is able to sustain profitability remains to be seen. However, if any ISP is able to lead the way to profitability, it is MindSpring.

Similarly, EarthLink provides specific operational statistics that are instructive: 60 percent of its employees are in customer service, and the company's churn rate is relatively low and dropping. The low churn rate increases the value of each customer.

AOL's success suggests that customers place a very high value on convenience. Despite AOL's service outages in 1996, the firm has continued to build its customer base because its service is designed to be the most convenient for the large portion of Internet users who care most about using technology to simplify their lives.

2. *Acquisitions are apparently a good way to add subscribers.* The prices and subscriber counts pertaining to MindSpring's smaller acquisitions have not been disclosed. However, it appears that the integration of customers into MindSpring has occurred smoothly. Whether the acquisitions prove to be a cost-effective way of acquiring new customers remains to be seen. AOL's acquisition of Netscape was clearly motivated by the desire to add eyeballs quickly and relatively inexpensively. Although AOL's gamble is likely to be successful, the outcome is unknown as this book goes to press.

3. *Managing costs is crucial to the survival of an ISP.* It may be that MindSpring finds it more cost-effective to increase profits per customer through excellent service than to spend heavily to get new customers who then switch to a new ISP as soon as a better deal comes along. By investing in excellent service while keeping its costs low, MindSpring is likely to earn sufficient profits to survive.

4. *The battle for leadership in market share consumes vast amounts of capital.* On the one hand, MindSpring weighs the incremental costs and benefits of geographic expansion. On the other hand, EarthLink has placed the goal of market share leadership at the top of its corporate hierarchy of needs. The result is that EarthLink is in constant pursuit of additional capital to fund its growth in subscriptions and increase its market share as quickly as possible. The implicit, still unproved, assumption is that although EarthLink shareholders sacrifice in the short run as the firm achieves its goals, the shares will be more valuable in the long run. By watching the fates of EarthLink and MindSpring, it will become clear which of these paths proves most profitable.

5. *Service packages must be tailored to the specific needs of different customer segments.* MindSpring has a good understanding of the specific expectations that consumers and small businesses have for their ISP. MindSpring therefore is able to increase loyalty by doing better than competitors at meeting customer needs, thereby building switching costs with its customers.

6. *Cultural issues can be very powerful barriers to realizing the full economic potential of a strategic alliance.* It appears that the partnership

between Betty and Dayton has worked well for EarthLink. Conversely, in the partnership between Sprint and EarthLink, the potential cultural mismatch could impede the ability of both firms to realize the full economic potential of the partnership. Given the challenges of implementing cross-selling arrangements, the ultimate gauge of the partnership's value will the extent to which cross-selling actually brings in a substantial number of new subscribers.

7. *Attempting to become a Web portal is a "me too" strategy that is only likely to work for ISPs with strong consumer marketing skills, such as AOL.* Netscape (prior to its acquisition by AOL) and EarthLink were coming from two very different strategic groups, yet they both appeared to be basing their hopes for profitability on competitive success in the Web portal space. As we will see in Chapter Ten, Netscape clearly lacked the media marketing expertise needed to achieve competitive dominance against the likes of Yahoo, NBC-Snap, and others. Whether EarthLink can do better than Netscape remains to be seen. And whether any of these firms can achieve substantial revenues from taking a piece of any e-commerce that occurs in their "online malls" remains unknown.

THE NET PROFIT RETRIEVER'S ASSESSMENT OF THE ISP SEGMENT

The ISP segment does not make the Net Profit Retriever bark three times. The industry lacks economic leverage, it offers no closed-loop solution, and its management varies in its ability to adapt to change.

1. *Economic leverage.* The ISP industry sells a commodity service. There are forty-five hundred competitors in the industry, and although demand is growing, these competitors are unable to raise their prices to cover the cost of adding the capacity needed to meet that demand. In addition, new technologies are creating pressure on incumbents to keep prices low as a means of deterring entry.

2. *Closed-loop solution.* Connection to the Internet is a necessary but insufficient condition for achieving the payoff from e-commerce or advertising. Such firms as MindSpring and EarthLink are demonstrating that they understand the important role that excellent customer service can play in contributing to the value of the Internet connection. Whether this understanding will enable them to offer customers a closed-loop solution remains to be seen.

3. *Adaptive management.* Although the telecommunications firms in the ISP business seem to have a particularly hard time adapting to change, not all ISPs are similarly sluggish. MindSpring has made a number of acquisitions and appears quite innovative in its efforts to enhance customer service. EarthLink has made several deals for financing that reflect the value of its customer service skills. Nevertheless, the prospects for many ISPs remain cloudy.

CHAPTER TEN

Web Commerce Tools:
Virtual Plumbing

J ust as the world's most glamorous homes need plumbing and electrical wires, Amazon.com and Yahoo require a complex and mostly unseen collection of tools that enable e-commerce to work. These virtual plumbing supplies include browsers, search engines, Web advertising management software, and e-commerce enabling software.

Many of the firms that sell these tools are not covered by the media. An exception that we discussed earlier is Netscape, the first firm to commercialize a Web browser successfully. Fewer people have heard of Inktomi, which develops Web search tools; DoubleClick, which manages Web advertising; Sterling Commerce, which provides b-to-b e-commerce software; or Macromedia, which makes tools for creative Web developers of video games, cartoons, and other content.

As we will see, it is somewhat artificial to group all the Web tools segments together as if they were one Internet segment. In fact, each set of products represents a unique subsegment with varying levels of inherent profitability, different sets of customer needs, and different requirements for competitive success. Nevertheless, it is useful to think of these subsegments as different tools that are intended to make the

Internet more useful for doing e-commerce. *Browsers* make the Web much easier to navigate by creating both a simple way to key in Web addresses and a very user-friendly way to see and hear the content on the Web. *Search engines* filter the hundreds of millions of Web sites down to the critical few that are most likely to meet a user's information needs. *Web advertising management* firms and software help Web advertisers account for their Web advertisements so that they can control their Web advertising expenses and assess the extent of the value that these expenses generate. And *e-commerce enabling* software lets companies build Web sites that display product information, take orders, and process the orders through their product supply systems.

In general, these firms compete in industries that are structurally unattractive. It is possible that some of these firms may be able to alter the structure of their industries to tilt the playing field in their favor, but they are certainly fighting some very powerful forces, the chief among which is Microsoft.

CAPITALIZATION AND THE MICROSOFT FALCON

Microsoft threatens the long-term survival of each of the firms in the Web commerce tools business, enjoying huge structural advantages over them. Its dominant position in PC operating systems and its growing market position in client-server operating systems give Microsoft tremendous leverage. Beyond Microsoft's technical leverage, Web tool companies must concern themselves even more with Microsoft's exceptional sales and marketing strength. The short-term solution for many of these firms has been to form partnerships with Microsoft, but Microsoft has not always proven itself to be the most pleasant partner in the business world.

The experience of Robert Glaser, CEO of RealNetworks, bears this out. Glaser is a former Microsoft employee who left the firm to start a company called Progressive Networks (later renamed RealNetworks), which makes a product called RealPlayer. RealPlayer can be downloaded free over the Internet. RealPlayer lets people view videos and hear audio on their PCs. Glaser formed what he thought was a fairly durable partnership with his former employer.

However, his feelings about the partnership changed, as he expressed in his testimony at a July 1998 hearing before the Senate Judiciary Committee. Glaser, who spent ten years at Microsoft before starting his own company, told the committee that Microsoft was using its dominant position to extend its grasp on the software market. Glaser told members of the panel and also demonstrated that Microsoft's software caused RealPlayer to crash when users tried to install it. In the meantime, Microsoft has introduced its own video player, NetShow.

An even more costly instance of Microsoft's use of its market power to diminish the fortunes of a Web tool company took place in the Web browser business. As we saw in Chapter Four, Netscape was one of the first highly successful Web IPOs. Netscape's huge market capitalization got Bill Gates's attention. Although Gates had been dimly aware of the Internet throughout much of the early 1990s, it was not until Netscape proved the Web could make money—for investors if not on an income statement—that Gates really decided to do something about the Web. Netscape, of course, introduced the first commercial Web browser. Netscape sold the browser for a nominal fee over the Internet, hoping to establish itself quickly as the industry standard. Netscape was enjoying tremendous growth in its stock price around the time that Microsoft was busy rolling out its Windows 95 PC operating system.

As soon as the Windows 95 operating system rollout was complete, Gates told hundreds of Microsoft programmers to drop what they were doing and start building a browser to compete with Netscape's. After three versions of the Explorer Web browser in quick succession, Microsoft's browser became so good and so popular that it seriously challenged Netscape's market leadership. And with Microsoft giving away its product free, Netscape felt compelled to cut the price of its browser to zero as well. Netscape's stock price—and its media cachet—collapsed with stunning speed. Netscape spent a few months struggling to rebuild itself into a Web portal and in November 1998 sold out to AOL.

These examples suggest the threat from Microsoft that any Web tool vendor may face. Over the long term, success on the Web depends heavily on the ability to turn the product or service into a leverage point. Although Microsoft has not succeeded as well in the world of online services, its dominance of the software business has not been seriously threatened. Any new entrant must find a way to overcome Microsoft's dominance in operating systems and its powerful sales and marketing force.

More important, a Web tool company must understand that Microsoft is predictable. As a large firm, Microsoft must grab big pieces of large, rapidly growing new markets in order to ensure the continued growth in its stock price. Microsoft assesses the emergence of such markets by looking for new companies that are building huge market capitalizations. The huge market capitalization signals an opportunity for Microsoft to gear up its programmers and marketers and attack the successful new company.

The attack follows a predictable pattern. Microsoft builds several versions of the new company's most successful product. Microsoft's first version is likely to be terrible, but by the fourth version, Microsoft has a product that is usually better than the new company's product. Then Microsoft uses its clout in the distribution channel to gain a huge share of the new market. The result is a massive transfer of wealth from the new company to Microsoft shareholders. In addition to video players and Web browsers, Microsoft has repeated this pattern in PC and client-server operating systems, word processing software, and spreadsheets.

It is obvious that any firm in the Web tool business needs to develop a strategy to keep Microsoft from doing the same thing to them. One possible strategy is to keep the industry so small that Microsoft decides it is not worth attacking. This strategy has two obvious flaws. One is that it assumes that a firm can limit the size of the market. The other is that most firms would not choose to place a cap on their potential profitability. Nevertheless, the "keep it small" strategy does have certain advantages. The most obvious advantage is that the small firm would be more likely to remain independent. At least it might have a chance to choose a strategic partner on its own terms rather than be driven into a quick acquisition after it has collapsed.

A more sustainable strategy would be for the Web tool firms to target markets in which Microsoft will have a difficult time competing—specifically, to participate in an industry in which software is not the driving force. For example, Microsoft has not excelled in businesses where understanding mass-market entertainment and information needs is paramount. Examples of less than stellar outcomes include the Microsoft Network and the BOB operating system.

From the inception of Microsoft Network (MSN) in 1995 to November 1998, Microsoft had invested about $1 billion. Although it grew to become the third most popular Web portal, MSN had never earned a profit. In November 1998, Pete Higgins, the vice president in charge of MSN, decided to take an extended leave of absence from Microsoft with the intent of returning to the company in a different role. So it remains unclear whether Microsoft will find a profitable formula for MSN or ultimately sell it to another firm that can.

BOB was a very simple operating system that was designed to encourage nontechnical people to use computers. According to *Overdrive*, it used cartoon characters to help make applications easier to use. BOB never achieved its objective of attracting a large group of new PC users who found traditional PC operating systems intimidating, and the team at Microsoft that was working on BOB was ultimately disbanded (Wallace, 1997).

Both of these examples reflect Microsoft's effort to develop consumer products and services that draw in the 50 percent of American homes without PCs. It is possible that there is something about Microsoft's culture that makes it impossible for the company to develop products that are popular among this less technically inclined majority. However, Microsoft's goal is a PC in every home and office running Microsoft software; it is unlikely that Microsoft will give up its efforts to succeed in this non-PC market segment.

BROWSERS

In our discussion of Microsoft's invasion of the Web browser business, we saw how quickly business models can evaporate. Two of the early leaders in the Web browser business, Netscape and Spyglass, have made attempts to reinvent themselves. Although people still use the Web browsers that these firms were the first to commercialize, they cannot earn profits off the browsers because Microsoft forced the market price to zero.

Browsers are a set of Web tools that clearly will never be profitable. Nevertheless, by giving away Web browsers, Netscape and Spyglass built up a collection of assets that they hoped to recast into profitable business models. Netscape tried to build a Web portal by taking advantage of the fact that so many Netscape Web browsers are automatically set to start with the Netscape Web site. Spyglass is trying to build a strategy around providing Web access software for an expected plethora of non-PC devices that will be used for accessing the Web. Both strategies have their advantages and disadvantages.

Netscape

Netscape's strategy was intended to give Netscape investors an opportunity to cash in on the high market valuations associated with Web portals. Nevertheless, the skills required to succeed in the Web portal business are very different from the skills that Netscape required to write browser and enterprise software. Given the intense rivalry in the Web portal business, it was not too surprising that Netscape did not significantly outperform its competitors. More specifically, Netscape faced challenges in developing the capabilities needed to establish market leadership: brand building, Web advertising sales, and converting visitors to purchasers.

Netscape's strategy started from a point of strength, but it was not clear whether Netscape's strength relative to competitors such as Yahoo and AOL (its current owner) would be sufficient to attain market dominance. According to the *Industry Standard,* although Netscape was generating $150 million in advertising revenue from its Web site, it was only in 1998 that Netscape's management focused on its Web site, Netcenter, as a significant business driver. In 1995 and 1996, Netscape management was reluctant to give the Web site priority, even though it generated substantial cash from willing advertisers. Instead, the management saw Netscape's enterprise software business (for example, software that does Web-based billing and ordering) as the primary source of future profitability (Lash, 1998).

Without even trying, Netscape received three hundred e-mails a day from people asking to do business with Netcenter. When Netscape finally decided to get serious about Netcenter, it assigned executive Mike Homer, who took charge of the service in an aggressive manner. In response to Microsoft's offer of free access to *Wall Street Journal Interactive* for Internet Explorer 3.0 users, Homer created In-Box Direct, a subscription service that delivered free newsletters from the *New York Times* and other top publishers to Navigator 3.0 users.

By July 1998, In-Box Direct had attracted about 1.8 million subscribers, and it subsequently continued to be an integral part of the Netcenter Web site. Unfortunately, In-Box Direct failed to generate direct revenue for Netscape, although it helped build Netcenter membership and relationships with media companies.

Netscape continued to experiment with ways of turning traffic into revenue; meanwhile, it was good at attracting visitors. For example,

Netscape's site recorded eighteen million unique visitors in June 1998. This placed Netcenter in third place behind Yahoo and AOL, according to RelevantKnowledge (Lash, 1998). But Microsoft's Internet Explorer had pulled nearly even in browser share, and Netscape was faced with the twin challenges of not only continuing to drive people to Netcenter but also making them stay.

Netcenter resisted marketing itself to "the masses," thus allowing Yahoo to become the top consumer portal brand. After Disney and NBC took control of smaller portals Infoseek and Snap, respectively, the need for Homer and his team to become media executives intensified. While Netcenter sought to hire a media executive to run content programming, Homer began to develop ideas about how to turn Netcenter into a consumer brand. Homer's ideas included an online sweepstakes and movie quiz for Netcenter's Web mail users, a Netscape-branded credit card, $10 million of TV and print advertising by November 1998, and long-distance phone discounts for Netcenter registrants (Lash, 1998).

Along these lines, Netscape announced a deal with Citibank in August 1998 that would give Citibank a major presence on Netcenter. The Netscape personal finance channel was intended help Citibank sell its financial services to Netcenter members ("Netscape and Citibank . . .," 1998).

The cumulative effect of such partnerships was not sufficient to make Netcenter the dominant Web portal, but it was sufficient to encourage AOL to pay $4.2 billion for Netscape in November 1998. Although the deal gave AOL control of Netscape's browser, portal, and e-commerce software, the real value to AOL was that the combined firms would reach well over half the total U.S. Internet population. The new entity would thus control $450 million of the $1.3 billion in online advertising revenues projected for 1998, or 35 percent. This was more than double Yahoo's 1998 estimated advertising level of $200 million. More important, AOL's fourteen million subscribers and Netscape's sixteen million monthly users would give AOL a reach of 61.2 percent of the online work audience and 58.4 percent of the total home audience (Weaver, 1998).

Whereas AOL had been able to turn its audience into revenues, Netscape had not. For example, in the third quarter of 1998, AOL's revenues from commerce and advertising grew to $102 million, up 133 percent from the previous year. By contrast, Netscape ad revenues for all of 1997 were $40 million and reportedly were flat for most of

1998. In acquiring Netscape, AOL was betting that it could take an undervalued asset—Netscape's sixteen million users—and use its marketing skills to convert that asset into much higher ad and e-commerce revenues.

Netscape's fate highlights the importance of matching a firm's capabilities to the requirements for competitive success in different industries. Netscape simply lacked the marketing skills needed to succeed in the Web portal business. Similarly, AOL lacked the skills to succeed in the e-commerce software business it was buying as part of its Netscape acquisition. Netscape's e-commerce software business had fifteen hundred employees who were slated as part of the deal to report to AOL's president, Bob Pittman, the founder of MTV. The basic skill that AOL lacked was the ability to sell Netscape's complex enterprise software to large corporations, such as CitiGroup and John Hancock. AOL formed a partnership with Sun Microsystems to help close this capability gap. A three-year agreement called for Sun to work with AOL to develop Netscape's software and service for online commerce. AOL in return agreed to buy $500 million of software and hardware from Sun through 2002.

Because of the different cultures at Sun and AOL, there will be significant challenges in getting the two firms to work together effectively in managing Netscape's e-commerce software business. According to *MSNBC,* one problem is simply geographic distance in the reporting structure. Barry Ariko, Netscape's software operations chief, will continue to work at Netscape's headquarters in Mountain View, California, while reporting to Bob Pittman, who works out of Dulles, Virginia. Furthermore, the help from Sun may not be that valuable. Sun sells hardware and lower-level systems software, focusing primarily on computers that run the Unix operating system. By contrast, Netscape sells software for all major operating systems, including Windows NT from Microsoft, Sun's rival. So the purchase of Netscape's software business may not offer AOL the kind of payoff that Netscape's portal is expected to generate (Crockett, 1998).

Spyglass

Spyglass's strategy of building Web access software for non-PC devices is similarly fraught with opportunity and peril. If Spyglass management is correct, the Internet device market is real, and Spyglass has a business model in place to capitalize on it. IDC and Forrester Research project that by 2002 more non-PC devices will be connected to the Internet than PCs and that the market for Internet appliances will grow to more than $16 billion in 2002 (Spyglass earnings release, July 22, 1998). For example, people might be able to use a wireless connection to connect Palm Pilots to the Web to download e-mail or surf the Web.

Spyglass has actually been performing systems integration work for companies in specific industries, including television, telecommunications, office equipment, and industrial controls. Because its employees are familiar with the operating systems of the most prominent non-PC devices, Spyglass has built many of the capabilities needed to be successful in this new market.

Nevertheless, Spyglass faces substantial risks. The most significant risk is that Microsoft may be well positioned to attack Spyglass's market. Considering that Microsoft already makes browsers and an operating system for a non-PC device, it would not be too difficult for Microsoft to develop a non-PC browser. Microsoft would be most likely to attack this business only if Spyglass began to experience significant success in the market.

Three Principles of Transformation

Although the browser market has evaporated as a source of cash, it produced assets in its wake that could be the basis for new businesses. The Web browser business was the first Internet business. Its transformation foreshadows the way subsequent Web businesses may be forced to adapt. Following are three principles suggested by this transformation that managers and investors in the Internet sector can use as they consider where to allocate their resources.

1. *Have a second act in mind.* Web business models rise and fall very quickly. In twelve to twenty-four months, a strategy that once looked great can become a disaster. Firms should be judged in part on the extent to which they are ready to roll out a new strategy if the one they are working on fails. For small firms, there is obviously not too much room for more than one or two backup strategies. The capital and the management talent are simply too scarce to support a significant number of alternatives. But the ability to hatch new strategies and make them happen is a critical determinant of a firm's long-term survival.

2. *Decide whether the second act will be in technology or in media.* Firms that start off with a technology-based business model are faced with two generic alternatives for the next act. They can move either into a new market where success depends on technical skill or into a market where success depends on media management skill. There are no clear answers regarding which strategy makes the most sense. To make the right choice, companies must get objective insights into how well they can perform the critical activities needed to succeed in the business relative to current and future competitors. Firms should pursue the market in which they can enjoy the greatest competitive advantage.

3. *If the market is crowded, acquire to dominate, or sell out.* In many Web segments, there is significant crowding and intense rivalry for industry dominance. Nowhere was this phenomenon more pronounced than in the Web portal business, Netscape's strategic destination. In theory, there are three strategies for building market dominance: growing internally, partnering with other firms that can help build traffic, and acquiring companies that can help build market share. Most firms are pursuing all three strategies in parallel, but acquisition is likely to be the most effective because it is by far the quickest way to build up relative market share. If a firm runs out of resources before it can reach market dominance, it should seek to be acquired. Netscape's fate exemplifies this principle.

SEARCH ENGINES

The aforementioned principles also apply to the search engine business. As with browsers, it is difficult to ascribe much revenue to search engines. However, several companies started out as search engines and succeeded in transforming themselves to some extent: these include Lycos, Infoseek, Excite, Inktomi, and AltaVista.

Adaptive Management in the Search Engine Business

Lycos, Infoseek, and Excite offer search engines, but their revenues from the business are minimal. These firms derive most of their current revenues from Web advertising, as we saw in Chapter Six. All these companies are trying to survive as Web portals. However, as we previously noted in Chapter Six, Excite will do so as part of At Home, and

Lycos may do so in a merger with USA Networks. Of the three, Lycos was the most aggressive in its acquisition strategy, ultimately choosing to merge with a media partner that would give Bob Davis, Lycos's CEO, a chance to continue in a deal-making role.

Inktomi actually earns most of its very limited revenues from licensing its search technology to other firms that use the search technology as part of a broader Web portal strategy. However, Inktomi is actively attempting to reshape itself into a firm that sells software to speed up the retrieval of information from the Web. Thus, Inktomi's second act is technology, not media.

The AltaVista search engine was originally developed to demonstrate the speed of the high-speed Alpha computer chip from Digital Equipment Corporation (DEC). Seeing the high stock market valuations of Internet companies, DEC thought it might be worthwhile to set up AltaVista as a separate subsidiary that could be taken public. This IPO attempt failed. Subsequently DEC (along with its still privately held AltaVista subsidiary) was acquired by Compaq Computer in 1998. Prior to the acquisition, AltaVista decided to reshape itself into a Web portal. These efforts resulted in AltaVista's addition of news content from ABC and a focus on attracting Web advertising.

Just as Inktomi's choice to become a technology business has had a direct impact on its revenues, so had AltaVista's choice to become a media business. According to *Computer Dealer News*, in June 1998, Yahoo announced that it would demote AltaVista from its previous position as Yahoo's primary search engine, changing AltaVista's status to that of an alternate source. Yahoo made the decision because, in part, AltaVista's new strategy put it in direct competition with Yahoo for advertising and e-commerce revenues (Woods, 1998). As of this writing, AltaVista continues to pursue its Web portal strategy, with lower revenues from Yahoo. As this book goes to press, Compaq had acquired shopping.com, an e-commerce site, and put all its Internet assets in an entity that it planned to spin off.

Inktomi's strategy fits more seamlessly into Yahoo's business ecosystem. Inktomi wanted to provide the technology for a "private-label" approach that would let Yahoo decide how to design the appearance of the search engine to the end user. For Yahoo, Inktomi's approach offered two critical advantages: its search technology was the most powerful on the market, and its business model did not put the company into competition with Yahoo's advertising and e-commerce initiatives (Woods, 1998).

Inktomi appears not to be betting its future on search technology. It is focusing on software that speeds up the retrieval of data over the Web. As Inktomi points out in its prospectus, there is a substantial amount of redundancy that takes place during the retrieval of information over the Web. A user seeking information typically sends out a request that is ultimately fulfilled by a central computer. To reach this central computer, the search process extends over several computer links that may be connected through paths of varying bandwidth. Each time the same site is accessed, this laborious path must be repeated. Inktomi is betting that Traffic Server, its "network caching" software for intermediate storage at certain sites, will eliminate much of this redundant searching and thereby make the Internet run faster.

Network caching software improves bandwidth efficiency and, consequently, profitability. Bandwidth savings may average 30 percent or more. An international company can spend up to $8 million a year for very high speed access to the United States. By spending around $500,000 to $700,000 for Inktomi's applications, a company might save as much as $2 million per year in access-line charges, especially for Internet content, which is predominantly based in the United States.

Inktomi's product is unlike that of other network caching competitors, such as Cisco Systems, which develop their applications in conjunction with proprietary hardware and operating systems. According to *InformationWeek*, Inktomi's Traffic Server application software stores copies of frequently accessed Web pages at dedicated storage points along the network. When the information is requested, it is distributed from the closest source. This reduces the amount of traffic on the network backbone. This reduction in backbone traffic benefits network operators, telecommunications companies, and ISPs. Because it is a software solution, the cost and time of implementation are much lower than with hardware solutions (Schaff, 1998).

New Technologies

People pay for answers and do not really care where or how they get them, as long as the answers are timely and accurate. The case of Inktomi shows how emerging new technologies can represent possible growth paths for firms that started as search engines. The new technologies may enable search engine firms to reinvent themselves while the firms continue to focus on the essential purpose for which they were created. Collaborative filtering, data extraction, and software agents all represent possible business opportunities for Web search companies that choose to expand by building a complete portfolio of tools that help end users find the information they need from the Internet more quickly.

Collaborative filtering offers recommendations to a user based on what other users have done. For instance, the Web site of CDNow, an online vendor of CDs, includes Album Advisor; when the customer designates his or her three favorite artists, Album Advisor suggests additional albums that may be of interest to the customer (Wiley, 1998).

Another example of collaborative filtering was rolled out in November 1998 by Levi Strauss's two online stores featuring its Levi's and Dockers brands. Levi's tested the dynamic profiling technology, developed with San Francisco–based Andromedia, for about six months. The Levi's store included a feature that helped consumers pick outfits based on their tastes in music and sports. The Style Finder used dynamic profiling to match consumers to clothes. Users told the site what type of music, sports, and "looks" they liked, such as grunge or hip-hop, and the site looked for what clothing choices have been made by other consumers with the same preferences. Levi's found that 74 percent of the people who went through the exercise said product suggestions were appropriate (Kane, 1998).

Data extraction draws on key pieces of data to answer a user's inquiry. The technology in this area grew primarily out of the intelligence community. The technology extracts the names of companies or individuals and then matches them with a centralized database of variant names. This enables users to find news articles or other information about a company or person, regardless of the name variant used.

Software agents easily replicate repetitive tasks. One type of software agent is the shopping agent, which combs the Internet comparing prices of specific products, such as books and CDs. For example, Acses compares prices and shipping charges for books at more than twenty-five online stores (Wiley, 1998).

Like browser companies, firms in the Web search segment need a next act to stay in business. The next act may be to turn into a media company, as Excite and Lycos have done. Or the next step may be to continue as a technology company that focuses on doing the best job of getting people the right information fast. For managers, the right decision depends on an objective assessment of what their firms do well and an understanding of the capabilities required to win.

WEB ADVERTISING MANAGEMENT

Web advertising management is a business that has not been around very long, and therefore few firms are very experienced in the field. Some Web advertisers actually hire a third party to manage their Web advertising. Others purchase tools for Web advertising management and build their own applications, often with the help of an outside firm.

As Chapter Six explained in more detail, Web advertising is fairly simple in concept. A company decides that it wants to place a banner advertisement on a Web site. It negotiates with the owner of the Web site. Usually advertising rates are set based on a certain cost per thousand impressions (CPM). These impressions are measured by the owner of the Web sites based on the number of times that the banner is seen by visitors. At the end of a period, the Web site sends a bill to the advertiser; it is calculated by multiplying the CPM by the number of impressions during that period. Once the bill is paid, the cash-flow loop for that cycle is closed.

The Outsourcing Model Versus the Tool Provision–Systems Integration Model

So far, the outsourcing model for advertising management is generating greater revenues and faster growth than the tool provision–systems integration model. For example, DoubleClick, a leader in advertising management outsourcing, generated $80 million in revenues in 1998, 162 percent more than the previous year. NetGravity, a tool provision–systems integration firm, generated only $12 million during that period, 81 percent more than the previous year. The stock market has rewarded these business models differently as well. For example, in March 1999, the ratio of market capitalization to most recent year's revenues was 45 for DoubleClick, 1.4 times greater than the ratio for NetGravity.

These different valuations reflect fundamental differences in business models. DoubleClick's revenues are received from the advertiser that orders the ad. DoubleClick pays a service fee, calculated as a percentage of such revenues, to the Web publisher on whose Web site the advertisement is delivered. This amount is included in DoubleClick's cost of revenues. DoubleClick is responsible for billing and collecting for ads delivered on the DoubleClick Network and typically assumes the risk of nonpayment from advertisers. After the initial sale, DoubleClick has the potential to enjoy an annuitylike stream of commissions.

DoubleClick is looking for ways to increase its commissions. As we saw in Chapter Six, advertisers are willing to pay more if their banner is targeted to individuals who are more likely to buy the advertised product. So DoubleClick is attempting to expand the market for a service that will match up advertisers and consumers with shared interests. As DoubleClick's matching business grows, advertisers should be paying higher rates, and DoubleClick's revenues should increase accordingly.

Nevertheless, DoubleClick has serious weaknesses in its business model. For example, as of June 1998, DoubleClick derived 49 percent of its revenues from one customer. This single customer was AltaVista, the search engine. Following DEC's acquisition by Compaq, the long-term future of the relationship between AltaVista and DoubleClick was unclear. In early 1999, DoubleClick announced that its AltaVista contract had been renewed.

The business model of NetGravity appears even weaker than that of DoubleClick. NetGravity's business model depends on selling software and services that advertisers can use to build their own advertising management capabilities. To succeed, NetGravity must convince potential customers that it makes more sense to build than to outsource. NetGravity must persuade them that the cost of building and maintaining their own advertising management systems is less than the benefit of greater control and potentially lower costs of outsourcing. In addition, NetGravity must convince customers that it offers the best tools and service in the industry. It takes time to win these arguments. If the arguments succeed, NetGravity increases the likelihood of its generating a steady stream of revenues from future product upgrades. However, the overall revenue stream may still be somewhat limited compared to that for the DoubleClick business model.

Both models currently are unprofitable. The profit potential of the Web advertising management segment is unclear. However, it appears more likely that the DoubleClick model will outlast the NetGravity one, and it is possible that DoubleClick's model will ultimately result in a profitable industry if the structure of the industry evolves.

Three Structural Changes to Watch

To gauge the future profitability of the advertising management segment, managers and investors should monitor three forces: the threat of new entrants, rivalry, and buyer power and new technology.

THREAT OF NEW ENTRANTS. Although the threat of new entrants is currently high, it is possible that entry barriers could rise. If DoubleClick or one of its peers establishes itself as a leading brand while using its size to lower relative unit costs, then the industry may become quite profitable. This change in industry structure would create high barriers to entry while encouraging long-term relationships between the industry leader, advertisers, and Web portals. And if the industry leader could make the targeting strategy work—in which advertisers pay higher rates to direct an ad at a customer group with a higher propensity to buy—revenues could increase rapidly.

RIVALRY. Because barriers to entry are low now, the level of rivalry is likely to intensify in the short term. New entrants will see the opportunity to gain market leadership in the Web advertising management business as a significant opportunity. They may battle each other through price competition, marketing and advertising spending, and acquisitions.

Acquisitions are the best hope for reducing the level of rivalry in the industry. As the number of firms diminishes, market power will become concentrated in the consolidators. As the consolidators achieve economies of scale in purchasing computer technology and network access, they will be in a position to lower unit costs. As their reach expands, they may be in a position to set high ad rates, or they may find ways to use data-mining technology to match up vendors and their Web advertisements with individuals who want to buy these vendors' products, in which case the firms can charge even higher rates for the targeted advertisements. Thus, the future could bring lower costs and higher prices, a prescription for rising profitability.

The firm called 24/7 Media is an example of such a consolidator, providing Internet advertising and online direct marketing services for advertisers and Web publishers. In August 1998, 24/7 Media became a public company operating acquired Internet advertising networks similar to that of DoubleClick. Its 24/7 network included eighty-five Web sites; its Cliqnow network had seventy-five Web sites; and its ContentZone network had two thousand small- to medium-size Web sites. From these assets, 24/7 extracted revenues of $5 million in 1997, losing $17 million in the process.

The reach of 24/7—the percentage of Internet users who view its ads—is considerable. According to *Red Herring,* 24/7's affiliated Web sites reached 36 percent of all Internet users in May 1998, compared to a reach of 29 percent in April 1998 for DoubleClick. The roll-up strategy of 24/7 Media depends on the company ability to use its stock price as a currency to acquire other industry participants and on its ability to cut deals. To be a credible participant in the industry, 24/7 must be able to integrate the acquired companies without losing key people. Furthermore, 24/7 must upgrade its somewhat deficient Web tracking software (Henig, 1998a).

BUYER POWER AND NEW TECHNOLOGY. The negotiating leverage of Web advertisers remains rather strong at this stage in the industry's evolution. The CPM rates have tended to remain fairly constant in the range of $20 to $25 per CPM (Cohen, 1998). Companies are not sure whether Internet advertising pays off (as is the case with many other forms of advertising as well).

However, as Chapter Six explained, technology is available that has the potential to measure the return on a Web advertisement. This technology could create a significant shift in the way companies think about advertising in general. The technology lets an advertiser follow the path that a visitor takes from the moment that the advertiser's banner advertisement appears in the visitor's browser. The technology can track whether or not the visitor clicked on the banner and ultimately purchased the product being advertised.

This information could lead to a fundamental change in the way advertising is priced. If the buyer and the seller have facts at their disposal, it may ultimately make more sense to pay for Web advertising in the form of a commission for sales generated as a direct result of the advertisement. Or the facts may indicate that Web advertising results in such a small volume of sales that the market will fall back on the traditional method of pricing advertising.

The technology for tracking the actual performance of Web advertising could be the force that drives the profitability of the Web advertising management business. There are two unknowns: (1) Will buyers and sellers of Web advertising actually allow the technology to be widely deployed? (2) If they do allow it, will they allow the power of the information that this technology generates have its "natural" effect on the way Web advertising is priced?

———∿∿∿———

The path along which these forces will evolve is not clear. However, if industry leaders emerge that can take advantage of economies of scale in purchasing computer equipment and backbone access, the profit potential of Web advertising could improve. This is the scenario on which such firms as DoubleClick and 24/7 are betting. In this scenario, tool vendors such as NetGravity could end up being acquired by the Web advertising management firms that emerge at the top of the heap.

E-COMMERCE ENABLING SOFTWARE

E-commerce enabling software enables companies to build and operate their Web sites. According to the *Wall Street Journal,* the market for this Internet-commerce software is expected to grow from $77 million in 1997 to $1.2 billion by the year 2000 (Hechinger, 1998). The software provided by Open Market, Sterling Commerce, Microsoft, Netscape, and others is used to "Web publish" product catalogs, to enable transactions over the Web, and to link the placement of an order with the back-end systems that fulfill the order after it has been placed.

Two firms—Sterling Commerce and Microsoft—are likely to emerge as winners in this arena. Many others may simply run out of cash before they can reach critical mass. Like Cisco Systems, Sterling Commerce is one of the most consistently and highly profitable firms that has anything to do with the Internet. With 1998 revenue of $490 million and a net loss of $61 million, Sterling Commerce has sustained a track record of revenue growth of 40 percent. Excluding a $116 million acquisition, Sterling Commerce was profitable in 1998. Despite the company's outstanding performance, few investors and managers are familiar with the company.

Sterling Commerce is based in Dublin, Ohio. It was spun out from Sterling Software of Dallas, Texas, in 1996. Sterling Commerce has about twenty years of experience in the arcane field of electronic data interchange (EDI). EDI is simply a way for businesses to exchange information with each other electronically. Having spent so many years building a business around EDI, Sterling has developed a business model that is advantageously balanced between software and services. For example, for the first nine months of fiscal 1998, Sterling Commerce generated 37 percent of its revenues from software, 43 percent from consulting services, and 20 percent from product support.

The company's business strategy has evolved over three decades, during which standards for EDI have changed. During this period, corporate technology architectures also evolved dramatically. In the 1970s, companies built their computer systems around the central mainframe. In the 1980s, client-server architectures emerged as PCs and servers became available. In the latter half of the 1990s, Web technology began to find its way into corporate networks. Each time, as companies changed their systems architectures, the role of EDI changed as well. Because Sterling Commerce started with such a strong market position in EDI, the emergence of Web architectures for e-commerce presented a natural opportunity for Sterling Commerce to exploit.

Sterling Commerce has a sober perspective on e-commerce enabling tools that few of its competitors share; two critical insights form the foundation of this unique perspective. First, Sterling Commerce does not start from the position of being at the cutting edge of technology. Sterling competitors, such as Open Market, started off by trying to develop the best technology architecture for Web commerce. Although this approach has generated many useful tools, it has not been quite as successful at creating solutions to business problems that result in higher profits.

This point leads to Sterling's second critical insight. Although e-commerce technologies are important, what is primary is that companies are buying tools and services because they are trying to solve a business problem. Through its years of experience with EDI, Sterling Commerce understands the problem of streamlining the process of electronic ordering and electronic order fulfillment; the company knows that to achieve tangible process improvements, technology must spur a new way of thinking about both the placement *and the fulfillment* of an order. In other words, Web tools for order entry alone will not create tangible process improvement. E-commerce enabling tools must be linked to the corporate systems that trigger the manufacture and delivery of the item that the customer ordered via the Web.

For example, in August 1998, Amazon announced that it had purchased Sterling Commerce's GENTRAN:Server to support its automated ordering of books and CDs. Amazon chose GENTRAN:Server because it perceived the application to be the industry leader. Amazon uses the program to format its outgoing purchase order data and incoming purchase order acknowledgment data according to industry standards. Sterling's product translates, manages, communicates, controls, and audits the functions needed to link business applications with customers and suppliers. The result is faster business information flows and more efficient processes.

Sterling Commerce is one of the most successful Web tools businesses. Ironically, one of the most important reasons for its success is that the company does not think of itself as a Web business. Sterling Commerce starts with understanding its client's business problem: how to streamline the flow of information associated with high-volume transactions between businesses. As a result of its long experience, the company is good at adapting the most practical solutions for its clients. Sterling Commerce also has accumulated specific expertise in its clients' industry dynamics and internal processes, which gives the company a sustainable competitive advantage.

CASES

There are other firms in the e-commerce enabling market whose strategies warrant further analysis. The purpose of this analysis is to highlight the strengths and weaknesses in the approaches that fairly recent start-ups are using to attempt to gain a foothold in the emerging e-commerce enabling market. This section analyzes the strategies of two competitors: Open Market, a Sterling Commerce competitor, and Macromedia, a firm that makes tools for people who create Web content.

Open Market: Too Far Ahead of Its Customers?

In many ways, Open Market is a typical East Coast Internet company. Founded in 1994 by Dave Gifford, a professor at MIT, the company obtained initial funding from Greylock Management, one of the leading financiers of niche technology companies, according to *Red Herring*. Gifford's goal was to create the infrastructure for managing transactions over the public network. Greylock brought in Shikhar Ghosh, a cellular telephone industry entrepreneur, to complement Gifford's technical skill (Claymon, 1997).

Originally positioned as a service company, Open Market expected to build the infrastructure for, and then open, an Internet shopping mall. However, in December 1995, the company shifted focus from storefronts to software and to building the tools, not the environment, for Internet commerce. In the process of transforming its strategy, a new CEO, Gary Eichorn, entered the picture.

By August 1998, Open Market had redefined itself as a provider of high-performance application software products and professional services. Open Market's intent is to allow its customers to engage in b-to-c and b-to-b Internet commerce, information commerce, and commercial publishing. In other words, Open Market is focused on delivering high-volume, large-scale application software specifically for publishing, b-to-b catalogue sales, and online retail.

Open Market sells software to such companies as office supply or wholesale plumbing supply firms, which distribute items with the accounting designation Maintenance, Repair and Other (MRO). MRO items include supplies and other goods and services that are not used in the manufacture of a company's product. MRO companies have traditionally promoted their products with catalogs. Many of Open Market's clients are distributors with thin margins. The advent of the Internet threatens these already thin margins by making it easier for people who buy supplies to bypass the distributors and purchase directly from the manufacturer that offers the best deal.

When distributors purchase Open Market's products, they are seeking to redefine themselves as "communities of interest" in order to keep customers from bypassing them. For example, a plumbing supplies distributor could purchase online catalogue software from Open Market to build a Web site that plumbers could use to purchase its supplies. The plumbing supplies distributor could then sell online advertising to plumbing supply manufacturers seeking access to all the plumbers who visit that distributor's catalogue (Gail Goodman, former marketing manager for Open Market, interview with the author, May 1998).

Open Market's results are much weaker than those of Sterling Commerce. Open Market claims that it has a deliberate strategy of losing money as it invests ahead of the market to build leadership. The results of this strategy for 1998 were grim. In 1998, Open Market generated revenues of $62 million and a net loss of $35 million. In contrast to Sterling Commerce, Open Market earns 70 percent of its revenues from software sales and 30 percent from services. In fact, Open Market's financial performance has been so weak that at the end of July 1998, the company announced the sale of 1.3 million un-registered common shares to CMG Information Services to raise $20 million in cash to finance its operations.

It is interesting to note that Amazon can announce the same objective of investing to build market share and experience very different stock price results. For example, on March 26, 1999, Open Market traded at 48 percent of its fifty-two-week high, and Amazon traded at 70 percent of its fifty-two-week high. The fundamental difference is that the Amazon business model is perceived as far superior to that of Open Market.

Part of Open Market's problem may be the extraordinarily high price that it charges for its products. For example, OM-Transact is transaction-processing software from Open Market that provides companies with access management, security, a secure Web server, Web publishing capabilities, and a server traffic analysis tool. The initial price for OM-Transact is $250,000. Additional programming, setup, and personnel for OM-Transact can cost an Open Market customer between $1 million and $10 million. Some analysts question whether Open Market provides enough of a technological advantage to warrant its high cost. In fact, they believe that customers can get much of what Open Market offers from Netscape and Microsoft at one-half to one-third the price (Claymon, 1997).

In addition to Open Market's high price for a fully integrated software package, there is a more fundamental problem facing the company. It is quite possible that the company will run out of cash before the market for its products gets big enough to generate positive cash flow. The hope for salvation in the medium term was the approaching Year 2000 and the accompanying frenzy of activity to deal with the Y2K problem. Some analysts had hoped that as companies dealt with the Y2K problem, they would choose to replace their legacy systems with e-commerce architectures. If this were to happen, Open Market would reap the rewards.

However, as of late 1998, it appeared that companies were not moving fast enough to make Open Market profitable. In October 1998, Open Market announced a loss that was worse than analysts had anticipated, along with a plan to restructure its operations in the fourth quarter at a cost of between $2 million and $4 million. The flaws in the company's strategy are thus becoming more painfully apparent. Like other East Coast companies, Open Market appears better at developing highly targeted component solutions than at building a robust business model. In focusing on building Web technology solutions, Open Market may be losing sight of the notion that has helped Sterling Commerce. The company needs to shift its orientation to understanding the customer's business first and only then pulling together the right tools and services to solve the customer's problem.

Macromedia: A Successful Reinvention

Macromedia focuses on providing tools that help developers create the content that enables e-commerce. In this sense Macromedia fits into the category of e-commerce enabling software, but it participates at a much earlier stage in the value system than does Sterling Commerce or Open Market.

Macromedia's mission is to bring life to the Web. According to *Presswire*, in the second quarter of fiscal 1999, Macromedia also earned profits *from* the Web. In that quarter, Macromedia revenues exceeded $35 million and its net income was $4 million ("Macromedia Reports . . .," 1998).

Macromedia's business focuses on three areas of opportunity: Web publishing, Web traffic, and Web learning. Web publishing tools let designers and developers create and distribute animations, applications, Web sites, and entire environments on the Web. Web traffic is covered by Macromedia's two Web sites, macromedia.com and ShockRave.com, which attract millions of visitors each month. Web learning focuses on using corporate intranets and the Web to train geographically diverse groups of people. Macromedia is focusing its attention for future sales on Web traffic and Web learning. The Web publishing tools constitute the bulk of current revenues (Macromedia 1998, Form 10K, June 25, 1998).

Rob Burgess, Macromedia chairman and CEO, and Norm Meyrowitz, president of Macromedia Products, believe that the company's three business areas are well positioned to take advantage of the opportunities presented by the growth of the Web. They point out that the Web has yet to realize its potential for enhancing people's lives. These executives envision a time when Web TVs will be "always-on" utilities; people will use the TV to do such things as browsing through headlines on the Web, picking the 25 percent of the stories that are of most interest to them, and printing out a customized newspaper to read while they are eating breakfast (Rob Burgess and Norm Meyrowitz, interview with the author, Apr. 1998).

Burgess and Meyrowitz also see the Web increasing the level of personalization and immediacy that people experience in shopping. They point out how the Web is transforming the CD business. On the supply side, artists can record their music and find audiences using the Web. The technology has the potential to shift the balance of power from the executives who control distribution channels to the artists who make the music. The Web has also empowered customers by letting them play snippets of CDs that they may purchase. This is a vast improvement over bricks-and-mortar retailing, where consumers traditionally have been forced to shop using the wrong sense—that is, by *looking* at the plastic CD cases.

In early 1998, Macromedia launched its ShockRave Web site to show how the Web could transform the relationship between creative people and their audiences. Using Macromedia authoring tools, cartoonists and video game developers can produce their work and show it to ShockRave's one hundred thousand visitors per day. If the visitor decides to purchase the work, Macromedia splits the revenues with the artists. So ShockRave is another example of how the Web can change the balance of power. It creates a new economic model in which artists seek markets for their work without submitting to the power of the middleman who chooses to promote only the top twenty sellers. And the new structure for creative markets opens up new opportunities for artists and their consumers.

Although Burgess and Meyrowitz are fond of today's Web, they are full of enthusiasm for the Web of the future. In particular, they see education as a tremendous untapped opportunity. With computer-based instruction, the small number of truly gifted teachers could reach the vast majority of students who suffer from mediocre learning experiences. Macromedia aspires to create a society in which these gifted teachers would have the same kinds of economic opportunities as rock stars or athletes. Macromedia could take advantage of the emergence of such a society by selling the software that would create and distribute the videos of these gifted teachers and host the Web site that would administer their viewing.

To realize the opportunities that Burgess and Meyrowitz envision, Macromedia is investing its research budget in technologies that will knock down the biggest technical impediments. In general, Macromedia plans to introduce products that systematically erode the technical barriers that keep the Web experience from being personalized and immediate. For example, such products might make more efficient use of available bandwidth to improve the speed and quality of multimedia images.

Introducing such products requires a new way of managing product development. Macromedia has developed a skill at managing geographically disparate teams of highly talented professionals. Macromedia finds the best people and manages them with great respect for their skills, while pushing them to produce according to very tight deadlines. The teams create prototypes quickly and get feedback on them from customers. The teams agree on general principles and then begin to produce. The loose confederation of talent perpetually changes its membership so that the best people are always working on the piece of the problem that they are best suited to solve.

For example, Macromedia created a hit program called Dream-Weaver, which was introduced in December 1997. Within three-and-a-half months it became one of the leading revenue-generating products for the company. It took ten months to develop from start to finish under the leadership of one twenty-nine-year-old who was able to motivate thirty people. The project leader was able to figure out a set of general principles on which everyone agreed, and the team executed those principles extraordinarily well (Burgess and Meyrowitz interview, Apr. 1998).

IMPLICATIONS

The foregoing analysis suggests four tests that investors can apply to evaluate Web commerce software companies.

1. *Is it relatively easy for Microsoft to replicate the firm's strategy?* We saw that the survival of firms such as Netscape and RealNetworks was substantially threatened by Microsoft. If a firm is engaging in a business strategy that appears to threaten Microsoft, staying away from it as a long-term investment may be a good idea. Our analysis suggests that Microsoft appears to be relatively vulnerable in businesses where understanding mass-market consumer needs is important for success; investors may therefore want to look harder at Web commerce software companies whose success depends on understanding mass-market consumer needs.

2. *Does the firm have a clear vision of how it creates value for customers?* Many firms in the software business have a tough time explaining how they create real value for customers. Investors must evaluate

whether a company can demonstrate that it understands how its product or service creates measurable value for customers. If a company has a difficult time articulating how customers will get a return on their investment in the firm's product, investors can take this difficulty as a good signal that they should shun the company. The examples of Net-Gravity and Open Market come to mind in this regard.

3. *Does the firm have the capabilities that it needs to create more value for customers than its competitors can?* Netscape tried unsuccessfully to compete with Yahoo and its peers. AOL's acquisition of Netscape makes it clear that Netscape lacked the marketing skill needed to beat Yahoo at building the leading brand in the Web portal business. If a firm cannot outperform its peers in the critical capabilities required to win, it is likely to end up an industry laggard or be acquired by a leader. Because the stock market places such a high premium on category leadership, it makes little sense for an investor to bet on a firm that is unlikely to dominate.

4. *Can the firm set prices that will leave ample room for profits?* If a firm passes all three of these tests but cannot set its prices high enough to earn a profit, then it is unlikely to be a good investment. This problem clearly beset Netscape in the browser business. Even though Netscape was setting its price very low to build market share, Microsoft was willing to give away the product to challenge Netscape's leadership. Investors should investigate pricing trends. If the trends indicate that the firm can hold prices at a profitable level, then it may make sense to invest.

THE NET PROFIT RETRIEVER'S ASSESSMENT OF THE WEB COMMERCE TOOLS SEGMENT

The Web commerce tools segment fails at least two of the Net Profit Retriever's three tests. Although there are several distinct industries within the segment, none of them has economic leverage. In most cases, companies do not offer closed-loop solutions. And in many cases, management does not adapt effectively to rapid change.

1. *Economic leverage.* Web commerce tools inherently lack economic leverage. There are many suppliers who spend heavily to convince companies to buy their product. The return on investment in their products is often difficult to demonstrate to senior executives.

2. *Closed-loop solution.* Most Web commerce tools are open-loop solutions. They help solve only part of a customer's problem. For example, Inktomi's search engine technology is valuable to Web portal firms, but it is only one of several components they need. Macromedia is an exception. By offering multimedia development tools and a place to sell creative content through its Web site, Macromedia is attempting to create a closed-loop solution for creative people.

3. *Adaptive management.* The record of adaptive management varies in the Web commerce tools segment. Macromedia and Sterling Commerce have adapted reasonably well to change. The management teams at Open Market and NetGravity have been somewhat less effective.

CHAPTER ELEVEN

What Have We Learned? Lessons for Present and Future Profits

T his chapter summarizes the prospects in existing Internet business segments and describes a new subsegment, matching, that has yet to be developed to its full potential. To begin, we will summarize what we have learned related to these basic questions:

- Which Internet business models are most profitable and why?
- Which Internet business models are most *un*profitable and why?
- What criteria can we use to screen for profitable Internet businesses?

To answer the first two questions, we will synthesize the findings of Chapters One through Ten. To answer the third question, we will distill the findings into a set of profitability criteria that can help screen new business ideas. After our summary discussion, we will explore some unmet needs that could be addressed through new processes enabled by Web technology. We will focus on the concept of matching, from which we'll extract several potentially profitable new Web business models.

WHICH SEGMENTS AND MODELS
ARE MOST PROFITABLE? WHY?

As we have seen throughout this book, Net profits are a function of two managerial or investment choices. The first is choosing the industry segment in which to compete. The second is choosing a competitive strategy within the industry segment. The Internet industry is plagued by uncertainty, but it is a mistake to respond to that uncertainty by keeping all bets constantly open. The most successful Web companies and investors resist this inclination to avoid choice. Instead, they focus their resources.

Economic Leverage

As we have seen in earlier chapters, there is a wide variation in profit outcomes *between* and *within* industry segments. The most profitable Web companies participate in industries with *economic leverage* and deploy competitive strategies within those industries that provide *closed-loop solutions* to their customers. As we saw in Chapter Two, leverage-point technology confers economic leverage because it controls customer access to a crucial channel of economic activity.

Economic leverage allows a firm or industry to negotiate high prices for its products, prices that far exceed their costs. That firm or industry can negotiate high prices because it controls a *product or service* the demand for which exceeds its supply.

ECONOMIC LEVERAGE POINTS. We have seen examples of economic leverage points in the Web world. For example, as we saw in Chapter Two, the major network equipment companies sell hardware that controls the flow of basic business information between the network nodes of large organizations. If the network hardware fails, the organizations cease to operate. By keeping up with the latest technology, network equipment firms become de facto systems integrators for their clients. The "promotion" from hardware vendor to systems integrator enhances the vendor's economic leverage over its customer. The customer buys more network equipment from that vendor, and the switching costs between the vendor and the customer increase.

As we saw in Chapter Three, the fixed time/price (FT/P) systems integration consultants enjoy a different form of economic leverage. They control a scarce resource that is valuable to a powerful decision maker. The FT/P systems integrators help executives achieve the promise of more effective and efficient organizations through the deployment of the right Web applications. By increasing the chances of successful implementation of a truly strategic Web application, the FT/P systems integrators can help increase their client's earnings growth. This earnings growth can help boost the value of the client executives' stock options. This connection between the work of the FT/P firm and the value of client executive stock options is the source of the FT/P systems integrator's economic leverage.

Along similar lines, as we saw in Chapter Four, the Internet venture capital firms provide the money that keeps Web start-ups going before they can generate enough revenues to support themselves. The venture capitalists draw on a network of experienced managers who can convert a new technology or innovative business model into a real revenue-generating operation. And the venture capitalists control access to a select group of stock underwriters who can determine whether or not shareholders in these small companies become wealthy. Thus the essence of their economic leverage is that they play a critical role in building companies that enhance the wealth of investors, entrepreneurs, and partners.

In Chapter Eight, we saw how general technology consultants, such as Gartner Group, occupy another important economic leverage point. The general technology consultants are objective analysts of technology from the perspective of a corporate purchaser. For a venture-backed technology firm, a positive report from the general technology consultant can help boost the prospects for an IPO. Conversely, a neutral or negative report can make corporate purchasers and IPO investors shy away. General technology consultants use these forms of economic leverage to keep their prices and profits high.

MANAGING TO CREATE ECONOMIC LEVERAGE. These most profitable segments of the Internet industry provide examples of how managers actively shape their firms to give them economic leverage. When the cofounders of Cisco Systems invented routers, they probably did not realize that routers would form the basis of an industry with such powerful economic leverage. But when John Morgridge and John Chambers took over the management of Cisco Systems, they harnessed the unique position of routers in a corporate network to build a powerful sales organization that could sell whatever new networking technology customers wanted. Morgridge and Chambers realized that the key to building negotiating leverage with customers was to offer Cisco's aggressive sales force a portfolio of technology that would provide Cisco customers the best-performing corporate network.

Similarly, among consultants, Sapient and Cambridge Technology Partners were able to enhance the economic leverage of systems integrators. By changing the paradigm from one of time and materials to FT/P, Sapient and Cambridge Technology Partners were able to offer companies a much better value proposition.

FT/P systems integrators began their task in a different way. Instead of passively interviewing clients to understand their needs, the FT/P systems integrators refused to continue work on a new project until client senior managers, system users, and IT managers all agreed on what they wanted the new system to do. This approach to defining project objectives helped reduce the risk that the client's commitment to the project would waver during the systems development process. Because they were willing to walk away from a project that they did not believe could be completed within a fixed time frame, FT/P systems integrators enhanced their negotiating leverage with clients.

Although venture capital was always an important industry, such firms as Kleiner Perkins were able to reshape the industry into a source of great economic leverage. Central to Kleiner Perkins's strategies to enhance the industry's economic leverage was building and sustaining a huge network of talented managers, marketers, and engineers. Kleiner Perkins used its stakes to encourage portfolio companies to work together. For example, Kleiner Perkins might encourage Amazon.com and Preview Travel to advertise on each other's Web sites. Such teaming up within the Kleiner keiretsu helped shape the evolution of the industries in which Kleiner Perkins invested. Through such techniques, Kleiner Perkins was also able to reshape the venture capital industry as well.

The strategies of these Net profiteers show us that a firm's or an industry's economic leverage is not something that simply happens. Companies must have the vision to see how they and their industries can evolve into a position of economic leverage. And then they must take action to make that vision real.

Closed-Loop Solutions

Even within Web industry segments that are inherently profitable, there are often wide differences in the returns that companies earn. The most profitable firms within these attractive industries pursue competitive strategies that reflect a deep understanding of why customers are buying the product and of how to outperform competitors in meeting customer needs. In many of these industries, customers are frustrated by the time it takes to evaluate different vendors, the uncertainty of whether the product or service will actually work, and the career risk of making the wrong decision. The leading Net profiteers have decided to help allay these customer fears by offering customers a closed-loop solution.

As we saw in Chapter Seven, Cisco Systems, the network equipment industry leader, has developed a Web site that reduces the cost to Cisco of making that incremental sale. The Cisco Connection Online not only reduces Cisco's incremental selling cost but also makes processing orders and providing technical service much more effective and efficient. Cisco thus takes away two potential sources of dissatisfaction that might make a customer think about switching to a different vendor, and thereby raises the customer's switching costs.

Providing a closed-loop solution is powerful for other Web business segments as well. For example, in the venture capital business, an entrepreneur can go to Kleiner Perkins and get capital, management, a network of partnerships to support their business, and access to the IPO market. In obtaining these resources from one venture firm, an entrepreneur frees up more time to make his or her business successful.

WHICH SEGMENTS ARE LEAST PROFITABLE? WHY?

Three brief examples of unprofitable Internet business segments highlight Internet business models that Internet investors and business managers should avoid.

In Chapter Eight, we examined CNET's strategy. CNET exemplifies the dangers of the *Field of Dreams* school of management in which the CEO decides that if he builds it, they will come. CNET decided to create a multimedia empire to provide Internet-only business coverage. The cost of building the multimedia infrastructure was not offset by the advertising revenues. Potential advertisers were skeptical that the audience for CNET's programming would be worth advertising to. Short on cash, CNET sold 60 percent of its Web portal, Snap, to NBC. As we also saw, CNET is evolving into a profitable e-commerce firm.

In Chapter Nine, we examined the powerful forces that suck the profitability out of the ISP business. Forty-five hundred competitors can charge no more than about $20 a month to provide what most people perceive as a commodity. Although the growth in demand is rapid, the cost of building the infrastructure to support that demand exceeds the incremental revenues from the new customers. Furthermore, new entrants offer connection technologies—cable TV, network TV, satellites, and so on—that put additional pressure on margins.

Two forces could help improve ISP profitability. Consolidation could provide industry leaders with enough negotiating leverage to raise the price of Internet access. Following MindSpring's example, ISPs could use excellent customer service to help lock in small business customers and could develop profitable ancillary services for them.

As we saw in Chapter Ten, Web browsers are exceptionally unprofitable. Browser technology was widely available, and Netscape, for example, sold its browser at a very low price in an attempt to create a dominant brand. Microsoft decided to compete by developing a competitive browser and giving it away. Netscape decided to match Microsoft's price. The company tried to reposition itself into a Web portal but quickly realized it could not succeed, selling out to AOL and Sun Microsystems.

CRITERIA FOR SCREENING INTERNET BUSINESS OPPORTUNITIES

The remainder of this chapter is devoted to a search for new, potentially profitable, Internet business opportunities. These opportunities could be exploited by financing the creation of entirely new Internet business segments, capitalizing and managing new Internet companies, or repositioning an existing company to take advantage of the new opportunity. We begin this pursuit by using the principles in Chapters One through Ten to develop specific criteria for screening Internet business opportunities. Next, we discuss significant unmet societal needs that could be addressed through the creation of new Internet businesses. We conclude with a description of new Internet business opportunities that could satisfy the screening criteria.

There are three clusters of criteria that we will use to screen Internet business opportunities. The first cluster helps us assess whether or not the Internet business segment has the potential to exert economic leverage. The second cluster contributes to understanding whether or not a specific company offers a closed-loop solution to its customers. The third cluster evaluates how effectively the firm's management team is likely to adapt to industry change.

Economic Leverage Tests

- Is there a large market for the product or service?
- Is the product or service so valuable that it will be possible to charge prices that far exceed costs?
- Are there clear opportunities to create switching costs with customers?
- Are there significant barriers to entry that can keep out potential entrants—both start-ups and existing companies?

Closed-Loop Solution Tests

- Do customers prefer to deal with a single vendor that offers a comprehensive solution?
- Does the company thoroughly understand the specific details of the customer's business problem?
- Can the company build or partner to get the full portfolio of products and services needed to solve the customer's business problem effectively?

Adaptive Management Tests

- Has the company's CEO learned from experience the importance of communicating frequently with customers?
- Does the CEO have a clear vision of where the company needs to go in order to lead its industry?
- Is the CEO willing to make acquisitions and partnerships that create customer value?
- Can the CEO hire and retain smart people who can help manage the company's growth?
- Does the CEO create compensation systems that lead employees to improve customer service and spend frugally?

UNMET SOCIETAL NEEDS: THE INTERNET'S POTENTIAL FOR MATCHING

Technology certainly has helped advance society, but there remain unmet needs that the Internet has the potential to address, as well as needs that it might serve more effectively than they are being served by other means. Although some of the needs we discuss in the sections that follow may not seem all that urgent, several of them do affect substantial numbers of people. Because the Internet offers inexpensive and relatively ubiquitous interconnection, it is uniquely well suited to solving problems of *matching*.

In life, there are several "matching processes" that have a tremendous amount of sway over how people's lives turn out. Matching processes result in people's getting married, choosing careers, taking jobs, investing in companies, and trading goods and services. In a matching process, people search for counterparties (mates, industries, companies, bosses, customers, suppliers, even organ donors) to fill various needs. During their search, people evaluate and reject many potential counterparties, and the counterparty that they ultimately select may or may not work out for an extended period of time.

When a counterparty does not work out, the costs of failure are sometimes high. A failed marriage results in divorce. A failed match between an employee and employer can lead to financial problems, stress, and frustration. Purchasing from the wrong supplier can cause the people who made the decision to lose their jobs. Selling to the wrong customer can cause a supplier to go unpaid or miss important insights into where the overall market is heading.

Even when successful, a matching process is often lengthy and expensive. A typical venture capital firm will receive two thousand business plans in a year, meet with the management teams of two hundred of these, and invest in twenty. Quite possibly, an individual seeking a mate in life goes through a process involving similar numbers.

In some cases there may be value in the process itself, but often adults simply grow accustomed to the costs of search, which are often at best a nuisance and at worst an emotional and financial drain. If people could reduce the costs of search in both personal and professional life, they would have more time and energy for making those matched relationships work better.

Better matching processes require more accurate and insightful information. For example, consider the process by which people choose a career. The ideal matching process would direct people to specific careers they have chosen in part on their inherent enjoyment of the work that the best people in that line of work actually do on a daily basis. Many people pick careers for which this fit is wrong or at best approximate, which leads them to failure. And in many cases, they keep failing until they stumble into the right career, or they simply run out of time.

Matching in Career Choice

There are two categories of information that could potentially be improved to create a more effective matching process in making career choices: self-assessment and opportunity assessment. Many tools have been developed to help people assess their skills and interests. The Internet might be able to help people self-administer and self-score these tools as their skills and interests change over the course of their career. The Internet might compare an individual's self-assessment scores with a sample of successful people in the same field. The Internet might also supply e-mail addresses of people who had volunteered to serve as mentors in each field. The Internet could facilitate more fact-based, accurate, and timely self-assessment.

The Internet could also help with opportunity assessment. The Internet already has a number of services that let people post their résumés for specific jobs. Other Internet services are communities of people with common interests, such as Korean-speaking Java programmers. The communities are set up to give members a chance to receive e-mails from potential employers anonymously. If a community member wishes to respond, they are free to do so. Such fledgling services could be the basis of a much more powerful matching industry.

In assessing career opportunities, people need to be able to separate fact from fiction. This need suggests an opportunity to modify current Internet career search programs to help job seekers make a more informed decision. Here is the problem: it is natural for informants to present information that serves their interests; receivers of the information need ways to figure out what is true, what is not, and what additional relevant information has not been offered.

In theory, the Web could be a useful technology for giving someone the complete picture of the person or organization with whom he or she is dealing, beginning with a checklist of the "right" information needed to make a fully informed decision. The next step would be to create a so-called Web bot, or personal agent, that could search information sources worldwide for all available information that the checklist required. The final step would be to present this complete information in a way that would make it easy for the individual to make a better-informed decision about whether or not to deal with the party in question.

Consider how this might apply to án individual seeking employment with a company. In general, the employer has the information advantage in such a situation. The employer is presenting a favorable impression of the company, the department, and the position. The employer may or may not present a complete picture of why the position is open or what happened to the previous occupant of the position. At the same time, the employer can obtain extensive information about the potential employee, including credit reports and detailed information about the potential employee's previous employment history.

But what if there were a way to level the playing field? For example, what if the potential employee could find out what current and previous employees within the company actually thought were the pros and cons of the company, the department, the job, and the boss? What if the potential employee could compare her own personal and professional attributes with those of the most successful employees in that company or department and try to assess her fit objectively? What if the person could gain some real insights into the political dynamics within the company, the department, and the company? What if the potential employee could find out what her compensation prospects really were before taking the position?

Cleaning up such matching processes represents a huge unmet societal need that could spawn many profitable Web businesses. Following are some additional speculations along these lines. In order for them to materialize, people will need to accept new ways of working together. They will need to be comfortable opening up and sharing information that heretofore has been considered "undiscussable." And technologists will need to invent new tools to make these businesses actually work. But of these three hurdles, the most significant one will be getting people to change the way they interact.

Although the ideas that follow are focused on business-oriented matching processes, the principles could be applied to personal matching processes, such as searching for a mate. There are many for-profit and nonprofit applications.

Matching in Employment

Continuing the career theme we have already introduced, let's explore how a profitable Web-based business could be built to help match people to jobs. In order to be profitable, this business would need to be structured in a way that would give the provider of the service substantial economic leverage. Leverage might accrue if the service were a unique source of proprietary information that was valuable to both the employer and the employee.

There are many Web sites now that try to match employers and employees. For example, there are hundreds of sites that let people post résumés for employers to review. And many employers have Web sites on which they post job opportunities for potential employees to browse.

Many of these sites are growing, but the fundamental problem they face is that their information is not proprietary and is not incrementally more valuable to both parties of the transaction. These Web sites thus must compete on the basis of their ability to provide much of the benefit of a "headhunter" at a fraction of the cost. My proposal for a profitable Web-based business is based on the company's coming up with much better insights about the employer and the employee. By offering a proprietary source of superior insight, the service could actually charge a higher price because it could offer both parties to the transaction a higher probability of a successful match.

The managers of the service could develop a business model based on its incremental value. The business would involve taking relatively nominal payment from the potential employee and a fee at the same rate as a headhunter from employers. The potential employee fee could be related to the value of the superior odds of a successful match. The employer would be encouraged to pay the higher fee by understanding that the service would cost the same as a headhunter but provide superior odds of a successful candidate.

The service would reinvest a portion of its revenues in its infrastructure and marketing. Its infrastructure would consist of an information base, a Web bot, and analysts who would collect and analyze information on the employers and the employees. The information base would involve getting the "right" information on candidates and employers, using the factors discussed earlier as criteria. The Web bot and the analysts would help employers and employees search the Web for matches between their needs and the available counterparties.

Some of the information would be developed through intensive interviewing of potential employees and employers. Information could also be gathered from company-sponsored Web sites, online discussion sites, newsgroups, industry-sponsored trade meetings, trade press, and industry association Web sites. Although the sources of information would evolve, the purpose would remain constant—to create an information base with the most relevant, insightful, and accurate information for making successful employer-employee matches.

The business would require extensive marketing. In order to sustain attractive prices, a firm would need to establish itself as the perceived industry leader in this unique category, through favorable coverage in the mainstream media. To fuel this media coverage, it would be helpful to keep track of market share statistics for the service. Perhaps more important, it would be useful to track the actual success rates of people who joined companies. This success could be measured in terms of turnover statistics, the rate of promotions, and the general level of satisfaction with the match from the employer's and the employee's perspectives.

This concept suggests several more specific business opportunities. Substantial consulting work would be needed to develop the research on which to base the indicators. Substantial ongoing effort would also be needed to build and maintain the database with accurate, relevant, and timely information. In addition, the technical infrastructure for the service would need to be built, including network equipment, servers, and data storage hardware, database and agent software, and a means of connecting with the Internet. Finally, the matching service itself would need to be built and managed.

Matching in Purchasing

Many of the businesses we have discussed in this book have aimed at improving the purchasing process. However, many of these businesses are not profitable. As we saw in Chapter Seven, in many of the examples, the fundamental reason for the lack of profitability is that the services alter bargaining leverage to favor the buyer. By distributing at no charge such useful information as the product's cost to the dealer, these sites gave purchasers a leg up in negotiating.

We found that the most profitable purchase-decision services were the general technology consultants. Such firms as Gartner Group succeed because they help people who make major investment decisions in technology make a better-informed evaluation. By generating high credibility with the purchasers, the consultants are able to create powerful incentives for technology vendors to sign up as clients.

The most profitable Web businesses to assist with purchasing are likely to be those with an attractive industry structure similar to that of the Gartner Group. In short, it makes sense to look for purchase decisions in which large amounts of capital and risk are involved. The business opportunity is to provide well-researched, objective analysis of these decisions from the perspective of the purchaser. To the extent that Web technology is a more effective means of delivering this information, so much the better. But the key to profitability in this business is not so much the technology used to distribute the information as it is the quality and nature of the information.

What kinds of purchasing-related businesses could emerge that involve high capital and risks? Any business that helped organizations evaluate the purchase of expensive assets would be a good candidate. Such expensive assets might include companies (as in mergers and acquisitions advice), large buildings, natural resource exploration rights, or complex financial assets (such as asset-backed securities).

A service that provided organizations with support for such purchase decisions would be able to charge a high price. The service would include specific insight, analysis, and detailed facts an executive needs to decide whether or not to purchase a specific asset and, if so, how much to pay. The high value of the service would make its users willing to pay a high price. They would also be willing to pay a high price for additional insights into business, legal, and regulatory risks; a well-researched second opinion; and help in fulfilling fiduciary responsibilities.

A potentially profitable service could evolve to support purchasers of commercial real estate, especially corporations seeking out new locations. It might also serve commercial real estate investors looking for bargains. The service would let users submit specific characteristics of the properties in which they would like to invest and receive a list of properties that matched the characteristics.

In general, the service would give a corporate real estate purchaser the information it needed to evaluate properties, calculate and submit bids, execute purchase transactions, and obtain financing. The service could also supply the client with data by which to evaluate the most interesting properties, including cash flow statements and projections for the property, tax records, appraisals, details of utility costs and contracts, title search results, sales prices for comparable buildings, terms of mortgages, and lease agreements. The service would also include specifically tailored spreadsheets that would be used in developing a bid for the property and that might be linked to standard forms for presenting a formal purchase offer to sellers. Finally, the service would provide links to sources of commercial real estate financing. These financing resources would take as input the user's criteria for the financial instrument and return a list of potential suppliers of the desired financial instrument along with the terms those suppliers had offered on similar deals in the past.

The service could be structured to generate very high profits. It could charge a high subscription fee to buyers, sellers, and financiers. It might charge a transaction fee to the seller that was a percentage of the purchase price. The service could charge a lender a percentage of the principal amount of the financial instrument. The price for the proposed service could be lower than that charged by corporate real estate brokers and real estate advisers whose high commissions constitute a price umbrella. The service could gain market share through a combination of somewhat lower prices and much greater convenience to the corporate real estate purchaser. The relatively low costs to deliver such a service and the magnitude of potential revenues make it likely that there would be ample gross profit available for building the infrastructure and for marketing.

As with the employment business model, two kinds of infrastructure would be needed. Most important, the information base would need to be built and maintained so that it could be the most comprehensive, accurate, and timely source of all relevant information on corporate real estate. To accomplish this goal, teams of experts in various aspects of corporate real estate would need to gather the information and maintain its currency. Part of the value of this information base would result from the centralization of previously dispersed bundles of paper. Additional value would come from the expert analysis and insight and the network of relationships of the analysts who write reports on specific properties. The second kind of infrastructure would be the system architecture required to deliver and collect this information quickly, cheaply, and reliably.

Significant marketing investment would also be essential. It would be important to inform commercial real estate buyers about the unique value of the service. Buyers would benefit because this service, unlike information services offered by commercial real estate brokers, would be developed with the buyer's economic interest in mind. Buyers would get a chance to look at all properties, not simply the ones that the broker decided to "dump" onto the computer system.

Commercial real estate brokers seek to earn the highest commissions with the least amount of effort. They therefore follow a non-Web process for brokering the sale of properties with the highest expected commissions. Properties that are more difficult to sell, or those with lower expected commissions, are more likely to end up being listed on the computer systems, and brokers devote little incremental effort to selling such properties. If the properties are sold via the online system, the firm gets the commission without having invested much incremental effort (Kevin Gray, managing director of Landauer Associates, interview with the author, Sept. 1998). The new service would capitalize on this state of affairs by initially listing the properties that were relatively difficult to sell. The greater convenience and lower price of the proposed service would help commercial real estate buyers and sellers to recognize the service's superior value. Once buyers and sellers became comfortable using the system, sellers would begin to list higher-quality properties. This would probably reduce the number of commercial real estate brokers to a small number of individuals with excellent industry contacts.

The marketing effort would focus on the unique value that the service provides for real estate buyers. As the service enlarges its share of the market, the marketing team would communicate that growth to all key market participants. As we discussed earlier, some sellers may be reluctant initially to list their properties with the service. Sellers might fear that by disseminating information to a wider audience, they would lose their bargaining leverage. However, the service would provide advantage to the buyer, and as buyers got greater leverage, sellers might find it increasingly difficult to avoid listing their properties on the system if they wished to reach the broadest market. Marketers would need to recognize that the service would fundamentally change the structure of the industry to favor the interests of the buyer. But they could argue that in the long run, buyers and sellers both would benefit from the streamlined intermediation process.

Matching in Investing

Investing is another process that could be enhanced through Web-enabled matching services. As we saw earlier, there are many online services available now for helping people pick investments and execute trades. There is some question as to whether the information these services provide actually enables investors to earn higher returns than they can by other means.

One kind of corporate information might be valuable to potential investors if it were available: specific information about who holds how much stock in a company, who is trading how many shares, and why they are making the trade. Although this information is quite relevant, there is no requirement to report this information to the public on a timely (for example, real-time) basis.

Passing SEC regulations that would require such reporting would be a huge challenge. The forces favoring the status quo would argue that the costs of such reporting would be too onerous. Underneath that argument is the concern that large shareholders would no longer be able to keep secrets that allow them to profit at the expense of less powerful and less informed market participants. To pass such regulations, the SEC would need to be convinced that if it defended the interests of the small investor, the overall market would be better off.

If such reporting did exist, there might emerge analytical methods for interpreting the information and using it to identify good investment opportunities. That information could be added to the data that investors receive from many of the Web-enabled investment sites discussed in Chapter Seven.

In the absence of such a change, there remains at least one important opportunity to transform an investment process through a Web-enabled business model: the process of matching entrepreneurs and venture capitalists. As we saw in Chapter Four, new venture creation is quite profitable for the venture capital firm. However, the process is inefficient and difficult for the entrepreneur. If there were a way to make the matching process more efficient for entrepreneurs while still profitable for venture capitalists, the more efficient process could prosper.

A firm called garage.com has actually pursued this concept in its own new venture. According to *Upside,* garage.com helps entrepreneurs searching for $500,000 to $2.5 million in seed money. The firm helps start-up founders prepare effectively for fundraising meetings with venture capitalists or angels. Although garage.com depends on technology, its ultimate success will depend on its ability to create a new "investment club" that rivals the current market structure (O'Brien, 1998a).

Garage.com's CEO is Guy Kawasaki, the Apple Computer evangelist who created enthusiastic demand for the Macintosh. Garage.com raised a total of $4 million from Compaq chairman, Ben Rosen; Silicon Valley Bank; Ron Conway, a prominent angel investor; PricewaterhouseCoopers; and Advanced Technology Ventures, a venture capital fund. In light of the threat that garage.com presents to traditional venture capital firms, no leading venture capital firms put money into it.

Garage.com uses its Web site to find leading entrepreneurs. The service prepares the entrepreneurs to sell their ideas to leading venture capitalists, angels, and corporations. In return for helping a start-up win funding, garage.com seeks as much as 5 percent of the start-up's equity at the very low prices at which founders invest. Garage.com also wants a "success fee" that equals 5 percent of the funds raised.

Garage.com is no less selective than venture capitalists. Even though anyone can click on the garage.com icon and write an abstract, only 20 percent of these start-ups are asked to fill out the long form, detailing their idea and business plan. If the garage.com people like what they read, then the entrepreneur will win a face-to-face meeting. Garage.com grooms only one entrepreneur out of every one hundred who write the initial abstract.

Once accepted into "the Garage" (a password-secured section of the Web site), the entrepreneur works on the business plan with the garage.com staff. When garage.com is satisfied that the start-up is ready to meet with the venture community, the deal is moved into "Heaven," where only venture capitalists, angels, and corporations with assigned passwords can review potential deals.

Traditional venture capital firms are not eager to fund a potential competitor, but they will watch what happens with garage.com closely. If the company succeeds, then traditional venture capital firms will need to offer a compelling response. For the moment, they appear skeptical. For example, Accel Partners is a traditional venture firm whose general partner Jim Breyer doubts garage.com's ability to succeed. Breyer suggests that garage.com must be able to recruit a team of managers and provide strategic insight; otherwise, entrepreneurs will not use the service. Breyer questions whether garage.com will have the necessary resources and expertise.

By the end of September 1998, free admission to garage.com's Heaven had attracted one hundred potential investors, including Adobe Systems, Sun Microsystems, Phillips Electronics, and Mayfield Partners. And despite the mixed reception that garage.com has received in the venture community, it has attracted prominent investors, board members, founders, and advisers, including John Dean, CEO of Silicon Valley Bank; Rich Karlgaard, publisher of *Forbes* magazine; Joe Grundfest, Stanford law professor and former SEC commissioner; Heidi Roizen, former Apple vice president of developer relations; and investment bankers Sandy Robertson and Frank Quattrone.

By the end of September 1998, garage.com had even completed one deal—a $500,000 investment in Reality Fusion, an interactive video software start-up. Investors included Joe Costello, former CEO of Cadence, and Federico Faggin, co-inventor of the microprocessor (O'Brien, 1998a).

SUCCESS IN MATCHING

Profitable businesses can be built by using the Web to enhance matching processes. As we would expect, the profitability depends on dominating a point of economic leverage and offering a closed-loop solution to customers. Three general principles are critical for managers and investors who are considering such businesses.

1. *A successful matching service will change the distribution of economic power in the industry.* Therefore, entrepreneurs will need to align themselves with the industry participants who are most likely to benefit from the service. And these entrepreneurs will need to anticipate—and find ways to overcome—the resistance of groups that will initially suffer as a result of the new service.

2. *The critical factor for success in a matching business is the information, not the technology.* The service must offer accurate, timely, and critical information. If that information is dispersed over a fast, secure, reliable, and inexpensive information pipeline, so much the better.

3. *Aggressive marketing is critical to survival.* Matching businesses must be marketed aggressively to key decision makers and influencers, and these businesses must develop new products and services to keep up with the changing needs of customers. The ultimate objective is to build the preeminent brand.

———

Entrepreneurs could create many new businesses by following the thought processes described in the preceding sections. In order to be profitable, new Web-enabled businesses will need to be focused on industries with high economic leverage. The most profitable companies in these industries will be the ones that offer customers a closed-loop solution. There continue to be opportunities to chip away at the inefficiency and ineffectiveness of many societal matching processes. By building Web-enabled business designed to make these processes more effective, managers and investors will achieve success and solve important societal problems.

CHAPTER TWELVE

Managers: Can the Web Improve Your Business?

T his chapter is intended for managers whose firms currently have nothing to do with the Web or who are beginning to use the Web as a new channel for conducting their business. The Web can help organizations become more profitable; however, managers will not be able to harness its power until they change their way of thinking about it. To put managers into the right mind-set, this chapter addresses several questions:

• What are the most commonly held myths about the Web, and what are the realities?

• What can managers learn from examples of successful and less successful organizational efforts to use the Web?

• How can managers evaluate whether it makes sense for their companies to use the Web?

• For companies that do have the potential to benefit from the Web, what should managers do?

• What kinds of challenges should managers expect if they decide to use the Web? How can they address and overcome these challenges?

WEB MYTHS AND REALITIES

The air is filled with myths about the power of the Web to fundamentally transform everything. These myths have enthralled their target audience—large organizations and consumers—while they have helped enrich a handful of venture capitalists and managers. To avoid becoming a victim of these myths, managers must parse them carefully. Managerial willingness to jump on the Internet bandwagon has helped investors and managers in the companies that sell Web products and services, but the same benefit has not always flowed to the organizations that have tried to use the Web.

Myth: *The Web will transform everything.* As was mentioned elsewhere, John Doerr of Kleiner Perkins thinks that, if anything, the Web is underhyped. Doerr has tremendous resources at his disposal for promulgating this message. He has had the ear of vice president Al Gore. He has influence in the high-tech and general business press and in many important Web news outlets. And he uses his access to these channels to communicate over and over a message that helps increase the value of his investments.

Reality: *The Web can help organizations become more effective if it is used appropriately.* As we have seen, the Web has created profit opportunities for some industries and some companies. If managers can find a way to use the Web to give them economic leverage within their system of value creation, then the Web can help enhance profits.

One example of the effective corporate use of the Web is General Electric (GE). GE and Thomson Publishing created a joint venture called Trade Processing Network (TPN). TPN helps companies use the Web to streamline corporate procurement of such items as office supplies. By increasing the percentage of corporate employees that buy office supplies through preferred suppliers, TPN can help a company reduce the unit costs of these supplies by up to 20 percent. For a large firm like GE with $5 billion in annual office supply purchases, a 20 percent cost reduction translates into $1 billion in annual savings.

But the TPN example is the exception that proves the rule. More frequently, managers get carried away by the superficial appeal of the technology: they often end up merely paving over the cow paths of their business with Web technology. Using this approach, it is easy for them to throw away $20 million on a systems project that delivers no payoff.

Myth: *Organizations that do not use the Web will soon perish.* This line of reasoning is a corollary to the basic message that the Web will transform everything. Salespeople often try to motivate managers by exhorting them not to be left behind. This message is directed most strongly at firms that are intermediaries. The reasoning goes that the middlemen will be squeezed out as the Web bypasses their role in the economic system.

Reality: *In many industries, the Web is unlikely to create much advantage.* In many industries, e-commerce start-ups are trying to use the Web to bypass intermediaries. However, many of these start-ups are losing huge amounts of money, and the incumbent intermediaries are not losing significant market share. Because the incumbents have greater financial resources, they may ultimately find themselves in a position to acquire the stumbling start-ups, and through these acquisitions, they may be able to add a complementary distribution channel that makes life a bit easier for their customers.

Myth: *E-commerce will become a huge factor in the world economy.* As we saw in Chapter Nine, countless pundits forecast trillions of e-commerce revenues by the year 2002. These projections do play an important role in raising capital for firms that have the suffix *.com* in their name. How these projections are derived and the assumptions on which they are based remain a bit murky. Nevertheless, the motivation for the projections is clear.

Reality: *E-commerce is likely to be a small part of the global economy at least through the year 2003.* According to an October 1998 study by the Organization for Economic Cooperation and Development (OECD) in Paris, e-commerce, especially in the consumer market, will remain a small percentage of overall retail sales for at least the next five years and will not have a significant impact on the global economy anytime soon. Including the more lucrative b-to-b e-commerce market, which the OECD predicted will account for about 80 percent of overall e-commerce through the next five years, global e-commerce revenues could reach $1 trillion by 2003, according to the *Industry Standard.* This figure is a mere 15 percent of the overall retail sales predicted for a selection of seven OECD member countries in 2003. And b-to-c e-commerce should account for just 20 percent of the total revenues generated by e-commerce in 2003, or $200 billion (Essick, 1998).

The OECD study says that the convenience and mass customization of b-to-c e-commerce are advantages, but adds that the success of b-to-c e-commerce suppliers is not assured. The report suggests that b-to-c e-commerce may become, like mail order, merely another channel for retailers, rather than a new dominant mode of commerce. The report notes that 80 percent of online commerce today is conducted in the United States. The OECD report also suggests that visions of global e-commerce must be tempered by the reality that half the world's population has never made a telephone call, much less accessed the Internet (Essick, 1998).

Myth: *The Web is the single greatest source of legal wealth creation in human history.* Venture capitalist John Doerr discusses the billions of dollars worth of market capitalization and hundreds of thousands of jobs created by Web companies. Although it is unclear how he arrived at the figures he cites, it is not difficult to concede that the levels of stockholder value and employment are tremendous. The question is, how has the wealth been created and distributed? And how real is it?

Reality: *The Web has enriched a very small number of investors and managers and has yet to realize its promise in terms of enriching organizations.* Venture firms are arbitrageurs. They purchase ownership of technology start-ups in one market, where they are cheap, and resell their stakes in another market, where they are dear. When a start-up is about to close down because it has run out of cash, a venture capitalist can purchase a big chunk of the company for relatively little money. And when the market for IPOs is strong, that same venture capitalist can turn around and sell the bargain-priced equity at ten to twenty times the purchase price. This is perfectly legal.

One of the reasons that venture capitalists can sell their shares in the public market is that they are able to include the names of large, prestigious organizations on the customer list of the companies whose shares the venture capitalists are selling. But unless the Web can create tangible value for these prestigious organizations, they will ultimately be pawns in the venture capitalists' arbitrage play.

LESSONS FROM EXPERIENCE WITH THE WEB

As we saw earlier, some organizations, such as Cisco and Dell, have profited from their use of the Web. Many of these organizations have achieved qualitative improvements in their operations, including the ability to solve customer service problems faster, or a reduction in the level of rework in order processing. It makes intuitive sense that if customers place billions of dollars worth of orders via the Web, the sales staff can be freed up to spend more time trying to close deals with new customers. Although managers perceive these qualitative benefits as real, potential e-commerce adopters should take a hard look at e-commerce's quantitative benefits as well. For example, while Cisco describes savings in the hundreds of millions, although most of the savings come from the ability to run a larger operation without needing to hire as many people. So the cost savings are quantified by comparing actual staff levels to a forecast of the number of staff that would have been on Cisco's payroll if the system were not in place.

These success stories highlight two organizational benefits of using the Web: The Web can increase the efficiency and effectiveness of repetitive operational processes, and the Web can help organizations set up processes that reduce errors in configuring orders even as these processes handle high transaction volumes. For example, Cisco's CCO helps customers configure their orders for new network equipment so that the product meets their needs and can be manufactured.

Although firms have used other means of performing electronic processing, such as Electronic Data Interchange (EDI), the Web is less expensive. EDI is a standard format for transmitting electronic documents such as purchase orders and invoices. It is very costly for companies with many suppliers to set up a system using EDI because they must change their systems and the systems of their suppliers to make all trading partners adhere to the EDI standards. Once firms have made the investment, however, they are reluctant to throw it out for the next new technology.

Nevertheless, a study by International Data Corporation indicates that 80 percent of the companies that use EDI are expected to shift 30 percent of their traffic over to the Web by 2003, because the Web is a cheaper way to transmit information. Using the hybrid of EDI and Web technology, these companies will be able to enjoy the cost advantages of the Web without overhauling the systems that are programmed for EDI.

The Web can also allow users to tap into a common experience base that helps them solve problems more quickly. For example, Cisco's CCO lets customers tap into the cumulative experience of Cisco's global customer base. A customer service person in California thus has access to the solution to an obscure technical problem that was solved by a service technician in Australia. Without access to that global experience base, the customer might have spent weeks reinventing a solution.

If managers find these examples helpful, they can understand the general lessons that they can apply to their own organizations. Specifically, managers should consider the following eight lessons gleaned from the experience of organizations that have used the Web.

1. *The CEO needs to be a Web user.* If CEOs do not have personal experience with the Web, it is difficult for them to understand how the technology can help their business. CEOs need to experience the power of the Web for such tasks as sending e-mail to friends and family, checking their stock portfolio, or getting information about a hobby. Once they have a feeling for what the Web can do at a personal level, they will begin to imagine how it can help improve the business.

2. *The Web-based solution must be driven by competitive strategy.* Managers must understand how the Web relates to competitive strategy. Making this connection is difficult in the absence of a commonly understood methodology for doing so, a deficiency we will address later in this chapter. With effective strategy, Net profiteers have used the Web to help them increase revenues as much as 70 percent a year while adding even more to their bottom lines. The source of these incremental profits is better customer service with the same number of employees.

3. *There should be a partnership between information systems (IS) and the business.* Unfortunately, many organizations have a long history of emotional volatility in the relationship between IS and business managers. The IS managers promise the business managers great results from a new technology but are unable to deliver. Dialogue lapses into blame and punishment.

In the organizations that have earned Net profits, the situation is different. In these organizations, there is a true partnership between IS and business management. Business managers bring up practical problems, and IS managers propose solutions. As the solution evolves, business and IS work together because the success of the enterprise (and the success of the stock options of both sets of management) depends on their teamwork. Both parties have a strong incentive to work together to overcome obstacles.

4. *Management has to set measurable objectives for the system.* A truism of management is that what gets measured gets done. Conversely,

what does not get measured does not get done. Different groups in an organization value different things, which leads to their using different performance measures. For example, IS may tend to measure itself in terms of how many people are working on cutting-edge technologies, whereas executive management is likely to measure itself on earnings growth and stock price performance. In order to make an e-commerce initiative work, management must set the objectives in a way that is meaningful for both the business and IS.

In short, management should define the problem in terms that matter to the entire organization, not just one part. The goal might be to have 50 percent of sales coming from the Web within two years, or to increase revenues 50 percent a year while keeping customer service headcount constant. Whatever the goal, it is important that it be specific, measurable, and understandable to all members of the team that is charged with achieving it.

5. *Management should direct the efforts of a cross-functional team to change the business process.* It is increasingly clear that using the Web to enhance corporate competitiveness is not something the CEO can delegate to middle management. The reason the CEO must lead the process is that the Web can be a tool for enhancing competitiveness only if the different functions within the company work together to create more value for customers. Unless the CEO creates strong incentives for such teamwork, the Web technology will not be a useful competitive tool.

6. *The back-end operations and systems must work together with the Web front end.* Consistent with the theme of teamwork among people is the need for teamwork among systems. The Web can make it very easy for a customer to place an order. This friendly front end creates an implicit promise that the order fulfillment process will be equally satisfying to the customer. If a company's fulfillment processes are inefficient and complex, then the customer's raised expectations for service will be ultimately disappointed. If a firm is going to invest in making its front-end operations very easy to use without simultaneously improving the back-end systems, the firm might be better off not using the Web at all.

Dell has figured this out. Even before it developed its Web site, Dell had an order fulfillment process that worked effectively. The company had created a "built-to-order" process for manufacturing and delivering computers, one that produced benefits for shareholders and customers. Dell shareholders were rewarded with higher profit growth because Dell did not incur the costs of carrying excess inventory. Customers were better off because they were able to purchase a computer that was configured specifically to meet their needs. And when they placed an order, it was delivered promptly and predictably.

Dell's Web site simply took advantage of the company's effective order fulfillment processes. The Web site made it possible for people to buy computers configured in a standard fashion at their desired price level. People could place their order over the Web, and Dell would take the order and fulfill it just as quickly and effectively as it had in the past. As of March 1999, Dell's success was evidenced by its $10 million a day in computer sales.

7. *In many cases, the Web is a parallel channel for exchanging information and distributing product.* Adding a parallel channel can be perceived as a threat to the hegemony of the existing channels. If a company has a direct sales force and a telephone sales force, these two groups will feel threatened by the addition of the Web distribution channel. The fear is that the Web will siphon away sales that might have been made by the direct and telephone sales forces. And because the Web does not need to receive sales commissions, the competing channels may see the Web as a threat to their long-term survival. There are no easy solutions to this problem, but if the CEO leads the cross-functional team, there will be a forum for addressing it.

Office Depot's recent addition of a Web-based distribution channel is a case in point. Office Depot worked closely with its customers to design a Web site that would be easy to use. Because Office Depot already sold office supplies through direct sales and telephone sales, the Web-based channel represented a potential threat. However, Office Depot's management made it clear to the incumbent sales channels that the firm needed to add a Web channel to sustain Office Depot's competitiveness and that the incumbent channels would need to develop new strategies to maintain their revenue growth. In response to their pressure, Office Depot's "channel managers" will need to achieve more ambitious sales targets.

8. *Regardless of other companies' experiences, each company must experiment and learn for itself how to use the Web.* There is very little established dogma about how best to use the Web to enhance a company's performance. This lack of experience is keeping many companies from using the Web. More adventurous companies have realized that this lack of certainty is a psychological barrier to entry for competitors. So the adventurous companies get started. They identify

pieces of a solution that they can implement and evaluate quickly. They do more of what succeeds and learn from what fails. Regardless of the outcome, they keep trying until they have achieved significant success, and this success emboldens them to try more.

SHOULD YOUR COMPANY USE THE WEB?

Perhaps the eight lessons we have looked at here are enough to scare you away from using the Web. Take heart. As Figure 12.1 illustrates, there is a pyramid of Web applications.

Whereas many companies have implemented applications near the base of the pyramid, very few companies have built the kinds of applications at the top. It is rare for a firm to start with Level III. More often, firms work their way up through the levels. They learn important corporate lessons at each level that enable them to perform more effectively when they move up.

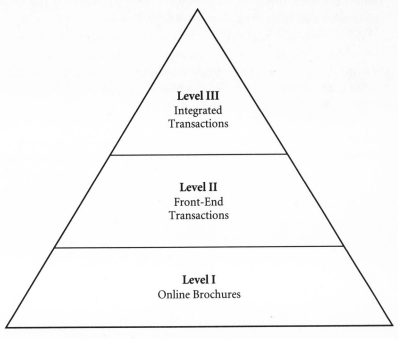

Figure 12.1. The Web Applications Pyramid.

Many companies are in the Level I, online brochure stage. They use their Web site to publish product literature, annual reports, and other information traditionally in print form. Some companies have begun to use the Web as a means of collecting order forms. They then print out the order information gathered via the Web and use it as an input into an unchanged order fulfillment process. Because these companies do not integrate the ordering information into their back-end processes, their use of the Web is referred to as Level II, front-end transaction applications.

A few companies, such as Dell and Cisco, have installed integrated transaction applications that tap into the full power of the Web. For example, these applications use the Web to exchange information with customers. The information is tightly linked with the internal operations of the company. As a result of this integration, the customer gets faster and better service at a lower cost. These applications are referred to as Level III, integrated applications.

How managers should go about evaluating the use of the Web in their firm depends on where the firm is positioned on the pyramid. If a firm is not using the Web at all, the factors that management should evaluate are quite different from those it should consider if the firm is at Level II and considering whether to go to Level III.

Managers should perform a cost-benefit analysis of a Web application depending on where they are and where they want to go in the pyramid. The cost-benefit analysis should compare the incremental costs and benefits of moving from where a company is now to where it wants to go. If the incremental benefits are higher than the incremental costs, then it makes sense to proceed. Table 12.1 suggests some benefits and costs that result from moving the firm to each higher level of Web investment. Some of these benefits and costs are likely to be difficult to quantify. However, we will explore ways to tackle some of these thorny analytical problems.

Approaching Level I

If a firm is not on the Web, it may consider the option of "getting its feet wet" by building an online brochure Web application. In theory, there is no reason why the firm could not go directly to Level II or III. However, there are significant benefits to starting at Level I rather than at a higher level. One benefit of starting at Level I is that it lets the firm's customers learn about the Web's value without threatening to disrupt

Status of Firm	Added Benefits of Moving Up	Added Costs of Moving Up
Below Level III	• Much higher sales • Lower fulfillment costs • More satisfied customers	• Integration of Web and back end • Better security • More site maintenance • Web site analysis
Below Level II	• More customer information • Increased sales • Lower cost to take orders	• Web site modification • Better security • More site maintenance
Below Level I	• Wider advertising reach • Lower printing costs • Current with technology	• Web site construction • Internet connection • Security • More site maintenance

Table 12.1.   Framework for Evaluating a Potential Web Application.

their current way of interacting with the company. Another benefit is that starting at Level I lets the firm's technical people learn about Web technology with less risk of crashing the firm's core computer systems.

Managers should conduct a more formal cost-benefit analysis. One common benefit that management would attempt to quantify is the growth in reach of the firm's advertising. The firm may expect a wider reach, because Web visitors may be different than the individuals reached by the firm's other media. One suggestion to help the firm develop reasonable estimates of this benefit is to research the effect that adding a Web presence has had on other firms in the industry.

Another quantifiable measure is printing costs, which should go down when marketing material is put on the Web. Of course the firm will achieve lower printing costs only to the extent that it stops printing and mailing paper marketing materials. Another benefit, one difficult to quantify, is that by going on the Web, the firm will create a perception that it is keeping up with changing technologies. Depending on the firm's customers, this perception could be important. For example, if a firm attracts a group of customers who use the Web, then the firm's failure to develop a Web presence could be costly. A corollary to creating the external perception of keeping up with technology is the internal benefit that the firm receives from beginning to get experience using Web technology.

There are several costs associated with going from no Web presence to a Level I application. First, the firm will incur the cost of purchasing the software to build the application. Perhaps a larger component of the construction cost will be for the time of outside professionals who will design and program the application.

The firm incurs a second incremental cost in getting connected to the Internet. This monthly fee is usually paid to an ISP that hosts the firm's Web site and keeps it connected to the Web. A third incremental cost is the software and service required to give management some assurance that the Web site is secure from external parties who may use the site as a point of entry into the firm's proprietary data systems. (If the firm's Web site resides on an ISP's network, these costs are bundled into the ISP's charges.) Finally, the firm may need to hire an internal Web master who is responsible for maintaining the site.

In general, it is easier to quantify the incremental costs than it is to estimate the added benefits from the system. One of the best ways to generate reliable estimates of the incremental benefits is to talk with other companies that have built similar systems. Through these benchmarking efforts, managers can develop more informed estimates of the benefits they can expect from the potential move to Level I. Once management has developed these estimates, it can compare the benefits and the costs. If the benefits exceed the costs, then it makes sense to proceed with the Level I implementation. We will discuss a CEO change agenda later in this chapter.

Approaching Level II

Once a firm has reached Level I, it may begin to recognize the inherent limitations of being able to broadcast information without receiving information back from customers. Moving to Level II creates the opportunity for the firm to begin to close the loop. A Level II application involves developing online input screens that let customers register with the Web site, state their interests, and even place orders for products or information about products.

A firm moving from Level I to Level II is likely to experience some important incremental benefits. If it adds online forms to the Web site, sponsors online chat sessions with customers, and enables visitors to send e-mails, then the firm will get a much higher level of customer feedback than it has ever had. Of course, the customer feedback is only valuable if management uses it. If management uses the feedback to create valuable new products and to improve the effectiveness of its internal processes, then it may be possible to quantify the benefit of the feedback; however, this particular benefit is likely to be most difficult to quantify.

In addition, managers can expect increased sales as a result of the Level II application. To estimate gains in sales, firms should study the experience of other firms who have gone from Level I to Level II systems to get a range of numbers on which to base their estimates. Another potential benefit may be a lower cost to process an order. To assess this, however, the firm will need to compare the estimated cost of partially processing an order via the Web to the actual cost of processing an order through whatever channel(s) it currently uses. Then the firm needs to estimate how many orders will be processed via the Web site. Whether or not it is possible to quantify cost savings, management must build the system to ensure that customers have an easier time placing orders via the Web.

There are several costs associated with going from Level I to Level II. First, the firm will need to build the technical infrastructure to let customers send information to the company and to store that information, analyze it, and use it in ways that add value. Second, the firm will need to reassess and reinforce its security policies and technologies. Third, the firm will incur additional costs to maintain a system that handles incoming data.

In addition to the quantifiable benefits and costs associated with the move from a Level I to a Level II system, there are important qualitative effects that management should consider in its decision-making process. One important benefit is the learning that the company will achieve from its efforts to process and analyze the additional customer information that will come in on the Web. One of the important insights that management is likely to gain is that the firm must follow through on its inherent promise to customers of a user-friendly means of placing orders and offering feedback. If the organization fulfills orders slowly, then putting a user-friendly Web point of entry is likely to increase customer frustration.

Approaching Level III

This disconnect between front-end and back-end systems is one of the principal reasons for making the transition from a Level II to a Level III Web application. Few companies have created such systems. The incremental costs of rethinking and redesigning many basic operational processes are very high, yet the expected value of the additional profits is also high. Unfortunately for managers, there is no way to reap the rewards without first taking the plunge.

A Level III Web application is a valuable step in the evolution of a company's basic business processes. Dell had already created a highly advantageous approach to the PC business before it began using the Web. For Dell, the Web was a way to make the front end of its fulfillment process as easy to use as the back end. For Cisco, the Web was a tool for enhancing customer satisfaction and holding its customer service headcount constant while the company grew rapidly. In short, Cisco used the Web as the technology for improving its order fulfillment and customer service processes.

As these examples suggest, Level III Web applications generate measurable benefits. One such benefit is incremental sales. In 1998, for example, Dell sales grew 60 percent while the overall PC industry grew 7 percent. To a large extent, Dell's additional growth was attributable to the way customers can place orders and have them fulfilled much more efficiently than they could if they had purchased from Dell's competitors.

And the more slowly growing firms, such as Hewlett-Packard, IBM, and Compaq, suffer from a competitive disadvantage relative to Dell. Because Dell always sold PCs directly to customers, it never had to contend with the channel conflict issues that beset its competitors. These Dell competitors cannot simply copy Dell's model: they are too dependent on their distribution channels. If the Dell competitors dealt directly with their customers, the distributors could retaliate by making private-label PCs. So the Level III Web application has the potential not only to increase a company's sales but also to create sustainable competitive advantage.

Level III applications also can help companies cut costs. As we saw in Chapter 2, the Cisco Systems Web application saved an estimated $500 million due to reduced call center volume, lower shipping costs, and other reduced expenses.

Electronic procurement, another Level III application, is expected to generate savings as high as 20 percent on annual procurement budgets for nonproduction items at such firms as GE, Bristol Myers Squibb, and Chevron. Web procurement applications transform the way a company purchases office supplies, for example. Electronic procurement uses the Web to let employees select what they want to buy from an online catalogue that contains items from approved suppliers. The employee fills up an online shopping cart, and the order is sent electronically to the appropriate supplier, who delivers the items to the employee's desk.

As we noted earlier, in some companies such as GE, the budgets for these items can reach as high as $5 billion, according to *TechWeb*. Thus the 20 percent savings could result in cost reductions as high as $1 billion. Most of these savings are a result of using electronic catalogues to increase the percentage of purchases that employees make with preferred suppliers from whom the company has negotiated volume discounts (Wilder, 1997). The savings from electronic procurement also include lower processing costs for the company and the supplier.

These benefits do not come cheaply. For a company the size of GE, the total cost of purchasing software and hiring systems integrators to help reengineer the company's processes and systems can reach the tens of millions of dollars, and the change can take years to complete. As we will explore later, these projects should be implemented in small pieces so that the company can achieve tangible benefits early in the process and thus sustain project momentum. The cost of these small projects should be included, with the appropriate timing, in the cost-benefit analysis.

Additional to the costs of rebuilding systems is the cost of changing the organization so that it will embrace the new business processes and new technologies. Management must devote significant amounts of time to communicating the importance of the new processes. People throughout the organization must learn how to use them. Incentives and objectives must reflect the increased importance of cross-departmental interaction. Management must create new organizational roles even as it phases out old ones. Many of these costs are qualitative, but management should nevertheless factor them into the cost-benefit analysis.

The foregoing discussion provides general guidelines for cost-benefit analysis. Each company that considers implementing a Web application will have its own unique issues to deal with. Despite the challenge, the analysis is worth doing. One important factor for managers to keep in mind is that companies tend to climb the pyramid of Web applications. In other words, once a firm gets started on the Web, it is likely that the incremental benefits of moving up to the next level will exceed the incremental costs.

A TEN-STEP MANAGERIAL
CHANGE AGENDA

Once a firm has decided to proceed with a Web application, management needs to make whatever changes are necessary to achieve the desired results; these changes will vary by project. Level I projects, for example, do not require as much process redesign work as Level III projects. Therefore, managers will need to evaluate what steps are appropriate for their particular project. Here is a relatively comprehensive ten-step process that managers can follow to realize the potential of their Web application.

1. *Build a Web application team.* To ensure success, the Web application must be led from the top. The leader is likely to be the CEO in a small organization and a business unit manager in a medium-size or large organization. The leader must form a cross-functional team and offer tangible incentives to motivate the team's drive to succeed. The team must be trained in the techniques it will need to do an effective job of Web-enabled process redesign. The team should consist of business unit managers, functional managers, and IS professionals. External stakeholders—such as customers and suppliers—should participate on the team where needed. The leader should direct a steering committee that offers advice and keeps the project on track.

2. *Set objectives.* The leader must set objectives for the Web application team. These objectives should be specific, measurable, and ambitious yet achievable. Web applications cannot be considered a success until they have produced measurable performance improvements in such areas as enhanced customer service, better quality, faster response time, and lower costs. As we mentioned earlier, setting big objectives is useful; however, the team should organize its work to achieve measurable results quickly rather than work on an ambitious project for two to three years with the hope of achieving the big results at the end.

3. *Benchmark peers.* The Web application team should identify other companies that have used similar Web applications. These benchmark companies should be inside and outside the industry. The benchmarking efforts should be highly focused on generating insights into what works and what does not work in process redesign.

4. *Work with customers and suppliers.* The Web application team should also work closely with relevant customers and suppliers. In

particular, the team should find out what these stakeholders like about the current processes and where they see opportunities for improvement. Working with customers and suppliers helps the Web application team create a new process that benefits these stakeholders.

5. *Map current processes.* The Web application team must then map the processes that are to be changed. Process mapping pays off by identifying opportunities for improvement. The Web application team can compare the insights from process mapping with the complaints of customers and suppliers and with the effective techniques of the benchmark companies. Areas in which all three of these analyses overlap are likely to contain the greatest potential for providing meaningful results.

6. *Envision the new Web application.* Once the team has collected all these data, it must envision a new Web application that will be radical enough to produce big performance improvement but practical enough to be achievable. To do so, all members of the team must review the results of the foregoing analytical steps. Then the team should brainstorm to develop ideas about what a new process would look like. Initially, the team should strive to generate a large number of new ideas and then criteria for ranking them. Criteria might include the ability of the process to achieve management objectives, its cost and time to implement, and its ability to use existing data, processes, and systems. The team should rank the ideas based on these criteria and then pick the best of the group.

7. *Design new processes and systems.* The team must now shift its focus to designing new workflows, new performance incentives, and new information systems. All these processes and systems must work together for reengineering to succeed. The team will work with whomever will be affected by the changes—people in departments throughout the organization, and external stakeholders—to design new ways for people to work together. The team will envision how performance measurement and incentives must change. And the team will design the new Web application that will support the new work processes.

8. *Sell to senior management.* At this point, the team needs to request resources from senior management. To do so, it will need to develop the business case for the project. The case should help persuade senior management that the resources required for the project will be more than offset by the benefits that the Web application will produce for the company. The business case should include specific project objectives, a description of the benefits that the project will

produce for the firm, highlights of how the new process will differ from the old one, an overview of the technical architecture of the new system, a project plan, and the anticipated budget required to achieve the plan.

If management approves the business case, then the team should present a detailed implementation plan to senior management and get its advice and consent to proceed with the project. (An important part of the implementation plan is the process of evaluating and selecting potential suppliers of Web tools and systems integration services for building the application. Given the importance of these inputs to the project, the team may decide to select suppliers before seeking the CEO's final approval of the project.)

9. *Roll out in phases.* As Pete Solvik, architect of Cisco's CCO, recommends in *Executive Edge,* teams should break a project into discrete phases that take no more than ninety days to complete. Each of these brief project phases should add a specific feature that is likely to produce measurable benefits. If the project phases actually achieve the anticipated benefits, then management will feel much more comfortable continuing to fund the project. The team should start with project phases that are most likely to generate big results quickly so as to build enthusiasm for the project (Graham, 1998).

10. *Measure, evaluate, and improve.* Finally, the CEO should recognize that the Web application process never really ends. The firm should evaluate the quantitative benefit of the project in relation to its ongoing costs. External and internal stakeholders in the Web application should give feedback to the company to identify what works and what needs improvement. Even after completion, new technologies are likely to emerge that could be incorporated into the system to make it more effective or efficient.

CASE
U.S. Cavalry: Building from Mail Order

U.S. Cavalry serves as an example of how companies are using the ten-step managerial agenda. As we will see, the company is following most of the ten steps, albeit in a way that is uniquely suited to its corporate style. Based in Radcliff, Kentucky, U.S. Cavalry is a retailer of military and law enforcement uniforms and accessories and has 290 employees. U.S. Cavalry also retails survival and outdoor clothing and equipment, action sports equipment, and collectibles. It was founded in

June 1973 to capitalize on the less-than-convenient service, restricted hours, and relatively narrow selection of uniforms and accessories available at military bases.

U.S. Cavalry started with one store in Kentucky and over the years opened four additional stores in Kentucky, North Carolina, Georgia, and Texas. In 1975, the company distributed eighteen hundred catalogues to potential customers. By 1998, it was distributing seven-and-a-half million catalogues annually. U.S. Cavalry listed forty-five hundred items in each of its 1998 catalogues.

In 1995, Randy Acton, CEO of U.S. Cavalry, decided to go online. He was convinced that the Internet was the wave of the future, and he wanted his company to be there. Acton registered the uscav.com URL and built a preliminary Web site. The site, a U.S. Cavalry home page, was a small version of the complete catalogue, with a toll-free number and an e-mail form that visitors could use to order the printed catalogue (Randy Acton, interview with the author, Oct. 1998).

At first, U.S. Cavalry still did not want its customers using the Web to place online orders, because Acton was concerned that the security issues had not been satisfactorily resolved. Customers who decided not to order the catalogue could use the Web site to decide what they wanted and place the order via telephone. The last thing he wanted to do was risk the excellent customer relationships that he had built up over twenty years by putting his business on an insecure Web site.

The Web site averaged five thousand catalogue requests a month. However, despite the additional cost of printing and mailing more catalogues, U.S. Cavalry was not getting many more orders. Acton realized that he needed to curb those people who ordered the catalogue without placing orders. So the site informed visitors that everything that was in the print catalogue was also on the Web site. Those who were more comfortable using the catalogue than using the Web to review the product information were free to order a catalogue. However, U.S. Cavalry instituted a new policy that required customers to pay for the privilege. As a result of this policy, only people who intended to place an order would order the catalogue.

In October 1997, U.S. Cavalry decided to take the next step in using the Web. Acton had been following the strategies of retailers whom he respected, such as L.L. Bean and Eddie Bauer, who were further along in building Web sites. When he was sure he could confidently put his business on the Web without risking his customer relationships, he moved forward. VeriSign's technology would enable his customers to secure their confidential payment information they would send to U.S. Cavalry's Web site. Acton now felt that customers would be confident conducting e-commerce at uscav.com.

When designing the site, he was determined to make the site fast, secure, and easy to use. These remained principle objectives. He made the site fast by cutting away unnecessary elements, such as heavy graphics. He made the site secure with the VeriSign technology. He made the site easy to use by installing a search engine that lets visitors seek out merchandise by using a variety of search methods, key words, and categories.

The individual members of the team involved in the project varied depending on the project phase. At the beginning, Acton and his director of marketing, Sam Young, developed ideas for how the Web site would operate. When they decided what they wanted it to look like, they coordinated an external programmer with an internal layout artist with HTML programming expertise. Once U.S. Cavalry built the site, the company received extensive feedback from customers that led it to change the system to make it easier to use and faster.

In October 1998, U.S. Cavalry was working on creating a linkage between its Web front-end ordering and its back-end fulfillment systems. Prior to initiating this linkage phase, U.S. Cavalry had simply printed out on paper the orders received via the Web and handed the paper orders on to the company's traditional order fulfillment department.

U.S. Cavalry has invested some people and analytical time into responding to and analyzing the data it gets from its Web site. For example, the company employs people specifically dedicated to responding to questions that customers pose via the e-mail system linked to the Web site. Customers tend to ask both technical product questions and general customer service questions.

In addition, U.S. Cavalry receives extensive information from its ISP pertaining to activity on its Web site. U.S. Cavalry is able to analyze these data to find out which products are selling the best, how customer preferences are shifting, and other important insights that help U.S. Cavalry enhance the ability of the Web site to generate higher revenues. One valuable insight that U.S. Cavalry has extracted from this analysis is that when a visitor to a Web portal conducts a search using keywords like *military,* the search engine will link the searcher to the U.S. Cavalry Web site, a practice we mentioned in Chapter Six.

U.S. Cavalry generated other valuable insights as a result of feedback from customers and its own internal brainstorming. For example, the company has learned that if it gives the customer something "free" with the order, the average order size increases. U.S. Cavalry's average Internet order of $105 is already higher than its average catalogue order of $79. A typical promotion to motivate higher average orders was to give a customer a $199 pair of leather boots if that customer placed an order over $500. In addition to increasing the size of the average order, this promotion allows U.S. Cavalry to promote new items to their customer base.

Acton recommends that any retailer considering a Web site be familiar with direct marketing. If a retailer is accustomed to selling its product in a store only, having to deal with direct marketing on the Web will come as a shock. The Web is much like selling a product on TV with an 800 number. To fulfill direct orders, a firm must have the ability to pick the item from the warehouse shelf, pack the order, and ship it from the warehouse very efficiently. Acton already had this experience because of his large catalogue business. Going on the Web only changed the medium by which the order was received.

Acton continues to get orders from both the printed catalogue and the Web. Each of these media promotes the other. However, U.S. Cavalry is having much better results with its Web site than a typical direct marketer gets from direct mail. Of U.S. Cavalry's orders, 50 percent come from new Web customers. The typical new-customer yield of direct mail programs is 2 percent (Acton interview, Oct. 1998).

OVERCOMING THE CHALLENGES OF IMPLEMENTING THE WEB

The ten-step managerial agenda we have described anticipates many of the challenges that a company will face as it tries to realize the potential of its Web application. Nevertheless, for such a methodology to be complete, we should also discuss some of the more common pitfalls and look at suggestions for how to overcome them. The success of U.S. Cavalry's Web site is partially a result of its ability to overcome these challenges. Following are four such pitfalls.

Lack of Management Commitment

Many corporate change initiatives follow a similar pattern. Management starts the initiative with fanfare and enthusiasm. A team is formed, and it begins work with ambitious goals and tight project plans. When the first deadline passes without the team's meeting the target, management distances itself from the project. The drive for success is replaced with a run for cover. The project manager disappears from the company, and the project is never discussed again. Soon thereafter a new fad comes along to capture the attention of senior management, and the cycle begins anew.

There is a real danger that a Web project will fall victim to this cycle. The best way to prevent this outcome is not to get started with the project until there are sufficient facts available to make reliable plans and to set realistic expectations. Fundamentally, if a project really will increase the value of the company's shares, senior management will have a personal incentive to ensure its success. It is the job of the Web application team to ensure that the project rests on a firm foundation of facts.

Unclear Project Objectives

If you don't know where you are going, any road will get you there. Many projects start off with great enthusiasm because they borrow their wind from the almost overpowering weather front of industry hype. Some projects therefore get started without a well thought out set of objectives that make sense in the context of the company. Sometimes this happens because people familiar with the technology allow their enthusiasm for the Web and its capabilities to overwhelm the voices that focus on business benefits.

The best way to overcome the problem of unclear objectives is for the CEO and the Web application team to assure themselves that the project objectives are specific, measurable, and ambitious yet achievable. The CEO can develop such objectives if other companies have achieved similar objectives and if the CEO believes that his or her firm has the ability and the desire to accomplish such objectives.

Absence of Internal Teamwork

If teamwork is a value that is not widely practiced within a company, then it will be difficult for the firm to embrace teamwork in creating a Web application. If a firm's departments are better at battling each other than at working together to create value for the customer, it may not make sense for the firm to undertake a Web application. If the CEO does not encourage departments to work together under normal business circumstances, it may be asking too much for the CEO suddenly to begin to encourage effective teamwork.

Therefore, a company should not undertake a Web application unless it normally encourages teamwork across the various operating units and departments of the company. Web applications tend to require very smooth interactions among different functions. If the firm is accustomed to such interactions, then implementing a Web application will proceed relatively smoothly. Even so, the CEO may need to offer specific incentives to Web application team members to encourage them to work on the team and to meet the project objectives that have removed them from their "normal" jobs or given them additional burdens.

Overly Ambitious Plans

Projects can founder if they try to do too much. For example, if a project team decides it will work for two to three years before a massive systems overhaul is complete, there is a danger that the company will spend too much money and achieve too little in the way of tangible benefits.

A company can overcome this potential obstacle by following the prescription from Pete Solvik outlined earlier. If the team rolls out the project in phases, each of which produces tangible benefits, then the project will be able to sustain momentum.

IMPLICATIONS

Companies have opportunities for using the Web to solve big problems. Managers need to evaluate whether the benefits of tackling such problems exceed the costs for their particular business. If such opportunities exist, managers must be prepared to sustain their leadership of the change initiatives that are required to achieve the objectives. If managers can overcome the challenges, the rewards from implementing Web applications can be substantial for shareholders, customers, and employees.

CHAPTER THIRTEEN

From Lossware
to Powerware:
Advice for Internet
Management
and Investment

F or managers of Internet businesses, this book has
one set of implications, on which we will now expand. For investors
in Internet businesses, the book has other implications that we will
develop here too. Many people wear both hats. To paraphrase Warren Buffett, stock is an ownership stake in a business. To evaluate
whether or not to buy the stock, the investor must understand the
business.

Web investors need to understand the challenges that Internet
business managers face and must be equipped to evaluate how well
the Internet business managers are addressing these challenges. Similarly, many Internet business managers own big chunks of equity in
their companies, so they are truly owner-managers. First, we will
draw further conclusions about Internet business management. Then
we will explore how investors can sort out the best investments, particularly in relation to stock valuations.

LOSSWARE, BRANDWARE, AND POWERWARE: RISING UP THE NET PROFIT PYRAMID

One central concept of this book has been that Internet business managers should choose the industry segment in which to compete. At this early stage in the industry's evolution, choosing the right industry accounts for most of the difference in performance. As we have seen, firms that participate in industries that enjoy economic leverage seem to have the greatest chance of earning exceptional returns.

A second central concept has been that the firm must choose a competitive strategy. We have found that within an industry, firms that offer their customers closed-loop solutions tend to perform better than firms that leave related needs unaddressed.

The most profitable business model is to participate in an industry with economic leverage and to offer customers in that industry a closed-loop solution. A firm's getting to this Web economic nirvana depends on where the firm is now. Figure 1.4 in Chapter One showed how we can view Internet business as a pyramid of generic models, each level in the pyramid containing several industry segments with similar profit potentials. We repeat that figure here as Figure 13.1 for your convenience.

At each level of the pyramid, managers have different strategic options. These options are outlined in Figure 13.2.

Strategic Options for Lossware Businesses

A Lossware business has the following characteristics:

- It is unprofitable.

- Its prices are very low, and its management is unable to raise prices without losing customers.

- It spends a large proportion of its available cash on trying to differentiate itself from many other competitors.

- It is difficult for management to explain in fewer than three sentences what the firm's product does, how it creates value for customers, and why it is better than the competition.

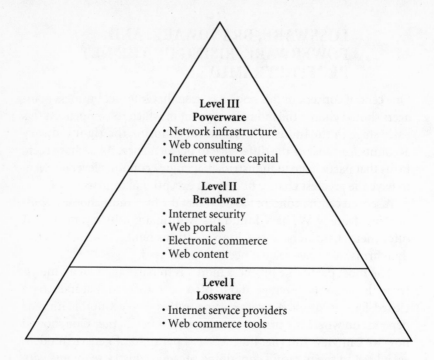

Figure 13.1.   Internet Business Segments and the Web Business Pyramid.

A lossware business has three strategic options.

1. *Leverage share into Brandware.* This means that the firm sells a product at a very low price to build de facto market leadership that becomes a Trojan Horse. The market leadership gets the firm embedded in customer organizations. Once there, the firm may be able to sell ancillary products and services that are important to the client's ongoing operations.

Microsoft succeeded with this strategy in a classic example of how a point product can evolve into Brandware. Microsoft licensed its PC operating system to computer manufacturers for a very low price. Consumers thus ended up purchasing PCs already equipped with the Microsoft operating system. To do anything useful with the computer, the consumer needed to purchase application software that was relatively expensive and profitable for Microsoft.

Thus Microsoft was able to go into markets that were created by other firms and ultimately create the leading product in that category.

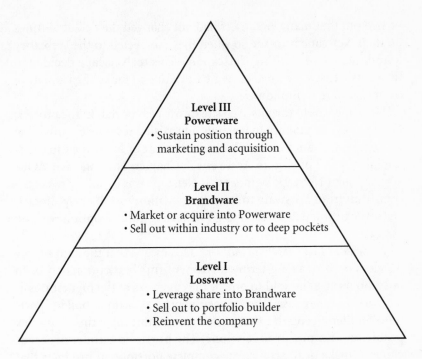

Figure 13.2. Strategic Options for Web Businesses.

Microsoft achieved this in word processing, taking the market away from WordPerfect, and in spreadsheets, taking the market away from Lotus Development. Microsoft purchased leaders in presentation software and PC database software as well.

After dominating individual product categories, Microsoft realized that it could offer customers a closed-loop solution by linking these programs together into office suites. The result was a powerful and profitable brand of application software that has fueled Microsoft's rise to the top of the corporate world.

Netscape tried unsuccessfully to execute the same strategy on the Web. As we saw earlier, Netscape sold its browser at a very low price to establish itself as the de facto standard. When Microsoft counterattacked by giving its browser away for free, Netscape felt obliged to match Microsoft's free offer. As a result of this price war, Netscape got the wind knocked out of its sails (and sales).

But, whether by design or chance, Netscape had an ace up its sleeve. Netscape's browser continued to hold its lead in market share. It turned out that many Web users had not changed the default settings on their Netscape browser, so when they connected to the Web, they found themselves visiting Netscape's Web site. Netscape decided to turn this situation into a strategic initiative to make the transition from Lossware to Brandware.

Netscape would turn its Web site into a Web portal. In the process, Netscape would attempt to generate advertising revenue by providing companies a chance to flash banners in front of Netscape's market-leading number of visitors. As we saw in Chapters Nine and Ten, AOL's acquisition of Netscape signifies that Netscape was unable to make the transition from Lossware to Brandware without AOL's help. In fact, Netscape ultimately decided to go with the strategic option we look at next.

2. *Sell out to a "portfolio builder."* This means that the firm simply decides not to be a long-term survivor. A firm's best option may be to position itself to be sold to one of the survivors at the highest possible price. In many cases, the survivor may be a portfolio builder. Portfolio builders recognize that customers cannot solve their complex problems with one product alone. The portfolio builder proceeds either to make or to acquire the complete portfolio of products that the customer needs. The Lossware company can maximize its value by focusing on developing products that will generate the most incremental revenue for the portfolio builder once they enter the builder's product portfolio.

This phenomenon is occurring in the Web security market. Companies are building Web sites. They are also distributing information internally via intranets and sharing information outside their firms via extranets. However, there is a very powerful force keeping the lid on the widespread growth of these applications: the fear of security leaks. Companies are reluctant to invest too heavily in Web sites, intranets, and extranets because they are afraid of the losses they will incur from breaches of information security.

Web security software and service providers have tried to address these concerns. The first wave of such firms sold products that addressed specific manifestations of the problem of information security breaches. For example, some firms made software to detect viruses; other firms sold firewalls, software that was designed to protect a company's information technology against unauthorized outside access. These point products were helpful but did not solve all the problems.

Companies began to realize that they needed a more comprehensive and integrated set of security services and software. Some vendors decided to position themselves to offer such solutions. In Web security, Network Associates is an example of a portfolio builder. In the last few years, it has acquired vendors of antivirus software, network security monitoring tools, and firewalls. Network Associates is attempting to knit these different products together into a system of network security management that will give companies a greater sense of security about their information assets.

The strategy of selling out to a portfolio builder is not limited to the security software business. The same phenomenon has taken place in the network equipment business. Cisco Systems has acquired thirty companies that make different kinds of network equipment and software that its customers need in order to operate their corporate networks.

This pattern may repeat itself in the Web advertising management software and service industry. As companies realize that technology can help them close a growing number of e-commerce transactions, they will seek out closed-loop solutions. These solutions will include software that can aggregate data about potential customers and analyze the data to pinpoint groups of customers with a high proclivity to buy. Closed-loop solutions will help companies get product information to their most likely buyers, provide a means for executing secure transactions, and transmit the orders to the companies' order fulfillment systems. Finally, these closed-loop solutions will pay the Web portals who enabled the placement of product information, update customer records, and refresh the analytical systems that track the most attractive customer segments. Firms selling pieces of this closed-loop solution may be able to sell out to the firms that stitch together the entire portfolio.

3. *Reinvent the company.* Reinventing the Lossware company means getting out of one product line and getting into a different one. The challenge in reinventing the company is that there needs to be some way of investing into the new strategy the resources generated by the old strategy. Reinventing the company works best if the customer relationships, strategic partnerships, or technical competencies developed under the old strategy can be used to create the new one.

We saw an example of reinvention in our discussion of Spyglass in Chapter Ten. Spyglass was one of the first Web browser firms. With the advent of Netscape and Microsoft, it became clear that Spyglass would not survive in their arena. Spyglass reinvented itself. But the reinvention was not a deracination. There was a clear connection be-tween the old Spyglass and the new one. The new Spyglass stayed in the Web browser business by developing software to give Web access to a variety of *non-PC* devices, such as handheld PCs, telephones, and the set-top boxes being used by cable companies for interactive tele-vision. Spyglass's burgeoning expertise in the development of non-PC systems may be shifting the firm from Lossware to Brandware.

Strategic Options for Brandware Businesses

A Brandware business has the following characteristics:

- It is marginally profitable.
- Its ability to charge high prices varies with its relative market share.
- It spends a large proportion of its available cash on trying to differentiate itself as a brand from a moderate number of relatively well financed competitors.
- Its customers are increasingly seeking to purchase the firm's product or service from the de facto industry standard supplier.

A Brandware business has four strategic options.

1. *Market into Powerware.* To market into Powerware, a firm in-vests heavily in marketing its product or service. This heavy invest-ment creates pressure on less well financed competitors to drop out or fall behind in the marketing warfare. At the same time, effective marketing helps the dominant Brandware firm gain a bigger share of the growing market. The growing share of the market leads to in-creased revenues, which help drive up the firm's stock price.

The most obvious example of marketing into Powerware is in the Web portal business. Here a handful of competitors are spending heavily to promote their brands so as to increase the number of visi-tors and to get those visitors to spend time on their sites. At the same time that these portals are marketing to consumers, they are selling hard to advertisers to close substantial promotional deals that give advertisers access to this growing number of Web portal visitors.

Fundamentally, Brandware is a transitional phase. There is typi-cally an endgame in which the most successful firms get bigger and the smaller firms drop out. The consolidation phase reduces the number of suppliers—one of the necessary conditions for Powerware. In order for the other condition to hold, growth in demand must remain strong even as the number of suppliers drops. Once these two conditions have been satisfied, the transition from Brandware to Powerware is complete. At this point, the firms left standing will reap the rewards of their protracted battle.

2. *Acquire into Powerware.* Another, possibly parallel way to become Powerware is to acquire companies that help the firm offer a broader set of services to its customers. To be deemed successful, the acquisitions need to offset their purchase price, which is possible when the firm adds new customers through an acquisition. As we saw in Chapter Six, Yahoo's acquisition of GeoCities exemplifies this strategic option

Another way that acquisitions can help Brandware firms in their quest to become Powerware is by raising their customers' switching costs. Web portal firms have made a variety of acquisitions specifically to achieve this objective. For example, Microsoft purchased Hotmail as a way to add free e-mail to Microsoft Network. Yahoo also acquired a company to give it free e-mail. The point of free e-mail is that it creates an incentive for the e-mailer to keep returning to the site. Another benefit to the Web portals is the potentially valuable information that customers provide when they register to receive free e-mail.

Acquiring the capability for free e-mail is one of many tactics that Web portal firms use to increase the number of visitors to their sites and to turn visitors into loyal customers. The long-term objective of these acquisitions is to increase the value of the brand in the minds of advertisers. If the Brandware firms can build a brand that represents a logical connection between Web advertising dollars spent and increased sales of the products or services being advertised, then they can acquire their way to Powerware.

3. *Sell out within the industry.* Not all Brandware firms will succeed in getting ahead of the power curve. When it becomes clear that a firm cannot raise the next round of capital needed to fund its place in the battlefield, then it must decide how best to salvage the shareholders' investment. In general, the goal is to get as many qualified purchasers as possible to place a bid for the company. Ultimately, the best deal will come from the firm who values the acquired firm's assets the most. In some cases the value will be highest for a portfolio builder within the industry.

4. *Sell out to deep pockets.* In some cases the Brandware firm will realize the most value by selling to a firm that is outside the industry and looking for a way to get into it. An example of this is NBC's acquisition of Snap, CNET's Web portal (Chapter Eight). NBC had the capital to acquire Snap at a price that looked reasonable to CNET. And more important for Snap's long-term survival, NBC appeared willing to spend the money needed to promote the site sufficiently to raise its market share. Given the stock market's reaction, it is unclear whether the USA Networks–Lycos deal was in the best interest of Lycos shareholders.

Strategic Options for Powerware Businesses

A Powerware business has the following characteristics:

- It is highly profitable.
- It can charge high prices for its services because demand exceeds the industry's qualified capacity.
- It spends a relatively large part of its resources on developing new capabilities to sustain its leadership position.
- Its customers are heavily dependent on its products and services.

Although Powerware businesses enjoy high profitability and significant economic leverage, their current positions do not guarantee long-term prosperity. Powerware businesses must guard against becoming arrogant and complacent. In industries that change as rapidly as the Web, a strong market position simply provides a firm with the resources it needs to try to keep ahead of competitors in the next round of competition. To sustain their market leadership, Powerware businesses have two strategic options.

1. *Sustain current position through marketing.* Powerware firms can sustain their position through aggressive marketing. Firms that choose this strategy hire the most aggressive salespeople and create a climate that encourages them to exceed very high quotas—by offering very high commissions to the top performers and by requiring the rest of the organization to stretch itself to give the sales force the products and services it needs to meet aggressive sales quotas.

2. *Sustain current position through acquisition.* At the same time, or as an independent strategy, Powerware firms can sustain their market leadership by acquiring new technologies needed to meet evolving customer needs. Chapter Two showed how Cisco Systems uses marketing and acquisitions to sustain its market leadership. The acquisitions help the firm give customers whatever products they need to build their corporate networks in response to changing business requirements. And Cisco's aggressive marketing force makes it very difficult for new competitors to gain access to Cisco customers.

FORMULATING WEB BUSINESS STRATEGY: A MANAGER'S GUIDE

The foregoing analysis may help managers think about their strategic options, but it is no substitute for a rigorous process of formulating Web business strategy. Although the generic Web business models and strategies can give some guidance, each firm has unique capabilities and therefore must develop its unique strategy. The seven-step process shown in Table 13.1 will help managers develop specific Web business strategies for their organizations.

Your firm should apply the seven-step process in a way that reflects the extremely rapid rate of change in the Internet business. Some people argue that an Internet firm must go from the conception of its strategy to full implementation in less than 120 days. If it does not, it will be left behind by faster firms. Such rapid implementation of strategy implies that rigorous analysis would be too time consuming. In fact, firms must apply the seven-step method described in the next sections rigorously *and* quickly, taking advantage of the Web itself to gather much of the market intelligence needed to formulate an Internet business strategy.

1. Build a Strategy Team
2. Map the Firm's Value System
3. Evaluate Customer Segments
4. Identify Requirements for Competitive Advantage
5. Formulate Strategic Options
6. Estimate the Net Present Value of Strategic Options
7. Develop an Implementation Plan

Table 13.1. Process for Developing Web Business Strategy.

Step 1: Build a Strategy Team

The first step in formulating a corporate strategy is to build a strategy team. The composition of this team will vary depending on the organization. For a company with several business units, the team would consist of the CEO, the business unit managers, and key staff executives from such areas as financial or human resources. For a firm with one business unit, the strategy team would consist of the CEO and the key functional managers from such areas as marketing, manufacturing, and engineering.

Having designated the team, the CEO needs to get the team members trained in the techniques they will use to develop the strategy. Furthermore, it may make sense for the CEO to retain a management consultant to help structure and facilitate the strategy development process.

This first step should accomplish three results. First, the team should identify and prioritize key strategic issues. Second, the team should develop measurable objectives that help the team agree on what the developing strategy is trying to accomplish. Finally, the team must agree on a specific work plan for developing the strategy.

Step 2: Map the Firm's Value System

A value map shows how a firm fits into its economic environment. The strategy team needs to think broadly about the various inputs to the firm and how the firm transforms these inputs into products and services that create downstream value. The value map should include the firm's inputs, including people, capital, and technology. The map should also include the firm and its partners and competitors, its customers, and its customers' customers.

Drawing the value system is an important process for the strategy development team. It helps team members develop a shared vision of the sources and uses of economic value in the firm's economic environment. The value map should give the team an opportunity to quantify the flows of cash, products and services, and intellectual capital through the firm's economic ecosystem.

Step 3: Evaluate Customer Segments

The strategy team should use the value map to help identify strategically distinct groups of customers. Segmentation criteria will vary depending on whether the customers are organizations or individuals. Having identified various segments, the team can rank them based on their attractiveness to the firm. Attractiveness criteria might include size, growth rate, profitability, and fit with the firm's strengths. The team should also research the key trends driving the future profitability of the most attractive segments. The outcome of this step is a list of segments that the team decides are worth further investigation.

Step 4: Identify Requirements for Competitive Advantage

The team then identifies the requirements for sustaining competitive advantage in the most attractive segments. To do this, team members must talk to customers and analyze competitors. From this analysis, the team can develop valuable insights that will help drive the strategy formulation process. For example, the team can learn more about how customers evaluate competing suppliers and what specific criteria they use to choose the winning supplier. The team can also gain useful insights into what specific capabilities the firm requires to do an outstanding job of outperforming competitors in meeting customer needs.

Step 5: Formulate Strategic Options

With the results of the foregoing analyses, team members can begin to formulate strategic options. The strategic options should reflect internally consistent choices about which segments to target, the specific customer needs on which the firm will focus, the products and services the firm will sell to meet those needs, the functional policies required to develop and deliver these products and services, and the strategic partnerships that may be required to implement the strategy.

Because of the dynamic nature of Web business, the team should develop a fairly broad set of scenarios and consider specific contingency plans for each. For example, it may be difficult to anticipate which of many competing technologies ultimately becomes the de facto industry standard. In such a case, a firm should consider developing product offerings that can work with several of the most likely standards. Then, as it becomes apparent which technology is going to emerge as the de facto industry standard, the firm is less likely to be caught unprepared than it would have been had it bet on only one technology.

The team should initially brainstorm a large number of strategic options that it then ranks based on criteria that it deems important. Ultimately the team should select two to three options that are worth analyzing further.

Step 6: Estimate the Net Present Value of Strategic Options

The analyses of segment profitability and the requirements for competitive advantage should help the team quantify the financial value of the top three strategic options. Given the many sources of uncertainty in the Internet business, some managers may view the effort to do a financial evaluation as futile. What matters for the strategy team is to remember why it is important to do such financial evaluation: the firm generally has limited financial resources and must therefore choose a strategy that the team believes is likely to be most valuable to the shareholders.

Bearing this point in mind, the team should proceed to develop pro forma cash flow analyses of the strategic options. The team should use the information gathered in the industry and competitor analyses as inputs to the financial models. These key assumptions will include market size, growth rates, prices, market share, operating costs, and capital investments, such as acquisitions and information infrastructure.

Given the huge uncertainties, the team may find it useful to look at different scenarios. Or the team may choose to quantify the probability estimates of different outcomes. If so, the team can calculate the expected value of the scenarios.

For all three strategic options whose net present value the team calculates, the team should use the same interest rate for discounting future cash flows. Having evaluated the three scenarios, the team must pick the one strategic option that has the highest net present value.

Step 7: Develop an Implementation Plan

The reason for all the foregoing analysis is to help managers take informed action, and this action should be reflected in an implementation plan. The team should develop a plan for executing specific strategic initiatives that will achieve the strategic option the team selected. The plan should include a more detailed series of action steps to implement each strategic initiative. Each action step should be accompanied by the name(s) of managers accountable for performing the step and the deadline for its completion. In addition, each action step should specify any additional resources required to implement it. Finally, the implementation plan should include a pro forma income statement, balance sheet, and statement of cash flows.

SIX CURRENT RULES FOR WEB INVESTING

Internet businesses span the spectrum of investment risk and return. Some Internet businesses have grown earnings rapidly, profitably, and predictably. Others will generate huge and growing losses far into the future. Ironically, some of the most attractive investments for the public investor have been in the latter category, and some of the more prosaic investments have been in the former. In short, the logical assumption that predictable earnings growth leads to consistent appreciation in stock price is turned on its head when it comes to Internet short-term investments.

The rules may apply somewhat differently depending on the nature of the investing. For venture investors, the strategies for finding good investment opportunities are different than for public equity investors. Nevertheless, there is significant overlap between the processes for finding good investment opportunities. Perhaps the biggest difference is that private equity investors are better positioned than public investors to take advantage of private-public arbitrage opportunities.

Many of the rules of thumb that investors use to make investment decisions may not apply to investing in Web businesses. Following are six current rules of Web investing. Because the Web industry changes so rapidly, these rules are provisional and subject to change. For each rule, we will look at some examples and then suggest some implications for investors. After presenting the rules, we will discuss both private and public equity investment in more detail.

Investment Rule 1

For Web companies, the market values rapid top-line growth more highly than it values predictable bottom-line growth. Figure 13.3 illustrates an example. Cisco Systems is a Web business that has grown earnings predictably while retaining high net margins. From the beginning of 1998 to mid-October 1998, Cisco's stock appreciated 45 percent. By way of contrast, Amazon.com is a Web stock whose net loss has tripled since it went public. And Amazon accomplished this while losing nineteen cents on every dollar of its sales. Has the stock market punished Amazon for its performance? No. Amazon's stock almost tripled during the same time period.

The most obvious factor that could explain the differences in stock price appreciation between Cisco and Amazon is the relative sales growth rate of the two companies. Because Cisco's 62 percent growth is far below Amazon's 316 percent growth, investors evaluate the two very differently. Unlike Amazon, Cisco can be evaluated with traditional investment valuation methods.

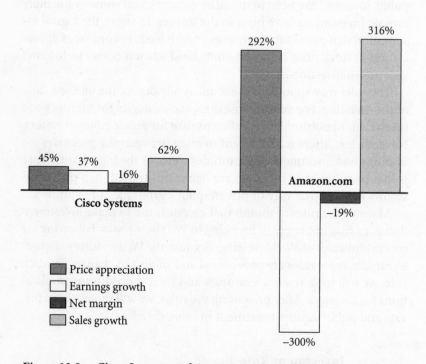

Figure 13.3.   Cisco Systems and Amazon.com: Stock Price Appreciation.
(January 2, 1998, to October 16, 1998) Earnings Growth
(CSCO, 1994–98; AMZN, 1997–98), Net Margin (December 31, 1997),
and Sales Growth (CSCO, 1994–98; AMZN, 1997–98).
Source: Cisco Systems Form 10-K; Amazon.com Form 10-K; www.pcquote.com,
author analysis.

Investment Rule 2

Web business offers significant private-public market arbitrage opportunities. In Chapter Four, we saw how venture capitalists exploit these arbitrage opportunities. As we saw in that chapter, the 1,100 percent increase in the value of Kleiner Perkins's venture portfolio between 1993 to 1997 attests to the extraordinary magnitude of these arbitrage opportunities. Publicly traded Web companies can exploit these opportunities as well.

Publicly traded Web portals have used their stock to purchase viewers from privately held firms. The public markets accord much higher valuations to the viewers of the publicly traded Web portals. This differential creates significant arbitrage opportunities between the private and public markets for viewers. For example, in June 1998, AOL paid $287 million for 6.8 million active users of a trial ICQ ("I seek you") instant communications and chat technology provided by Mirabilis. This amounts to a purchase price of $42 for each Mirabilis user. By contrast, on October 19, 1998, the stock market valued AOL's fifteen million subscribers at $23.8 billion, or $1,599 per subscriber. As we discussed in Chapter Eight, advertising rates are set on the basis of cost per thousand impressions. By acquiring Mirabilis, AOL added 45 percent more new visitors for its advertisers to target, at a cost per new visitor that was less than 3 percent of the stock market's valuation of AOL's own fifteen million subscribers.

Not all these arbitrage opportunities work out quite so well. For example, in February 1998, Lycos purchased Tripod, a privately held "Web community" of about one million registered users, for about $63 million. This purchase price compares rather unfavorably to the $1,074 million market capitalization associated with Lycos's 17.7 million users. In short, Lycos paid $63 per registered user for Tripod, whereas the stock market valued Lycos's user base at $61 a user. One could argue that Lycos overpaid.

Investment Rule 3

The volatility of a Web stock increases with the extent of its private ownership. As we saw in our example of Amazon in Chapter Six, if only a small percentage of the total shares in a firm's stock are publicly traded, then the firm's stock price is likely to fluctuate widely. The fluctuation is due to the market dynamics that occur between amateur short sellers and the rest of the market participants in that stock. If a firm has very few shares traded, the behavior of short sellers can cause the stock to swing widely. If amateur traders begin to sell the stock short, they may not realize that they are taking on a great deal of risk—that they will be forced to buy scarce shares very suddenly in order to cover their short position in the event that the stock begins to rise.

Figure 13.4 shows this principle at work. It compares the volatility of four Web portal stocks. Yahoo and Excite have heavy inside ownership, whereas AOL and Infoseek have relatively limited inside ownership.

As the figure illustrates, the higher the share of insider stock ownership, the greater the stock's volatility. Volatility here is defined as the variance of the firm's stock price returns relative to the S&P 500 index; this variance is known as the stock's beta. By definition, the beta of the S&P 500 is 1.0. So Yahoo and Excite are more than three times as volatile as the market, whereas AOL and Infoseek are a little

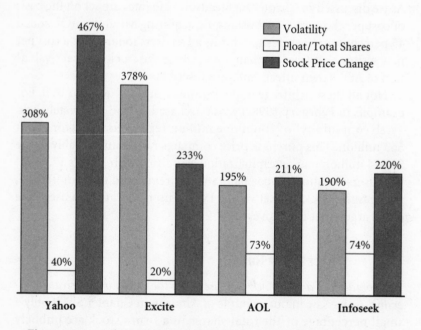

Figure 13.4.   Yahoo, Excite, AOL, and Infoseek: Volatility, Float/Total Shares, and Stock Price Change, January 2, 1998, to November 20, 1998.

less than twice as volatile as the market. The chart also indicates that insiders own about 60 percent of Yahoo shares and 80 percent of Excite shares, whereas the figures for AOL and Infoseek are a little over 25 percent. In the Web portal business, the higher the proportion of the company's stock owned by insiders, the greater the stock's volatility.

Investment Rule 4

Internet stocks appreciate much more than NASDAQ in a market upturn and decline about the same as NASDAQ in a downturn. At least this was true during much of 1998. As Figure 13.5 indicates, Internet stocks rose 59.3 percent from the beginning of 1998 to the July peak. From the peak to October 16, 1998, Internet stocks lost 18.6 percent of their value. During these same time periods, NASDAQ stocks rose 27 percent and declined 18.8 percent; the Dow Jones Industrial average rose 17.7 percent and declined 9.7 percent.

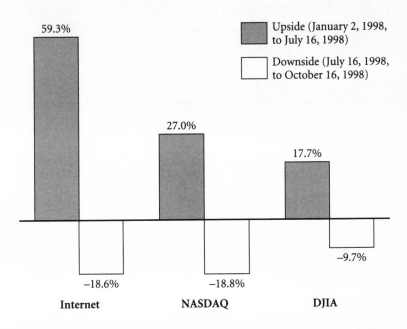

Figure 13.5.   Average Percentage Changes for Internet Stocks, NASDAQ, and the Dow Jones Industrial Average.

Investment Rule 5

Web stock returns vary by industry segment. The returns for Internet stocks tend to vary by industry segment. As Figure 13.6 illustrates, between October 19, 1997, and the same date in 1998, an index of Web portal and ISP stocks increased 168 percent and 60 percent, respectively. During the same period, e-commerce and network hardware stocks actually lost value, 16 percent and 23 percent respectively.

The point of this example is not to suggest that these particular segments will underperform or lead the market in the future. The pur-

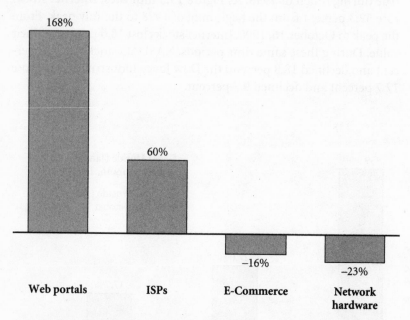

Figure 13.6.   Percentage Change in Stock Indices for Web Portal, ISP, E-Commerce, and Network Hardware Firms, October 19, 1997, to October 19, 1998.

Note: Web portal index includes Yahoo, Lycos, Excite, Go2Net, and Infoseek. ISPs include AOL, MindSpring, Exodus, Verio, PSINet, IDT, EarthLink, Metricom, At Home, and Concentric Network. E-commerce index includes Amazon, CDNow, Onsale, Preview Travel, N2K, E-Trade, and Sportsline USA. Network hardware index includes Cisco Systems, 3Com, Ascend Communications, Broadband Technologies, Cabletron, and Pairgain.

pose is to suggest that from an investment perspective, Internet stocks should not be viewed monolithically. Potential investors should carefully analyze the differences among industry segments before making their decisions.

Investment Rule 6

Web investors and the stock market reward market leadership. The stock market also rewards market leadership. There is a big difference in stock market returns for investors in firms that are clear leaders in their industries. As Figure 13.7 illustrates, this principle applies to the Web portal business. The stock price of Yahoo, the market leader, has appreciated far faster than that of followers Lycos and Excite. Furthermore, the market values each dollar of Yahoo sales at a multiple of seventy-one, whereas the market values each dollar of Lycos and Excite sales at a multiple of about eighteen.

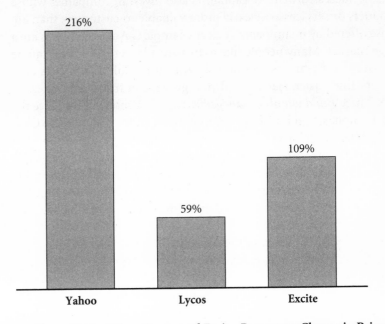

Figure 13.7.   Yahoo, Lycos, and Excite: Percentage Change in Price per Share, January 2, 1998, to October 19, 1998.

TIPS FOR PRIVATE EQUITY INVESTMENT

For private equity investors, there are six tips for making excellent investments. Before launching into a description of these tips, it is important to note that investors must do their homework in order to be successful. Doing the homework is difficult because it entails resisting the powerful pull of "pack emotions" that produce cycles of greed and fear, but the payoff is that investors become aware of important changes in technology, customer needs, and competitor strategies.

- Tip 1: *Look for big markets.* One of the most common mistakes that venture investors make is falling in love with a technology. When they do, they begin to imagine a myriad of market opportunities in which to sell the product. The most successful venture capitalists usually avoid this error. Instead, the winning venture capitalists invest in companies that are taking share in very large markets, often over $100 billion. Such large markets leave more room for the inevitable mistakes.
- Tip 2: *Invest in products and services that will create value for customers.* Successful venture capitalists also invest in companies whose products or services are clearly more valuable to customers than are those offered by incumbents. A clear example is Amazon. Books are a huge market. Many people like to browse a larger store than can be surrounded by bricks and mortar. Amazon's solution makes customers' lives easier. Hence the firm is growing at triple-digit rates.
- Tip 3: *Build winning management teams.* Venture firms place the most emphasis on building winning management teams. The CEO should have previously built companies from the ground up to $100 million or more in sales; the CEO also ought to be able to hire people who are smarter than he or she is in such functional areas as engineering, sales, and marketing. The team should be able to work together well and meet demanding growth objectives; it also should have both the persistence to stick with a business strategy during difficult times and the flexibility to change the strategy if it is not working.
- Tip 4: *Forge strong partnerships.* New ventures are often quite strong in one link of the value chain. To offer the complete set of activities that customers need, however, the new ventures must find partners that are strong in complementary activities. When ventures have strong partnerships, they can more easily build a closed-loop solution for customers, which affords a greater chance of gaining economic leverage and high returns for investors.

• Tip 5: *Get sufficient cash to protect against down cycles.* The time to raise cash is not when the new venture needs it. If a firm waits until it is short of cash, the next round of investors will be in a stronger position to ask for a bigger stake in the company in exchange for a smaller cash infusion.

The time to raise cash is when cash is amply available. For example, in the last few years, venture capital has hit record levels each quarter. Venture capitalists are very eager to put that cash into excellent companies. If you are an early-stage investor in a new venture, try to raise as much cash as possible when it is in ample supply. When public markets crash, the IPO exit door slams shut. When the exit is closed, investors in venture capital limited partnerships yank their money as well. The result is that unprepared companies become starved for scarce capital when they need it most, which can lead to unpleasant consequences for early-stage investors.

• Tip 6: *Be flexible about the exit strategy.* Venture firms must be open to the notion that going public is not always going to be a viable exit strategy. At times it may make sense to seek out a firm that has had experience with acquiring start-ups before they go public, such as Cisco or AOL. These acquisition exits are frequently less profitable than the IPO route. Sometimes the ventures run out of cash at a time when acquisition is the only option. In these situations, it is obviously better to accept a lower sale price for the company than to liquidate.

SCREENING A PUBLIC EQUITY INVESTMENT

For public equity investors, the means of finding great investment opportunities are different. The investment screening process described here is designed to weed out potential investment candidates at each step. The survivors of this winnowing are most likely to generate high investment returns.

• Screen 1: *Identify fast-growing industry segments.* As we saw earlier in this chapter, the market drives up stocks that are in fast-growing industries. Public equity investors should seek out the fastest-growing industries, preferably those with annual growth rates in excess of 100 percent.

• Screen 2: *Find the market leader within that industry.* Our earlier analysis also indicates that the stock market drives up the stock price of the dominant firm in a fast-growing industry segment. Investors should rely on industry analysts, the trade press, and the Web as sources for figuring out which company is the market leader.

• Screen 3: *Assess customer satisfaction with the leader's product.* One way to assess the durability of the advantage of the leading firm is to see what customers think of its product. The trade press in many Web segments provides objectives reviews of products and services. Investors can read these reviews and assess whether a firm with leading market share also sustains high levels of customer satisfaction.

• Screen 4: *Analyze the strength of the management team.* By studying the biographies of key members of the management team, investors can assess management's ability to grow the company profitably. Investors should look for management's prior track record in handling similar situations. And as our earlier analysis points out, high inside ownership of the stock can often bode well for the growth in the stock price. High inside ownership increases the likelihood that short sellers will drive up the stock price rapidly. More important, high inside ownership suggests that the management team will be more highly motivated to do what is necessary to get the stock price up.

• Screen 5: *Compare the company's stock price to its value.* Figuring out the value of a company is a complex art, about which many books have been written. Because most Web companies do not have profits, it is not useful to use the price-earnings ratio as a valuation tool. Internet stock analysts tend to use the company's price-sales ratio as a guide. They look at the price-sales ratio of companies in the industry and compare that ratio to the companies' sales growth rates. This comparison yields industry benchmark valuations that can help the analysts spot potentially under- or overvalued stocks. Some analysts also try to guess at the value of the company by forecasting its future revenues and profits many years into the future. This screen is the most difficult to do correctly. One rule of thumb is for investors to look at market dips as opportunities to buy the stock of companies that pass the first four screens.

—⁓—

Although the real world of Internet business has many unique characteristics, it is still subject to certain fundamental rules of economics. For the manager or investor, the most important of these rules is that economic leverage goes to the firm that can deliver a product or service that is both in short supply and critically important to a powerful decision maker. If the manager can build a company that supplies this commodity, that manager will sustain high Net profits. The investor who buys shares early in that company's history will be amply rewarded.

⎯ᴧᴧ⎯ References

Aley, J. "The Heart of Silicon Valley." *Fortune,* July 7, 1997, p. 66.

"America Online Briefing Book." *Wall Street Journal Interactive,* Nov. 30, 1998.
 [http://interactive.wsj.com/inap-bin/bb_idd?sym=AOL&page=4].

Barnett, M. "Users Prefer Portals to Online Brokerages for Managing
 Finances." *Industry Standard,* July 23, 1998.
 [http://www.thestandard.net/articles/article_print/1,1454,1196,00.html].

Borland, J. "Rivalry in ISP Market Heats Up." *Red Herring,* Jan. 1, 1998.
 [http://www.herring.com/mag/issue50/rivalry.html].

Boslet, M. "Security-Software Market Is Razor Sharp." *Wall Street Journal,*
 May 15, 1998, p. B7A.

Byron, C. "Seeking the Source of Amazon.com's Recent, and Continuing,
 Stock Surge." *MSNBC,* July 17, 1998.
 [http://www.msnbc.com/news/178410.asp].

Center for Responsive Politics. "Individual Donor Search on 'John Doerr.'"
 Nov. 8, 1998. [http://www.crp.org/indivs/].

Claymon, D. "Open Question." *Red Herring,* Feb. 1997.
 [http://www.redherring.com/mag/issue39/open.html].

"CMP Media Leads All Technology Media Companies in U.S. Ad Page
 Growth and Market Share at the Close of First Half of 1998."
 Business Wire, July 29, 1998. [http://www.pcquote.com].

"CNET, Inc. Reports Profitable Fourth Quarter Results." *PR Newswire,*
 Feb. 10, 1999. [http://www.pcquote.com].

Cohen, J. "Internet Navigation." *Merrill Lynch,* Apr. 13, 1998, p. 6.

Crockett, B. "AOL's Software Challenge." *MSNBC,* Nov. 24, 1998.
 [http://www.msnbc.com/news/218028.asp].

Dalton, G. "Stiff Competition in the ISP Market." *InformationWeek,*
 Oct. 6, 1997, p. 50.

Doerr, J. "Outlook for the Net, New Ventures, and the New Economy."
 BASES, Stanford University, May 1, 1998.

Essick, K. "E-Commerce Will Play Small Part in Global Economy,
 Report Says." *Industry Standard,* Oct. 2, 1998.

[http://www.thestandard.net/articles/display/0,1449,1853,00.
html?home.col2.1].

"E*Trade Expands Marketing and Commerce Agreement with Yahoo!;
Signs Exclusive Marketing Agreement with ZDNet."
PR Newswire, Aug. 6, 1998. [http://www.pcquote.com].

Foster, C., with Pitta, J. "Watch Out Charles Wang." *Forbes*, Aug. 24, 1998.
[http://www.forbes.com/forbes/98/0824/6204093a.htm].

Franson, P. "The Market Research Shell Game." *Upside*, Mar. 1, 1997a.
[http://www.upside.com/texis/mvm/story?id=34712c1924].

Franson, P. "Who Are These Guys?" *Upside*, Mar. 1, 1997b.
[http://www.upside.com/texis/mvm/story?id=34712c1918].

Gomez Advisors. "Internet Broker Scorecard." *Gomezwire*, Oct. 15, 1998.
[http://www.gomezwire.com/brokers/scorecard].

Gove, A. "American Keiretsu." *Red Herring*, Feb. 1998.
[http://www.redherring.com/mag/issue51/american.html].

Graham, A. "The Cisco Kid Grows Up." *Executive Edge*, Sept. 1998, p. 48.

Harrison, A. "CheckPoint Sets Boundaries." *Software Magazine*, July 1997,
p. 114.

Harvey, P. "Striking It 'Rich.'" *Upside*, Nov. 23, 1998.
[http://www.upside.com/texis/mvm/story?id=36/59e82b0].

Hechinger, J. "Heard in New England: Open Market May Not Belong
on Investors' Stock Shopping Lists." *Wall Street Journal*, Apr. 22,
1998, p. B10.

Heilemann, J. "Letters from Silicon Valley." *New Yorker*, Aug. 11, 1997, p. 34.

Henig, P. "IPO Update: 24/7 Does Better Than Expected."
Red Herring, Aug. 14, 1998a.
[http://www.redherring.com/insider/1998/0814/247ipo.html].

Henig, P. "Nexabit Claims Terabit-Speed Routers." *Red Herring*,
Nov. 6, 1998b.
[http://www.redherring.com/insider/1998/1106/nexabit.html].

Henig, P. "At Home Gets Excited." *Red Herring*, Jan. 19, 1999c.
[http://www.redherring.com/insider/1999/0119/news-athome.html].

Hoffman, D. "Internet Commerce: The Ever Changing Landscape."
Fortune Conference Presentation, May 14, 1998, p. 24.

Intindola, B. "FOCUS—Barnes & Noble Buying Ingram; Steps Up Book
Wars." *Reuters*, Nov. 6, 1998.
[http://investor.msn.com/news/pressrel.asp?SYMBOL=
amzn&ARTICLEID=RTR,1998/11/06,N06288908].

Jeffers, M. "None of Your Business! There Was Nothing Public About These
Private Fortunes . . . Until Now." *Forbes ASAP*, Oct. 6, 1997.
[http://www.forbes.com/asap/97/1006/087.htm].

Jubak, J. "Jubak's Journal: Counting Those Internet Chickens." *Microsoft Investor,* July 28, 1998. [http://investor.msn.com/prospect/articles/jubak/774.asp].

The Jupiter/NFO Consumer Survey, Volume 1. Figure v.19: "Churn Patterns Among Online Households," *Jupiter Communications,* Oct. 1998. [http://www.jup.com/store/studies/jup_nfo1/tof.html].

Kane, M. "'Tis the Season to Go Shopping." *ZD Network News,* Nov. 9, 1998. [http://www.zdnet.com/zdnn/stories/news/0 percent2C4586 percent 2C2161757 percent2C00.html].

Keegan, P. "Can Bob Pittman Make AOL Rock?" *Upside,* Oct. 14, 1998. [http://www.upside.com/texis/mvm/story?id=362390460].

Kelleher, K. "E-Trade Delays Launch of Portal Site." *Industry Standard,* July 10, 1998. [http://www.thestandard.net/articles/article_print/1,1454,1025,00.html].

Komando, K. "When Cable Modems and DSL Compete, Consumers Will Win." *Los Angeles Times,* Feb. 16, 1998, p. D1.

Kornblum, J. "USA-Lycos Deal Treads on Heels of Internet Gold Rush." *USA Today,* Feb. 10, 1999, p. 2B.

Krantz, M. "Click Till You Drop." *Time,* July 20, 1998. [http://www.pathfinder.com/time/magazine/1998/dom/980720/cover2.html].

Lash, A. "Mike Homer: Netscape's Media Mogul?" *Industry Standard,* July 27, 1998. [http://www.thestandard.net/articles/article_display/0,1449,1156–5,00.html].

Littman, J. "The New Face of Venture Capital." *Electronic Business,* Mar. 1998, p. 72.

"Macromedia Reports Record Revenues for Second Quarter Fiscal 1999." *Presswire,* Oct. 30, 1998. [http://www.pcquote.com].

"McAfee to Combine with Network General; Two Companies Join to Form Network Associates World's Largest Network Security and Management Software Company; Tenth Largest Independent Software Company." *PRNewswire,* Oct. 13, 1997. [http://www.networkassociate.com/about/news/press/1997/101397.asp].

McGarvey, R. "Infonauts." *Red Herring,* Aug. 20, 1998. [http://www.herring.com/mag/issue57/infonauts.html].

"Mecklermedia, 'The Internet Media Company,' Reports Operating Results for Third Quarter and First Nine Months of Fiscal 1998." *Business Wire,* Aug. 4, 1998. [http://www.pcquote.com].

Media Metrix. "New Media Highlights." [http://www.mediametrix.com]. May 1998.

Mehling, H. "Madhavan Rangaswami." *Computer Reseller News,* Nov. 17, 1997, p. 157.

"MindSpring Announces Second Quarter Results: Continuing the Commitment." *Business Wire,* July 22, 1998. [http://www.pcquote.com].

"MindSpring Says to Buy AOL's SpryNet." *Reuters,* Sept. 10, 1998. [http://www.pcquote.com].

"Money Tree Report: 1998 Results." Pricewaterhouse Coopers, Dec. 1998. [http://204.198.129.80/reportq398_highlights.asp].

Nesdore, P. "ISPs See Managing Growth as Their Greatest Challenge." *Web Week,* Dec. 8, 1997, p. 1.

"Netscape and Citibank in Online Deal." *Reuters,* Aug. 11, 1998. [http://www.msnbc.com/news/187240.asp].

"Network Associates' Acquisition of CyberMedia Closes—McAfee Software Division Expands Comprehensive Product Line." *PRNewswire,* Sept. 10, 1998. [http://www.networkassociate.com/about/news/press/1998/September/091098a.asp].

"Network Associates Company Background." *Wall Street Journal Interactive,* Nov. 6, 1998. [http://interactive.wsj.com/inap-bin/bb_idd?sym=NETA&page=4].

"Network Associates to Acquire Dr. Solomon's; European Anti-Virus Software Vendor to Join Preeminent Network Security and Management Company." *PRNewswire,* June 9, 1998. [http://www.networkassociate.com/about/news/press/1998/June/060998a.asp].

Nocera, J. "Cooking with Cisco." *Fortune,* Dec. 25, 1995. [http://www.pathfinder.com/fortune/magazine/1995/951225/cisco.html].

O'Brien, T. "Out of the Garage." *Upside,* Sept. 30, 1998a. [http://www.upside.com/texis/mvm/story?id=361168d40].

O'Brien, T. "Save Bill Clinton." *Upside,* Sept. 9, 1998b. [http://www.upside.com/texis/mvm/story?id=35f580970].

"Online Insecurity." *BusinessWeek,* Mar. 16, 1998. [http://www.businessweek.com].

Pang, A. "E-Commerce Bonanza: Is It Real or Imagined?" *Internet Computing,* Feb. 2, 1998. [http://www.zdnet.com/icom/content/anchors/199802/09/ecom.bonanza/3.html].

Peltz, M. "High Tech's Premier Venture Capitalist." *Institutional Investor,* June 1996, p. 92.

Rafter, M. "EarthLink Connects." *Industry Standard,* May 28, 1998.
[http://www.thestandard.net/articles/issue_display/0,1261,436,00.html].

Rendleman, J. "Connecting on the Net." *PC Week,* Feb. 16, 1998, p. 14.

"Responding to Rising Security Breaches, Companies Spend More, Plan Less." *EDP Weekly,* June 15, 1998, p. 7.

Robb, J. "Why E*Trade Will Recast Itself as a Financial Destination." *Gomezwire,* July 15, 1998.
[http://www.gomezwire.com/GomezWire/Analysis/98.html].

"Sapient Acquires Studio Archetype; Industry Leaders Combine to Create Best-in-Class Internet Consulting Firm." *Business Wire,* Aug. 25, 1998. [http://www.pcquote.com]

Schaff, W. "Inktomi Isn't Just Hype—Inktomi's Distinctive Feature: It Focuses More on Technology and Applications, and Less on Branding Its Own Name." *InformationWeek,* Aug. 3, 1998, p. 94.

Schoenberger, C. "Relying on Self-Reliance." *Boston Globe,* Sept. 6, 1998, pp. E1, E7.

Sinton, P. "Venturing into the Record Book: Kleiner Perkins Leads the League." *San Francisco Chronicle,* Mar. 7, 1998.
[http://www.kpcb.com].

Speiss, N. "Home Theater: How to Get Started." *Fortune,* Jan. 1, 1998, p. 168.

"State of the Networking Equipment Market 1998 Abstract." Cahners In-Stat Group, Apr. 1998.
[http://www.instat.com/abstracts/cn/98/cn9809ms_abs.htm].

Stubbs, C. "RELOAD: The Heavily Hyped Revisited: EarthLink and Hotmail." *Red Herring,* Apr. 1998.
[http://www.herring.com/mag/issue53/reload.html].

Surkan, M. "The Nasty Truth About ADSL." *PC Week,* Feb. 9, 1998, p. 100.

Tully, S. "How Cisco Mastered the Net." *Fortune,* Aug. 17, 1998.
[http://www.pathfinder.com/fortune/1998/980817/cis.html].

U.S. Department of Commerce. "The Emerging Digital Economy." April 1998. [http://www.doc.gov/ecommerce/ederept.pdf].

"VCs Face Increased Competition." *Red Herring,* Dec. 1997.
[http://www.herring.com/mag/issue49/top/9.html].

Wallace, J. *Overdrive.* New York: Wiley, 1997.

Warner, M. "Cool Companies 1998: CheckPoint Software." *Fortune,* July 6, 1998.
[http://www.pathfinder.com/fortune/1998/980706/coo3.html].

Weaver, J. "Merged AOL-Netcenter Could Draw $450 Million in Spending." *MSNBC,* Nov. 24, 1998. [http://www.msnbc.com/news/217639.asp].

Wilder, C. "GE to Move Purchasing to the Internet." *TechWeb News,*
    June 26, 1997.
    [http://www.techweb.com/se/directlink.cgi?WIR1997062611].
Wiley, D. "Beyond Information Retrieval." *Database,* Aug.-Sept. 1998, p. 19.
Woods, B. "Competition Between AltaVista, Yahoo Leads to Inktomi Corp.
    Deal." *Computer Dealer News,* June 8, 1998, p. 37.
Wyatt, J. "E-Trade: Is This Investing's Future?" *Fortune,* Mar. 3, 1997.
    [http://www.pathfinder.com/fortune/1997/970303/inv.html].

⟶ Subject Index

Company Name Index